HIDING FROM LOVE

✜

WE ALL LONG TO BE CARED FOR, BUT WE PREVENT IT BY...

HiDING *FROM* LOVE

HOW TO CHANGE THE WITHDRAWAL PATTERNS THAT ISOLATE AND IMPRISON YOU

DR. JOHN TOWNSEND

Co-director of the Minirth-Meier Clinic West, California

NAVPRESS ◗®

A MINISTRY OF THE NAVIGATORS
P.O. BOX 6000, COLORADO SPRINGS, COLORADO 80934

The Navigators is an international Christian
organization. Jesus Christ gave His followers
the Great Commission to go and make disciples
(Matthew 28:19). The aim of The Navigators is
to help fulfill that commission by multiplying
laborers for Christ in every nation.

NavPress is the publishing ministry of The
Navigators. NavPress publications are tools
to help Christians grow. Although publications alone cannot make disciples or change
lives, they can help believers learn biblical
discipleship, and apply what they learn to their
lives and ministries.

Unless otherwise identified, all Scripture in
this publication is from the *New American
Standard Bible* (NASB), © The Lockman Foundation 1960, 1962, 1963, 1968, 1971, 1972,
1973, 1975, 1977. Other versions used include:
the *Good News Bible: Today's English Version*
(TEV), copyright © American Bible Society 1966,
1971, 1976; the *Holy Bible: New International
Version* (NIV). Copyright © 1973, 1978, 1984,
International Bible Society. Used by permission
of Zondervan Bible Publishers; and the *King
James Version* (KJV).

Printed in the United States of America

FOR A FREE CATALOG OF
NAVPRESS BOOKS & BIBLE STUDIES,
CALL TOLL FREE 1-800-366-7788 (USA)
or 1-416-499-4615 (CANADA)

Contents

To Naomi Lamm Barnes
(1889–1972)
She loved without hiding.

Author

Dr. John Townsend was raised in Wilson, North Carolina. He attended college in Raleigh at North Carolina State University, where he received his B.A. in psychology with honors. He then attended Dallas Theological Seminary, where he received his Master of Theology degree, also with honors. He went on to California, where he completed further studies at Rosemead Graduate School of Psychology, and received his Ph.D. in clinical psychology.

Both a licensed clinical psychologist and a marriage, family, and child counselor, John is Co-Director of the Minirth-Meier Clinic West, a Christian inpatient treatment center group. John has an extensive background in both inpatient and outpatient treatment programs, and has a private practice in Newport Beach. In addition to his clinical work, John is a popular speaker and specialist on such topics as developmental models of spiritual and emotional growth and the integration of Scripture and psychology. He is coauthor of *Secrets of Your Family Tree* with Dave Carder, Dr. Earl Henslin, Dr. Henry Cloud, and Alice Brawand (Moody Press, 1991).

Dr. Townsend lives in southern California with his wife, Barbi, and their son, Ricky.

For information on materials, tapes, seminars, or speaking engage-
ments, write:

Dr. John Townsend
260 Newport Center Drive, #450
Newport Beach, CA 92660

For information on the treatment programs of the Minirth-Meier
Clinic West, call 1-800-545-1819, or write to the above address.

Foreword

I first met John Townsend in the 1970s when I was a Dallas Seminary professor and John was one of my top students. Even then, John had a passion for truth and a sincere goal for applying the practical applications of God's Word to our lives. After graduating with honors from Dallas Seminary, John diligently pursued his doctorate in psychology at Rosemead. This was followed by private practice, when he effectively and very successfully applied the wisdom, knowledge, and passion for people that God had gifted him with.

Over the years since our initial professor-student contacts, our relationship has grown and developed to friendship, colleague, partners in Minirth-Meier West, and now I often go to John to teach me the latest research findings on developmental issues. He has come full circle and become my mentor in enhancing my own understanding of the developmental injuries we humans all suffer in our childhoods and how we can overcome them to be the most effective and efficient servants of Jesus Christ we can possibly be. I have seen the wonderful effects of John's thoroughly scriptural therapy programs on the hundreds of fellow-believers who have come through our Minirth-Meier West hospitals. Many of our patients have personally expressed their appreciation for his love and compassion as well as his wisdom during their time of crisis.

In fact, John has been so busy ministering to individuals over our years together as partners that I have been prodding him repeatedly to share with the masses the valuable principles he has learned. An ounce of prevention is worth a pound of cure. So Dr. Frank Minirth and I have continually encouraged Christian therapists to always put ministry first and foremost. We want to do everything we can to equip our brothers and sisters in Christ before they come to our counselors to work out the finishing touches.

I am personally thrilled that John has shared his heart and wisdom in this book, *Hiding from Love*. As you take your own personal journey through the pages of this book, be prepared for a roller-coaster ride into your own soul.

Jeremiah the prophet told us over two thousand years ago that our human hearts are very deceitful, hiding the truth from our conscious awareness. But God's Word is powerful and sharp. It can cut through our defenses to expose the naked truth about our thoughts, feelings, and motives.

In *Hiding from Love*, John's love for people and passion for truth come through as he teaches us about the various developmental injuries that hinder us from fully experiencing the abundant life Christ wants us to have. He exposes our specific methods of self-deception that hinder us from intimate bonding and establishing biblical boundaries.

John compassionately reveals ways to biblically fill the developmental holes in our souls so we can overcome the sins and addictive tendencies we erroneously use to fill those vacuums. God doesn't want us merely to quit sinning. He loves us and wants to meet our emotional and spiritual needs in ways that sin never can. *Hiding from Love* teaches us ways to cooperate with God in our own sanctification process—a process that never ends until we get to Heaven.

—Paul Meier, M.D.
Executive Vice President
Minirth-Meier Clinics

Acknowledgments

This book is the fruit of God working through many people in my life. Personally and professionally, they have helped me come out of hiding to grow in the grace and truth of Jesus Christ. I would like to recognize their ministries here.

My wife, Barbi, has provided a safe place in which to live and work. Her gentle encouragement is a constant source of God's love and acceptance for me. She was also my first "editor," and her contributions have been valuable. In addition, it has been a privilege to be a part of the growth process of my wonderful son, Ricky.

Dr. Henry Cloud, my friend and associate, has been instrumental in the formulation of this material. His theoretical and clinical thinking have made a profound difference in the concepts presented here. Henry's heart for the hurting and his allegiance to Scripture have also made significant impacts on my own life.

Dr. David Cabush and Dr. Barbara Laier have provided professional, supervisory, and personal input, for which I am grateful.

Dr. Frank Minirth and Dr. Paul Meier have had primary roles in my work. I appreciate their mentorship and colaborship.

The faculty of the Rosemead School of Psychology was instrumental in my learning to integrate psychology with theology. Dr. John Carter helped me learn the alliance of the Scriptures and psychology. Dr. Phil Sutherland helped me greatly in understanding the therapeutic implications of hiding.

ACKNOWLEDGMENTS

Guy and Christi Owen have been models of the unhidden life. They impacted my understanding of the Christian family.

Tom McCall and Rev. Ben Patterson have spent many hours with me in making counseling relevant to the Body of Christ.

The staff of Minirth-Meier Clinic West has been a source of inspiration for me as they daily implant God's love in the lives of struggling people. I'd like to single out my associates Dr. David Stoop and Bob Whiton for their part in this process. In addition, the clinical staff at Community Hospital of Gardena, including Dr. Tom Okamoto, Linda Auth, and Michelle Boswell, were a support in understanding the psychiatric implications of defenses.

The members of Community Bible Chapel in Richardson, Texas, have spent time investing in me. I'm grateful for Mike and Cindy Fannin, John and Marcia Davis, Dr. Gary and Vickie Boatman, Rev. Bob Deffinbaugh, and the Lakewood Ministry Group.

Chuck Minchew, Gordon and Brenda Van Amburgh, Rev. Calhoun Johnson, Rev. Jim Dethmer, and Rev. Roy Zinn played a large part in helping me conceptualize what true ministry is.

Pastor Gary Richmond allowed me to test my material on his Single Parents Fellowship at First Evangelical Free Church in Fullerton, California. I'm grateful to him and to his wife, Carol, for their belief in this book.

Dave Carder, Pastor of Counseling Ministries at First Evangelical Free Church, provided a field of reference so I could present this information in his lay counseling training classes.

My editor, Steve Webb, showed a personal as well as a professional interest in the material. His editorial skill shows, and the book is better because of him.

The faculty of Dallas Theological Seminary provided me with the much needed tools to become an independent student of Scripture. Dr. Howard Hendricks and Dr. Frank Wichern encouraged me to think of sound theology in terms of its relevance to real needs.

Sharon Kinard prayed diligently during the most difficult months of writing.

My parents, Jack and Becky Townsend, and my sisters, Lynn Dealey, Susan Holt, and Cris Townsend, helped me understand how love should look. I am grateful for their lives.

PART ONE

The Hiding
Dilemma

CHAPTER ONE

Jenny's Story

❖

TO JENNY'S nine-year-old mind the butterfly she gazed at was the most beautiful thing she'd ever seen. She felt so happy and comfortable here in her meadow, knowing Mother and Father were just over the hill, gathering vegetables from the garden. She loved her parents so much—they always showed her the love and warmth every little girl or boy wants.

Growing up in her small, European country village was also a delight. Whenever she and her folks went on a trip she always remembered her butterfly back home in the meadow, and her dolls in her room, and the vegetable garden and small playground just beyond that Father had built for her.

And she would remember her dear friend Officer Josef, the neighborhood policeman, who always brought her candies that came from his brother's little shop in the village. She liked his big brown uniform and his officer's hat. But mostly, she liked his kind face and their long chats on the street corner.

Often, after a long time of playing with her dolls or helping Mother and Father in the garden, Jenny would take a long walk with her parents in the Deep Woods that lay just beyond the meadow behind the house. Jenny's life was full of joy and comfort; she felt especially secure.

One day, though, a terrible thing happened: *War!* It broke out in Jenny's country only a couple of months after her ninth birthday. A neighboring country attacked hers, and the streets rang with the sounds of gunfire, explosions, and fighting.

Jenny's little country lost the war and was occupied by the enemy forces. Only a few days after the occupation, she saw several strange men walking up the gravel path to her house. At first, Jenny thought they were friends, because of their military uniforms. Their outfits looked very much like Officer Josef's. But she was wrong. The men in the friendly looking uniforms were from the occupying forces. They crashed through the front door of Jenny's home and began to ransack the house.

"Run, Jenny! Run to the Deep Woods!" her father cried out. Racing out the back door, wearing only a dress and sandals, Jenny looked back at the house just in time to witness a terrifying sight. The soldiers were roughly dragging her parents toward a big black car. They pushed and shoved them into the back seat.

Jenny's heart was filled with terror. Sobbing, she raced into the Deep Woods behind her meadow.

THE HAVEN OF THE DEEP WOODS

To a stranger the Deep Woods might have seemed thick and impenetrable. But to Jenny they were an old friend. Her walks with her father had filled her with knowledge about the forest. She had spent many pleasant days there with him and her mother as well, exploring streams, hills, and the underbrush rustling with scurrying animals. Her parents had taught her how to make friends with the animals, so she wasn't afraid of them.

Even now in her frightened state, Jenny quickly found one of her favorite spots in the forest where she could hide. It was a small cave near a stream. Still sobbing, she collapsed to the ground, confused and exhausted from her ordeal. Her energy consumed by terror and flight, Jenny fell into a deep sleep.

When she awoke the next day, Jenny still felt frightened and a bit confused, but her need for survival was strong. After she thought for a long time, she knew what she had to do. *I'm alone now*, she said to herself. *Mother and Father are gone. The scary men in uniform will catch me if I return home. I guess home isn't home anymore.* Jenny sighed as she sadly decided that her new home would be the cave in the Deep Woods. It had always been her friend; now it was her only safe place.

Over the next few weeks, Jenny made the Woods her home . . . far away from the men in uniforms. She grew lonely after a while—so lonely that she began to wonder if she had even existed in that past life at all. Her memories of her parents and her former safety kept her longing for her old life. Then she would relive her day of terror and feel deep confusion. But in spite of her conflicting emotions, she still felt safe in her Deep Woods.

LEARNING TO LIVE ALONE

In the weeks following her parents' arrest, fear and loneliness became Jenny's constant companions. She hated being alone, but she was more afraid of exposure, especially to the men in uniform.

During her worst moments, the little lost girl thought her heart would break from the sadness. She missed Mother and Father *so much!* During these sad times, Jenny learned to comfort and soothe herself with warm memories of the old days at home. She replayed favorite scenes, of love and safety, over and over, gathering as much warmth from them as she could.

In one of her favorite scenes, Jenny was sitting in her mother's lap by the fire on a quiet night. Her father read stories to her from his chair nearby, while her mother rocked her until drowsiness turned into sleep. Then she was gently carried off to bed and lovingly tucked in.

Jenny longed for those times in her life when she'd had no reason to hide. But now, she thought, her hideout in the Deep Woods was the only thing keeping her safe.

The Woods were her safety, but memories kept her going. She would cry herself to sleep each night and then wake up the next day and get on about the business of surviving. She found the best places in the stream to get fresh water; she learned where the best berries and food plants were. Once in a while she would sneak back to her old vegetable garden just after dark and take a few potatoes or turnips. She knew how to build a fire and where to find warm places in cold weather.

Jenny was making a place for herself in the forest. Food and shelter weren't problems anymore. She began to feel that she was out of danger—at least for now.

But something was different inside the little girl's heart. Her heart had been broken, and it did not mend while she was busy learning how to live in the forest. The part of Jenny that had trusted, had longed for caring, had reached out for a warm embrace or a kind word, became still and quiet. It was replaced by a dull, painful emptiness. She had felt it shriveling up inside, until now there was nothing. Jenny hadn't wanted that part of her to break. But it just did, anyway.

Survival is a difficult task, even in familiar places. Jenny managed the immediate necessities, but her biggest problem was facing all the decisions that were now left up to her. She didn't feel grown-up enough to make them.

Jenny didn't have ready answers for everything that confronted her. When she made her snap decision to live in the cave, she hadn't felt confident about it. Even now she wondered if a tree house would be better—but then, she didn't know how to build one. Which plants would provide good leaf cover, and which would fall apart after a rain? Which berries were safe to eat, and which were poisonous?

Jenny felt too small to confront these questions all by herself. Yet they had to be answered in some way for her to make a life for herself in the Deep Woods.

Whenever Jenny felt inadequate to solve a problem or make a decision, she would think back to Officer Josef's kind face. He had helped her with so many grown-up questions when she was back home. He'd helped her get to her friend's house. He told her the best way to catch crickets and had taught her to ride a bicycle.

Now what would Officer Josef say I should do about this? Jenny would ask herself. On many occasions this would help her come up with solutions to her problems. And sometimes she'd remember her mother's or father's wise advice about things.

But at other times, Jenny would sit on the ground and weep. She just felt too little and too overwhelmed for all these questions and decisions. Her aloneness had become deeply painful.

About the only thing Jenny could look forward to now were her walks in the Deep Woods. If there weren't any humans around, at least she could be with the plants and animals. For hours at a time she would greet the deer, watch the badgers and snakes and foxes on their way here and there, even glimpse a small black bear.

Jenny wasn't sure if the animals recognized her, but they didn't seem particularly bothered or afraid when she passed by. She was careful not to make sudden movements toward them, as her father had taught her. Now, she understood very well why that was so important. She was well-acquainted with being frightened.

TERROR STRIKES AGAIN

One day during one of her long walks, Jenny was surprised to hear a man shouting. Looking back over her shoulder, she was horrified to see four uniformed soldiers—the same ones who had broken into her home and taken her parents! It was obvious that they also recognized Jenny. Breaking into a run, they spread out to catch her.

For a split-second, Jenny was paralyzed with fear. Then her brain told her feet to *move* and she was off. She quickly scanned the pathway through the brush, trying to remember where she had been on her walk.

The ancient oak tree saved her. Hundreds of years old, with a massive trunk that even her father had never been able to get his arms around, the ancient tree had always been Jenny's marker for a small fork in the path that she headed for now. The turnoff was almost invisible, but she knew the mark well and veered sharply to her left.

Darting behind the oak, Jenny plunged into deep, almost impenetrable brush along the narrow pathway toward a little tunnel that ran through the briers. It was barely big enough even for her to get through. She knew the foxes and badgers used this path often. She ran silently, although she could hear her heart pounding.

The soldiers ran right past the hidden path and rushed down the larger one. Perplexed and confused, their voices echoed off the surrounding oaks, sounding like bloodhounds losing a scent. Then their sounds died off in the distance.

Jenny waited for a while before she returned to her friendly cave, just in case they might have found it. She thanked the oak tree for being just where he was supposed to be.

Jenny had used her months in the Deep Woods well. Her understanding had helped her escape the soldiers. Silently, she began to thread her way back through the trees to her shelter.

TROUBLING CONVERSATIONS

Being so alone gave Jenny a lot of time to think. Since she had no one to talk to, she conducted conversations with herself to make her day a little more interesting and a little less lonely. She conjured up two imaginary friends: Big Jenny and Little Jenny.

Jenny repeated one particular conversation over and over again. It was a discussion about a very important question: *Why am I here?* Jenny would sort out all the reasons why she had ended up in the Deep Woods all by herself. Then Big Jenny and Little Jenny would try to make sense of the sad situation.

As the weeks dragged on, the conversation began taking an unpleasant turn. It would sound like this:

BIG JENNY: Why are you here?
LITTLE JENNY: Because the bad soldiers took my parents and they were coming to get me.

BIG JENNY: You're sure of that?

LITTLE JENNY: Yes, I'm sure. But what do you mean?

BIG JENNY: Could there possibly be another reason?

LITTLE JENNY: No—well, could there be?

BIG JENNY: Of course! Remember the time you were sick and had to stay in bed for a week?

LITTLE JENNY: I remember. It was awful! I felt terrible.

BIG JENNY: That's not all. Do you remember what your parents did when you were sick?

LITTLE JENNY: Mother took care of me during the day and Father stayed with me in the evening when she was tired.

BIG JENNY: Yes, they took care of you. And did you notice how tired they both were? After *all* they had to do, then they had to play nursemaid to you!

LITTLE JENNY: They did look pretty worn out.

BIG JENNY: You bet they did. And that's really why you're here.

LITTLE JENNY: I don't understand.

BIG JENNY: Of course you do. Your selfishness was too much of a drain on them. You exhausted them. Your demands kept them from being able to prepare a getaway plan for when the soldiers came. If you hadn't asked for so much, you'd be safe with them today.

LITTLE JENNY: I did complain about my tummyache—maybe more than I should have. . . .

These conversations troubled Jenny, but they didn't stop.

ANOTHER CHASE

Jenny would sometimes find relief from these discussions by sitting quietly beside the stream that ran through the Deep Woods. It had taken her a long time to find it, because it was hidden in a remote part of the Woods. It had always been a safe place for her. She loved listening to the musical language of the water as it rushed over the smooth stones in the stream bed.

One afternoon Jenny's reverie was shattered when the sound of shouting again broke into her seclusion. Less than a hundred yards away was another group of several uniformed soldiers. Just as she spotted them, they noticed her and began shouting and running toward her.

The last frightening experience with soldiers had taught Jenny a lesson. Even during her meditation by the babbling brook, she had kept one eye on her possible escape routes. This time, though, her reactions were much faster.

Without stopping to deliberate, the little girl moved into a dodge-and-weave pattern, running away from the soldiers and straight for the thickest part of the brush. Stooping over, she disappeared into the dense foliage.

As she scurried through the brambles, Jenny stopped every few seconds to listen for the men's voices. Once again, they grew fainter and eventually died off.

After losing her, the soldiers stopped to rest. Jenny was much too far away to hear their conversation.

"Are you sure it was her?" gasped one of the older men, out of breath.

"Absolutely," replied the second soldier, obviously the leader of the group. "Jenny's here and she's alive. Her parents were right about her escape route."

The first soldier stooped to take a drink from the stream. As he stood up he said sadly, "Jenny must not realize that we have turned back the enemy invaders, that our land is safe again. And if that's right, then she wouldn't know that her parents sent us to find her."

A third soldier turned to face the commander and asked, "There's something I don't understand, sir. Why did she run? We're her countrymen. We're here to bring her home. Why would Jenny be panicked by *us*?"

The leader remained thoughtfully silent for a moment. Then, raising his eyes to the brush where he'd last seen Jenny, Officer Josef said quietly, "A uniform is a uniform." Turning toward the last rays of sunlight that bathed the edge of the Deep Woods, he led his men out of the forest.

JENNY'S SAFETY IN HIDING

By now Jenny had learned how to keep her life orderly and safe in the Deep Woods. Her daily routine included waking up at about the same time each morning, washing in the stream, eating, walking, and exploring.

Jenny's routine also included all kinds of rules, even for the little things. *Wash in the stream until you count to two hundred, then come out,* she would remind herself. As she set out to explore she would recite, *Explore the Deep Woods one hundred more steps than the day before.* These rules became rather fixed and rigid, but they helped give her a sense of control over her life. She didn't feel quite so helpless inside now.

At the same time that life in the Deep Woods seemed more familiar and routine, Jenny's heart was changing toward her memories of home and family. At first they had felt sharp and painful, and then receded into a dull ache. Now she had a new feeling—an emotion of pushing away.

Each day now, Jenny felt less and less that she needed her old relationships, even with her parents and Officer Josef. The growing distance was replaced by a kind of strength, but with a hard edge to it. It gave her thoughts such as, *I never really needed them anyway.* Or, *I'm better off than I was before; we were never that close.*

Jenny was somewhat concerned that the distance was widening between her formerly sad, needy feelings and her newfound strength. But it did seem to make things more peaceful in her heart.

Eventually, Jenny became aware that the pieces of her broken heart were slipping away. Not that she wasn't doing well in her task of survival. In fact, if anything, she was more competent at finding food, catching fish, locating shelter, and staying warm. But the feelings that she had felt all her life were becoming more and more faint. Emotions such as love, tenderness, and joy seemed like words written in stone.

It wasn't just the good feelings that had left. Even the bad ones—terror, panic, rage, and sadness—were a dull memory for

Jenny. She never thought she would miss those feelings, but when they went, she knew something was wrong. Jenny was aware that feelings tell people they are alive.

Now Jenny had become merely a creature of empty habits. She went through her routines of survival sluggishly, without the sense of spontaneity that had characterized her early days in the forest. She felt almost dead.

RESCUED FROM HIDING

There it was again: "Jenny! Jenny! Where are you?" When she heard the man's voice calling her, Jenny crawled to her safest spying tree and scurried up to her well-concealed lookout post to watch. This was the twentieth day in a row—why did this same soldier keep coming back every day?

Jenny didn't know much except that he was one of the terrifying men in uniform. That was reason enough to stay away. She recognized him from the last scare. But for these last several days, he'd always come alone to the Deep Woods, which was no small feat. The Woods weren't especially friendly to strangers.

Today, something was different about the soldier's approach. Jenny noticed that he didn't seem in any particular hurry. His voice and mannerisms seemed appealingly calm to her. He just sat there in the same place, near a large maple tree, calling for her every few minutes. After about an hour he left.

The soldier returned at the same time the next day. Now Jenny felt that he appeared kind and patient. And strangely enough, the animals were befriending him the way they had befriended her when she'd first come to the Deep Woods. The squirrels, rabbits, and deer slowly approached him as he sat under the maple, eventually coming close enough for him to touch them.

After thirty consecutive days of the soldier's appearing, Jenny decided to take a small risk. She positioned herself about a hundred feet away from him, next to a secret entrance to the deepest part of the forest. Poised to melt instantly into the woods, Jenny coughed in the soldier's direction.

As he peered toward her, Jenny caught her first full glimpse of his face. It seemed vaguely familiar. The solider began to smile without making a move or even getting up. Jenny's dim recollections of him began to well up inside until she recognized the kind face of her old friend.

"Jenny," he called out warmly. "It's me, Josef. I've come to take you home."

"I don't have a home," she replied. "Didn't you know about Mother and Father being taken away? I live here now. I live in a cave. It's my home."

"It's true," Josef went on, "your mom and dad were taken away by soldiers from another land. But your countrymen fought back and freed our land. Their soldiers are gone. The whole country is safe now and so are your parents. They're in the hospital, but they're doing very well and will be home soon. They want you to come to see them. Your mother and father miss you very much, and they sent me to find you."

Hearing this news created a multitude of mixed emotions in Jenny. Conflicting feelings surged through her. She felt a tremendous sense of relief at knowing her parents were safe and wanted her back. Deep within her was the little girl who longed to be held in their arms again.

But Jenny also felt a sharp tug of fear at the prospect of leaving the safety of the home she'd made for herself in the Deep Woods. For many months now, the dark places had been good to her. They had kept her safe and protected during her times of sadness and moments of terror. They had been her only comfort in endless lonely nights.

Jenny realized that staying in the Woods meant being alone forever. "Should I go with Officer Josef? Or should I stay here?" The difficult dilemma brought back her old confusion.

To make matters worse, there was the problem of Officer Josef's uniform. For so long, the sight of military-style outfits had kept her terrified, reminding her of the horrible day her parents had been taken away. For Jenny, seeing a uniform had become a warning signal for danger.

Jenny gazed at Officer Josef's uniform, then looked at his kind face. Back to the uniform, and again to his face. The kind features and warm smile brought back memories of their close times in the village, their talks on the street corner, and their laughter together on her small playground. The memories flooded back.

Jenny waited, agonizing. *His face*, she told herself. *I think I remember his face.* Then she took a deep breath and made the hardest decision of her life. She slowly approached Josef and took his outstretched hand. Together, they walked out of the Deep Woods. Toward home.

❖ ❖ ❖

Jenny's story is a fictional tale that illustrates for us the reality of hiding. We all hide in various ways. Now let's move on and discover more about the hiding process and how it affects us emotionally and spiritually. As we do, we'll learn more about Jenny *and* ourselves.

Chapter Two

Our Two Biggest Problems

M Y OFFICE was silent for what seemed like an eternity. Only a few seconds had passed, however, since Sally, an attractive woman in her mid-thirties, had opened up her session with three words: "Dan's leaving me."

Sally's husband of seven years had called her from work, less than an hour before her appointment. He'd told her that he didn't want to stay married. There was no other woman. It just wasn't working out. He was apartment hunting, and would leave a phone number with her.

Dan's leaving was quite painful, but no real surprise to Sally. She had felt him slipping away since the first few years of the marriage. "There's always been a distance in Dan that I could never get past," she said sadly. "It's as if there's a wall around him. I don't even think he's really aware of it."

Sensing Dan's isolation, Sally had made many attempts to become closer to him through the years. She had discussed the problem with him, read books, gone to marriage seminars.

Dan, however, had shown little interest in the various methods Sally used. The only problem he could see was Sally's constant dissatisfaction with their relationship. Obviously, her unhappiness had become a big problem for him.

Dan did leave Sally. He also left a question in her mind for a long time afterward: *Why did Dan hide?* What would possess him to conceal his heart from Sally, who would have cherished it? Why avoid the very closeness that he needed from a wife?

PEOPLE IN HIDING

Answering this question of why we hide from the very relationships and truths we need is one of the purposes of this book. For a variety of reasons, all of us to some extent live two lives: an external life, in which we learn the feelings, attitudes, and behaviors that are "safe" to express; and an internal life, in which we closet away our "unsafe" traits, which exist isolated and undeveloped.

Our tendency is to keep the "unloved" parts of ourselves forever under wraps, with the hope that in time, they will go away and not cause us more pain.

This pattern is like the frightened man who goes to see his doctor for an annual physical. He's been having sharp back pains for some time, and he's terrified of the prospect of back surgery. So, as the doctor probes and prods, he bites his lip on the pain, murmuring to the doctor, "Nope—no pain there, either," in hopes that nothing will be discovered. He tries to distract his doctor by listing off his great energy level, good diet, and general fitness. All the while he desperately wishes that he'll get off without a diagnosis.

Jesus referred to our reticence to reveal our pain in one of His many confrontations with the Pharisees. He spent a great deal of time with hurting people. Once He had dinner with a tax-gatherer named Matthew—in our day, the equivalent of eating with an unpopular government official. Criticized for His choice of relationships, Jesus said,

> "It is not those who are healthy who need a physician, but those who are sick. But go and learn what this means, 'I desire compassion, and not sacrifice,' for I did not come to call the righteous, but sinners." (Matthew 9:12-13)

Jesus' point was that we all have problems and needs to be looked at, understood, loved, and helped by Him and His resources. But revealing these problems is often the *larger* problem.

We can call our efforts to conceal these problems *defenses*, which are anything we use to protect ourselves from danger. We put them up as spiritual and emotional "shields" to keep from being exposed or hurt.

This isn't to say that we have only one shield. Most of us use a variety of hiding patterns in different situations. We tend to select certain shields depending on two factors:

(1) what injured part of ourselves we're protecting;
(2) who or what we're protecting ourselves from.

For example, some people find that they have one defense at work and another at home. At work, an executive might hide feelings of rage and frustration behind a mask of compliance and high performance, especially when there is an authoritarian or critical boss. The *compliance* defense keeps the executive from speaking the truth about how he really feels toward his boss's critical nature.

Then when this executive walks in the door of his home, a shift often occurs. He may continue hiding his anger but may also be feeling ashamed of his encounter with the boss. This can easily lead to his withdrawing to the television or newspaper: a *withdrawal* defense. Worse, he may blame his rotten day on someone in his family: a *displacement* defense.

Notice the difference between home and work. At home, the overworked executive no longer protects himself from his rage at the boss; instead, he shields feelings of shame and worthlessness from the family.

What is it that sends us into hiding? To understand this pattern of building defenses we must go back to foundational issues. I think life is basically about *solving problems*. We need to do some problem-solving at the roots in order to understand what's going on above ground.

I believe that the reason why we tend to hide our problems and struggles can be traced to two basic problems in life:

(1) we're unfinished people;
(2) we fear the very things we need to restore us.

Let's take a closer look at these problems that cause us to become *people in hiding*.

PROBLEM #1: WE'RE UNFINISHED

Our fundamental problem is that *we are an unfinished people*. As Christians, all of us are somewhat like a beautiful but damaged home under restoration.

Have you ever walked past a house under renovation near your neighborhood—one that was close enough to your usual pathways that you could see it in its various stages of development? I can remember such a home when I was growing up. Though I wasn't aware of it at the time, it had been a grand mansion. Years of weather and neglect had sent it into disrepair.

Then new owners bought the house with the idea of restoring it to its former glory. These "house lovers" poured large amounts of time and money into rebuilding the mansion with materials as similar to the originals as possible.

Several times a week, I'd pass the large lot where the building activity went on. I always made sure I looked at the house from the same spot on the sidewalk (a little to the right of the front door) and at the same time of day (late afternoon). The process of gradual change and growth were a mystery to me. I was fascinated to watch the step-by-step changes in the home as it "grew" over the months. It was like having little sequenced snapshots of the building in my mind.

What struck me were the tremendous variations in the house's appearance *over time*. Some days it looked like a burned-out bomb site, with piles of lumber and sacks of concrete surrounding truckfuls of dirt; yet on others I could glimpse the heartbeat of its architect in its lines, its grace, its columns, and its large bay windows. And then there were days when both the breathtaking beauty as well as the fragile incompleteness of the site would stand out.

That unfinished home had a wonderful past, and a hopeful future upon completion. Its past was rooted in the dreams and desires of the family who had bought it, as well as the vision and skill of the architect who designed its renovation. Its future—which is now its present—has been a good one. It has stood tall and beautiful for a long time now, a host to several families over the years.

This process is similar to how God sees us. Like the mansion, we have a past of wonder. Chosen and designed by God "before the foundation of the world" (Ephesians 1:4), we have been created to take on certain aspects of His character, such as being loved and loving, and being productive. This is what it means to be created in His image. We all have an Architect's blueprint inside our hearts. This blueprint is in the process of being developed.

Like the mansion, we also have a future of hope. Our destiny is to one day be like God in our character: "We know that, when He appears, we shall be like Him, because we shall see Him just as He is" (1 John 3:2). The Bible calls this maturity: "until we all attain to the unity of the faith, and of the knowledge of the Son of God, to a mature man, to the measure of the stature of which belongs to the fulness of Christ" (Ephesians 4:13).

But what about the present? Like the mansion under construction, we are all in various stages of spiritual and emotional immaturity and disrepair. At times, we may feel like a burned-out bomb site; sometimes we can see a glimmer of the image of God in us. And sometimes both are apparent.

We have both a heritage established and a future planned by One who loves us as a parent. And our present is the link between the two. Our present is the time period in which the development and restoration of essential parts of our soul is to occur. It's that season in which blueprint (past) is supposed to become a completed project (future).

For most of us, the present can be a painful time of struggle. It's a period of being "under construction," and sometimes the process hurts. The Bible compares this pain to what a woman experiences in childbirth:

For we know that the whole creation groans and suffers the pains of childbirth together until now. And not only this, but also we ourselves, having the first fruits of the Spirit, even we ourselves groan within ourselves, waiting eagerly for our adoption as sons, the redemption of our body. (Romans 8:22-23)

People who have suffered great loss in their lives understand this passage. Being "under construction" means having to endure much.

Our basic problem in life is that we are an unfinished and damaged creation, somewhere in between the blueprint and the final whisk of the cleaning cloth. Just as a contractor provides labor and materials to build the structure, we are to be active participants in our own growth. The solution to our problem is to find our areas of spiritual and emotional immaturity, and to enter into the process of restoring those parts to their renovated condition.

THE UNFINISHED BUSINESS OF RELATIONSHIPS

The fundamental problem of being unfinished has many kinds of effects in our lives. One area of growth that many of us struggle with is a need for genuine, deep, warm personal relationships. Sometimes this need is manifested in a deep sense of not "belonging," of not "fitting in." It seems there is a void inside our hearts that just will not be filled.

The Bible proclaims our need for connection. At the deepest spiritual and emotional level, we are beings who need safety and a sense of belonging in our three primary relationships: God, self, and others. We begin life in a terrified and disconnected state. Disconnectedness is the most destructive result of sin's entrance into the universe. It is the deepest and most fundamental problem we can experience.

This disconnectedness is a violation of the very nature of God, of what He holds primary. God created us for a life of closeness and attachment. Jesus declared that the entire Hebrew Scriptures rested on loving God and people. Perhaps the number one root of emotional disorders is that some part of the self is isolated from relationship.

Jesus referred to our need to be close to Him in His picture of the vine that nourishes the branches:

> "Abide in Me, and I in you. As the branch cannot bear fruit of itself, unless it abides in the vine, so neither can you, unless you abide in Me. I am the vine, you are the branches; he who abides in Me, and I in him, he bears much fruit; for apart from Me you can do nothing." (John 15:4-5)

The Bible teaches that we are to form attachments with people, not only with God. We are to learn how to feel loved and experience a sense of belonging by being in relationship with others. That's why John emphasizes our people-to-people relationships:

> If someone says, "I love God," and hates his brother, he is a liar; for the one who does not love his brother whom he has seen, cannot love God whom he has not seen. (1 John 4:20)

John is declaring that our closeness to people is a measuring stick, to some extent, of our closeness to God. It is the rare person who can be deeply intimate with God and yet isolated and disconnected from His incarnate Body.

We are left with what may appear to be a simple formula:

Problem—our need for attachment.
Solution—find intimate relationships.

To the casual observer, this might seem uncomplicated. "Just find a good church with supportive people and begin to get involved; it can't be that difficult," one might conclude.

It's a different picture, however, for those who have had painful experiences or little experience of close involvement with others.

In many cases, believers suffering from isolation may even attend growing, healthy, biblically oriented churches that put a premium on caring relationships. They may be quite active in their fellowships, spending a great deal of time, effort, and money to be involved in a community of believers. Yet these same folks also report feeling disconnected, detached or "dead" inside, often while engaged in "fellowship activities."

"I tried changing churches," one person told me. "I thought if I got around different groups, I'd develop closeness. But the problem was the same at all the churches. I never really felt a part of things. So I decided to get in a good church and settle in—you know, make a commitment. I was at that church for five years. And now, half a decade later, I still feel on the outside. I thought at first it was people. Now I'm begining to think it might be me."

Meeting our emotional and spiritual needs is not as simple as it looks. This "added complication" in God's growth process is the essence of Problem #2: In many ways, *we hide from what we need to be whole.*

PROBLEM #2: WE FEAR WHAT WE NEED

One night, a policeman walking his beat encountered a man on his knees underneath a bright street lamp, desperately scouring the sidewalk.

"What's the matter?" the policeman queried.

Without looking up, the man cried, "I lost my wallet!"

"I'll be glad to help, sir," replied the patrolman. "Give me an idea of the area where you lost it."

"Oh, that's easy," said the distraught searcher. "It dropped out of my pocket about halfway down the block." The man pointed to another part of the street.

Puzzled, the policeman asked, "I'm confused—then why are we looking over here?"

The man answered without hesitation, "The light's better."

This story sums up the essence of the problem of hiding. The poor man who found himself walletless was frantically looking in the wrong place for the right thing. We have a similar malady. For a variety of reasons, many of us are afraid of exposing and repairing the broken parts of our souls.

That's Problem #2: Though we are an unfinished people, we fear and avoid the very things we need to restore us. We hide parts of our soul from love.

Notice I said "parts," not "part." Just as our bodies have many different muscles and bones that can be hurt, God has created us with different aspects—parts—of our souls. These various aspects can be loved and developed. They can also be isolated and immature. Each of us is a complex arrangement of such "parts" that together create a unique whole.

We will be dealing with our varied spiritual and emotional developmental needs later in this book, but it's important for each of us to realize that we're not the product of some cosmic cookie-cutter. We're *individuals*. David affirms this when he thanks God for supervising his own creation:

> For you created my inmost being; you knit me together in my mother's womb. I praise you because I am fearfully and wonderfully made; your works are wonderful, I know that full well. My frame was not hidden from you when I was made in the secret place. When I was woven together in the depths of the earth, your eyes saw my unformed body. All the days ordained for me were written in your book before one of them came to be. (Psalm 139:13-15, NIV)

Because of the effects of Adam and Eve's fall from innocence into sin, those "inward parts" made by God have been damaged in their ability to function in some way. Let's face it, sin injures us! And untangling the combination of "what's broken and why" is a major task we must undertake if we're to see those injured parts healed.

WHAT ABOUT ME?

Someone might ask at this point, "How does this describe me? I really try to be open and honest. My problem has more to do with relationships in which the other person is hiding."

I have a couple of answers to this. First, hiding isn't always a conscious process. Sometimes, our deep hurts and immaturities have been isolated from relationship for so long that we no longer have access to certain thoughts, feelings, or memories. In this case, hiding is a device used to protect us from overwhelming pain when we aren't ready for it.

A few verses after his prayer of thanks, David now asks God for more access to his "hidden parts":

> Search me, O God, and know my heart; try me and know my anxious thoughts; and see if there be any hurtful way in me, and lead me in the everlasting way. (Psalm 139:23-24)

David prayed for awareness of the truth about himself that he needed to look at. He didn't want to walk off a cliff blindfolded.

A second answer to the question of how this fear of exposure applies is that *different people hide different parts of the self.* Some struggle with being open about their needs to be loved. Others have difficulty bringing their more autonomous, self-directed parts into the light.

Sally, whom we met at the beginning of the chapter, didn't consider herself to be a withdrawn person. She was outgoing and expressive. Yet as she began working on important personal issues in counseling, she began realizing that an aggressive, decision-making part to her personality had been lost years ago. For Sally, this independent part of her soul was hidden from love and truth.

I'm writing to those of you who are hiding parts of yourself from relationship, whether or not you're currently aware of it. I want to help you uncover and bring before the grace of God and His people the wounded aspects of yourself that have been in darkness. God Himself and the Body of Christ can heal your hurt places.

Think over the past few years of your life. Review the "regrets": those relationships or opportunities that you wish had turned out positively. Many of us can date our problems in important relationships to a point at which we began to conceal parts of ourselves from God, self, or others.

HOW DO I KNOW WHAT I'M HIDING?

Many of us, like Sally, often don't truly know whether or not we're being defensive in some way. But we have a genuine desire to mature and develop the relationships we've been missing. Then how do we become aware of what's hidden?

A scriptural teaching can help us here. It's the principle of roots and fruits. God has designed the universe so that we can identify problems based on their effects on our lives.

For example, suppose you discover water dripping from the ceiling in your living room, ruining the carpet. You'll probably respond to this problem in one of two ways. One way is to engage in damage control. You'll keep empty pots and pans wherever the water is leaking and scurry around to keep them emptied. If you live in a rainy climate, this could become a full-time job. Plus it's hard to cook without cookware.

The second method of response that you might choose is to hire someone to come in and fix the leaky roof. This may cost more, but it will truly solve the problem.

The soggy carpet is the evidence or "fruit." It tells us that there's a serious problem in the structure of the house. The "root" is the leaky roof. If we don't pay attention to the root, we're likely to have much more bad fruit, such as thousands of dollars of damaged carpet and flooring.

Jesus talks about the principle of roots and fruits in Matthew 7:17-18:

> "Every good tree bears good fruit; but the bad tree bears bad fruit. A good tree cannot produce bad fruit, nor can a bad tree produce good fruit."

In other words, *results always point to causes*. Children are a good example. A family with loving, successful children is generally a sign of some good roots, such as parenting style, environment, and support. The family with troubled children is often a sign of some sort of struggle in the parents' lives.

The same is true in our lives. Our spiritual and emotional fruit points to our roots.

Let's look at another term to describe fruit: *symptoms,* a word used by physicians and therapists to mean the same thing: results or effects. Symptoms point to a root cause.

Hiding always has some fruit, or symptom. In other words, you and I can detect hiding in our lives by the problems it causes. When we hide, a part of our character is pushed away from relationship into a spiritual darkness called isolation. *The isolation of some part of our soul from love will always produce a problem.* This makes sense, because whatever is isolated from nourishment remains broken and undeveloped. In the physical world, we call this malnutrition. Spiritual and emotional malnutrition are just as destructive.

Symptoms can range from a failed marriage—like Sally's—to depression, anxiety, guilt feelings, shame, eating disorders, substance abuse, career conflicts, physical ailments, and many others. Remember, however, that symptoms can be our friends. They're doing the job that God intended for them, which is to tap us on the shoulder and say, "There's a problem—it's time to take a look at it."

But suppose there are no detectable symptoms in our life? Should we take a look at our defenses anyway? Certainly, prevention is better than cure. Recall David's prayer in Psalm 139. He asks God for awareness without mentioning any symptoms. It's likely that he's taking a preventive look at himself. So even if we appear to be without symptoms (which really isn't possible in a fallen world), we're wise to stay awake, spiritually and emotionally.

Awareness is not all we need, however. We require an environment of safe relationships in order to come out from hiding, no matter how much insight and information we have about our spiritual and emotional makeup. This is how God designed it.

This point is often missed in our Christian circles, where it is often assumed that doctrinal exposure to the truths of the Bible is sufficient to ensure solutions to all problems. Yet Jesus Himself stressed the necessity of relationship in order to take in truth. His statement "I am the way, and the truth, and the life" (John 14:6) is one indication that knowing a person is necessary to knowing his truth. To know here means to understand personally, not just intellectually. This "knowing" applies to relationships with people as well as with God.

The heart of God places great value on our needs being met. Jesus' anguish over His people's turning from His provision is a poignant picture:

> "O Jerusalem, Jerusalem, who kills the prophets and stones those who are sent to her! How often I wanted to gather your children together, the way a hen gathers her chicks under her wings, and you were unwilling." (Matthew 23:37)

God wants to help His people in their struggles. James tells us God is a gift-giver:

> Every good thing bestowed and every perfect gift is from above, coming down from the Father of lights, with whom there is no variation, or shifting shadow. (James 1:17)

The Bible presents God as a Father who is anxious to see His children taken care of. He delights in helping us, in providing for us.

Then why do we feel so bad so often?

That's the irony of the hiding problem. We all have needs; we're all unfinished. God has provided what we need to enter the healing and maturing process—becoming like Him. Yet in many areas of life, many of us feel spiritually and emotionally bankrupt, in pain, and unable to cope with life as we would like to. We're inherently unable to see what God has provided as good. It's as if He has laid out a banquet table for His children, inviting us to fill up, but something inside sees danger in the invitation and causes us to turn away.

This danger signal is the same one operating in our illustration at the beginning of the chapter: It caused Dan to turn from his need for caring, and Sally to avoid her need for autonomy.

Eating problems provide us a helpful example of the hiding dilemma. Several years ago, I was working in our hospital program with Rachel, a young woman with an eating disorder. Rachel had almost died from malnutrition several weeks before coming for help. She exercised obsessively, ate almost nothing, and worried that she was too heavy—at only eighty-five percent of her normal body weight. All of her family's and friends' efforts to get her to eat had failed.

Rachel's obvious problem was malnutrition. The "simplicity formula" would say: *Problem*—Rachel suffers from malnutrition. *Solution*—She needs a lot of good food. Yet she could not make herself take in the meals provided.

As I got to know Rachel, it became obvious there was much under the surface between her and her food. Let's go back to Problem #1: We are an unfinished people, in need of maturing. Rachel had come from a well-to-do, high-achieving Christian family. She was expected to follow her parents' lifestyle and career leanings. Her family had provided a safe structure of providing for her physical needs, but had placed little value on teaching Rachel the concept of thinking for herself. They had done too much for her and at the same time kept a tight rein on her behavior.

Over the years, Rachel had begun to symbolically equate relationship with food (love can also be symbolically confused with many things besides food, such as sex, performance, and admiration). She had begun believing that all people were as tight-reined as her parents were. In Rachel's words, "For me, to eat was to allow more of their control inside me. To refuse to eat was the only way to have any sense of control over my life. Food became the enemy."

Rachel came by this concealment of her own needs naturally. It's inbred in all of us. To understand the roots of our two biggest problems, we need to go back to the very first story in the Bible.

OUR DEEPEST ROOTS

Adam and Eve planted those first roots that keep sprouting into our hiding problems. When they ate from the forbidden tree of the knowledge of good and evil, they became acquainted with evil. This experiential knowledge of evil was something we weren't meant to have. That's the essence of Problem #1: a break in relationship with God, self, and others.

The roots of Problem #2 were planted shortly thereafter:

> Then the eyes of both of them were opened, and they real-
> ized they were naked; *so they sewed fig leaves together and
> made coverings for themselves.*
> Then the man and his wife heard the sound of the LORD
> God as he was walking in the garden in the cool of the day,
> and they hid from the LORD God among the trees of the gar-
> den. But the LORD God called to the man, "Where are you?"
> He answered, "I heard you in the garden, and *I was
> afraid because I was naked; so I hid.*" (Genesis 3:7-10, NIV;
> emphasis added)

Adam and Eve hid from God's restoring, forgiving, healing love. Notice the emphasized phrases. Adam and Eve had just moved out of a state of perfect attachment and obedience to God and into a state of separation and sinfulness. Yet the power of sin was already at work, shown in the solutions they conceived. First, they covered themselves. They put on the appearance that they did not have private parts. Second, they withdrew.

Why didn't they run to God, tell Him what they'd done, and ask Him to help them? They mistakenly saw God as someone who would hurt and not heal them. So they hid.

The story of the Fall presents a picture of the two main problems of living: the *task* of growing up, and the *obstacles* to growing up.

We can all relate to the conflict of our original parents in our sense of having a "secret," which is either our own fault or our own shame, so frightening that it would be inconceivable to tell another about it.

The writer of Hebrews calls us out of our life in hiding:

> Let us also lay aside every encumbrance, and the sin which
> so easily entangles us, and let us run with endurance the
> race that is set before us. (12:1)

Our subject is those encumbrances to our growth: where they come from, how they operate, what they tell us, and what we can do about them.

The process of spiritual and emotional maturing is difficult enough in itself, even without hindrances. Near the end of his life, Paul called himself "foremost" among sinners, an indication of how much work goes into anyone's growth.

But this difficult process is paralyzed when—because of past experiences, fears, shame, and pride—we withdraw from the very relationships and truths that would mature us. Our "fig leaves" keep us isolated from God, self, and others. They perpetuate not only our destructive patterns of living, but also our symptoms.

The safety of the walls we build as children can become a trap in our adult lives, as what was once a protection now becomes a prison. We build a safe place for ourselves when we hide, but those walls can prevent us from entering into the good things God has for us.

REMEMBER JENNY

Ideas are like prescription pills. They go down better with some sort of coating. Jesus explained many important spiritual issues in parables. His tales helped people understand concepts in terms of pictures.

The "coating" for our exploration of hiding from love is Jenny's story. Jenny represents all of us. She'll appear at the end of each chapter, fleshing out the truths we're learning. I hope that as you get to know Jenny, you'll recognize your own hiding process in her story.

We all have parts of our character that, like Jenny, have retreated deep inside the Deep Woods of our hearts. There those parts remain. For decades, perhaps, these hidden parts have been kept safe from abandonment, ridicule, or annihilation. Yet they have also remained frightened, disconnected, undeveloped, and unloved.

Jenny is a picture of the state of humanity since the Fall—desperately needing restoration, but terrified of exposure. We'll discover in the next chapter how these problems can open up opportunities for growth.

CHAPTER THREE

"This Wasn't in Plan A"

✛

"IT'S AMAZING," mused Sherri one afternoon during our discussion. "I never realized how much peoples' backgrounds mattered." Sherri was referring to what she had begun learning about herself and her husband of fourteen years.

After beginning treatment for a chronic depression that had lasted several years, Sherri gradually realized that much of her struggle had to do with her own hiding patterns. She was constantly on guard against making mistakes and being "found out" by others. Because of this fear, Sherri found herself spending a great deal of time and energy constructing an image of herself to her friends that seemed happy and problem-free.

Sherri's defensive fears were so pronounced that when she was asked to meet with her boss without knowing what it was about she experienced heart flutters, lightheadedness, and body tremors—all signs of a panic attack. Sherri identified the source of her anxiety as her projection that her boss was going to expose and criticize her mistakes on the job. Actually, the boss wanted to ask Sherri's advice on a budgeting plan.

Sherri had spent the majority of her life hiding her mistakes and failures from others. The "false self" she had created had finally taken its toll on her, and her depression was a symptom of the isolation and exhaustion she felt.

Sherri had never been able to understand her husband, Bill. His resiliency and openness had both drawn her to him and made her envious of him since their dating days.

Bill's mistakes and failure were parts of himself to which he'd always readily admitted without shame or fear. Bill had been fired from a job several years ago. After a short period of being upset, he told her one day, "Actually, they were right—I'm not the right person for their line of work."

"I'd never be able to say that—the firing would devastate me," Sherri admitted. "I guess Bill's never pretended to be anyone he's not. Yet I'm constantly checking to see if anyone's found out my bad points. Why am I so scared—and yet he's so relaxed—about who we are?" Sherri queried.

As she explored and contrasted her own family background with Bill's, Sherri reached some startling conclusions. Failure had been a taboo topic in her family. As a young girl, whenever Sherri had earned a poor grade in school, she met an icy silence from her parents. Spilling her milk at the dinner table required her to clean up the mess quickly while the rest of the family looked on uncomfortably, waiting for her to finish before resuming conversation.

Sherri had learned to experience mistakes as painfully uncomfortable—something to avoid and hide from, even if it meant changing her own personality. And so she learned to protect herself from the dreaded discomfort.

In Bill's family, no one took failure very seriously. In fact, much of the dinner conversation involved telling tales on themselves in which the teller was the foolish one, who then joined in the family's warm laughter. They laughed with, not at, each other. Mistakes were treated as part of life. Something to learn from. Definitely not something to fear.

These insights helped Sherri understand how the differences between herself and Bill could be traced to different family backgrounds: one that encouraged hiding and one that had little need for such defenses.

THE WAY IT WAS SUPPOSED TO BE

The story of Sherri and Bill provides a good introduction to a crucial principle: *God never intended hiding to be a part of our lives.* It wasn't part of His own "Plan A."

If it weren't for the Fall, there would have been no Problem #1: that is, no sin—no need for our restoration into the image of God. And there would have been no Problem #2: we would have no need to hide.

God had a "Plan A" for us: a life of unbroken connectedness with Him and each other. Not only was there to be unbroken attachment, but we were also to experience a deep, satisfying sense of purpose and accomplishment in performing the task that He gave to us:

"Be fruitful and multiply, and fill the earth, and subdue it; and rule over the fish of the sea and over the birds of the sky, and over every living thing that moves on the earth." (Genesis 1:28)

The two verbs *rule* and *subdue* summarize any job we now have. The subduing function refers to the more entrepreneurial, pioneering, groundbreaking tasks of life. Starting a business can be a subduing role. So can some aspects of motherhood. The ruling function has more to do with running an already-operating system. Administrative and managerial duties are part of the ruling category.

In other words, our lives were meant to be filled with relationships and activity, or love and work. This doesn't mean that Adam and Eve weren't intended to learn, mature, or grow. *Perfection doesn't exclude growth.* A gardener who raises perfect roses begins with perfect seeds. Perfection simply means that *things are as they should be at a given stage of development.*

The last time you began a new job you probably endured some sort of apprenticeship or training period. During that time you were exposed to the duties of the position, tried them out, made mistakes, and tried again. Then, over time, your skill increased and you became competent. Or it didn't, and you changed jobs.

If you were in a wise company, your mistakes were expected. Your superiors knew that the term *training* meant just that. There was no penalty for failure, except failure to learn from mistakes. The slogan, "The only dumb question is the one you didn't ask" is the sign of a good business.

SINLESS IMMATURITY

The idea that sinlessness and immaturity might go together may be confusing for some. One might ask, "Immaturity, imperfection, are they the same? Most of the immature people I know are definitely imperfect." The term *immature* does conjure up negative images in most of us – the self-centered man, or the woman whose emotions easily go out of control. And actually, those *are* images of immaturity.

What makes them seem wrong, however, is that immature adults present both *mature* parts of their character along with *immature* parts at the same time. They don't fit together. Have you ever encountered a person who has a problem with immature reactions – say, a temper tantrum? Often, the explosion occurs only during certain periods of loss or stress, when the possibility of regression is greater. At other times, the individual may appear adult and reasonable.

Immaturity, then, only means that a goal has not yet been reached for something. For example, Adam was created perfect. But he was not mature. Had he been mature, he would not have needed God's instruction – he would immediately have begun subduing and ruling. He wouldn't have needed lessons from God on how to rule the earth.

Also, being fruitful and multiplying speaks of the reproductive cycle in which little ones learn how to become adults. We were never intended to be born as adults.

We find another indication that learning and growth existed before the Fall. The Hebrew word for "subdue" implies that the one being subdued is resistant to the subduer.[1] In other words, Adam and Eve were to learn how to cultivate an undomesticated, young planet. Parents understand the taming process of "subduing." Anyone who has ever seen the intense emotions of a baby has seen a picture of uncultivated, raw joy, love, tears, anger, and fear. Over time, with proper care, these become more manageable and mature.

Jesus Himself also experienced growing, practicing, and learning. The Scriptures tell us that He "kept increasing in wisdom and stature, and in favor with God and men" (Luke 2:52). Jesus put Himself through the same on-the-job training that we go through to learn about life, yet without sin. In fact, like His mother's husband, Joseph, Jesus had a profession: carpentry (Mark 6:3). Perhaps He winced through a few mashed thumbs on the way to becoming proficient.

THE TWO TYPES OF GROWTH

It's important here to distinguish the two types of growth that we constantly deal with in the process of becoming mature Christians. We have been talking about one of these that existed before the Fall. From eternity past, God designed this type of growth as a process of moving from undamaged, perfect immaturity to adulthood. That is, Adam was just as he should have been, yet not who he would be later. This type of "pre-Fall" growth is called "maturing growth."

Maturing Growth
In the maturing growth phase, we learn to develop those aspects of God's character that He imparted to us. Recall our reconstructed mansion in chapter 2. In one sense, it was actually a "new" building, in the process of moving from incompleteness to completeness. Like that building, our maturity is part of the completion process.

If you've ever noticed the delight that a one-year-old has in touching, tasting, and banging objects, you've observed maturing growth. The baby is excitedly learning to relate to his world, what it's made of, how it operates, and how he can impact it.

A perfect rose comes from a perfect rosebud. The bud isn't

what it will be yet, but it's perfectly as it should be in its present stage of development.

Maturing growth moves us from a young "good" place to a mature "good" place. This is the process Paul referred to in 2 Corinthians 3:18:

> But we all, with unveiled face beholding as in a mirror the glory of the Lord, are being transformed into the same image from glory to glory, just as from the Lord, the Spirit.

Theologian Charles Ryrie says that the phrase "from glory to glory" refers to a state of "from one degree of glory to another."[2] It's moving from a good place to a better place.

Maturing growth means that if we find someone in our life we care deeply about, our love can deepen further. If we have a passion for a job that means something to us, we can deepen our satisfaction in it. That seems to be the reason why people who have had the benefit of several long-term relationships in their lifetimes look back fondly at their lives. They were able to enlarge their hearts with these relationships over time, "from glory to glory."

On the other hand those who have been less fortunate in relationships and have had a lifelong string of failed relationships tend to end their years with regret and bitterness. For whatever reason, maturing growth wasn't something they were able to experience.

One struggle many Christians experience related to maturing growth is a lack of patience with themselves or others in not being "instantly finished." One patient I saw married in his late thirties. Since Jack's and his wife's friends had mostly been married in their mid-to-late twenties, suddenly he was exposed to the fact that many of the marriages around him had answered questions that he and his bride were still dealing with.

Yet it was difficult for Jack to see that he had a "baby marriage" and his friends had "older marriages." "I should be able to solve the conflicts that my friends can solve," he would say. An inability to deal with the process of maturing caused him much guilt, frustration, and shame. The difference in years of practice was the reason the marriages were different.

Restoring Growth

Jack's example pictures an undamaged but young marriage. That's maturing growth. The second kind of growth is different: I call it "restoring growth." This part of the mansion was damaged in our earlier illustration. There had been some improper caretaking done to the structure by weather and neglect, and it had been bought and revamped by the house-loving couple.

Restoring growth means that there is a problem. Something is broken and needs fixing. We are unable to move out of our damaged position by ourselves. The brokenness is a result of a combination of our own sin (see Romans 3:9-20,23) and someone else's sin against us.

Let's understand "sin against us." Christians usually see quickly how our own innate sin leads us into painful consequences. In fact, I've seen a great deal of abuse of this principle by well-meaning friends of hurting people who blamed all of the hurting person's depression, anxiety, or other symptoms on "unconfessed sin."

This thinking can be destructive for a couple of reasons. First, it's not always true. Many emotional and spiritual struggles have nothing to do with someone's choices to rebel. God presents this principle in the second commandment:

> "You shall not make for yourself an idol . . . for I, the LORD your God, am a jealous God, visiting the iniquity of the fathers on the children, on the third and the fourth generations of those who hate Me." (Exodus 20:4-5)

In fact, this could have been what Jesus' disciples were thinking of when they saw the man blind from birth and asked Jesus, "Rabbi, who sinned, this man or his parents, that he should be born blind?" (John 9:2).

The point here is that damage comes from more than one direction: ourselves, and those who have been destructive to us.

The Bible addresses these two aspects of the sin problem in the same place: "The heart is more deceitful than all else and is desperately sick; who can understand it?" (Jeremiah 17:9).

The term *deceitful* refers to our own sinful parts. It comes from a Hebrew word meaning to be crooked, or supplant. "Desperately sick" refers to a wounded state, indicating our damaged condition rather than our evil nature. God wants to help us deal with both kinds of problems.

Child abuse is a good example of the "sinned against" problem. The adult who was mistreated in his early years had some violence done to his soul at a point where there was no choice given to him. In fact, Jesus angrily denounced the hurtful influence that others can have on us: "But whoever causes one of these little ones who believe in Me to stumble, it is better for him that a heavy millstone be hung around his neck, and that he be drowned in the depth of the sea" (Matthew 18:6).

Jesus is stating a principle here: *We are an injured, as well as a sinful, people.* Not all of our scars from the past are self-inflicted.

The second problem with pointing blame at the wounded person is that this absolves the helper of a hurting person of any responsibility. If the depression or eating disorder continues after the "sin" has been confronted, the counselor can simply say, "Well, I told him to stop. It's up to him to listen to my advice." That's an easy out for the helper. This is a source of much destructiveness in Christian circles today.

MATURING VERSUS RESTORING GROWTH

We'll deal later with those specific parts of the soul that become injured and go into hiding. For now, it's important to understand the relationship of maturing growth to restoring growth. Fundamentally, maturing and restoring growth involve the same process. There is no qualitative difference between the two.

The only real difference between our normal spiritual growth and our growth out of damage is their relationship to time. Maturing growth deals with our "on schedule" parts. Restoring growth deals with our "behind schedule" parts. Maturing growth is developing the undamaged aspects of the soul, while restoring growth concentrates on those parts that are damaged—that is, still lost in the past in an undeveloped state.

God's process of spiritual growth is to reach into the soul, where the hurt parts of the person have been stuck in their injured place. With love, truth, and people, He helps bring those parts of the personality that are younger than the rest of the self back into sync with the whole.

Think of a garden producing different seasonal vegetables. Spring may bring lettuce; autumn may produce corn. Around April, the spring vegetables will appear much more mature than the autumn plants. The fall vegetables cannot "catch up" to the spring ones.

Chuck, a forty-five-year-old Christian businessman, left his wife and family and bought a new wardrobe, a red sportscar, and a membership to a singles' club all in the same four months. His friends were at a loss to understand the radical changes in this otherwise stable, responsible family man. This didn't seem to be a "part" of him.

After a year of adolescent living, Chuck suffered a nervous breakdown and was hospitalized for depression. As he began working on his struggles, he realized that forty-five was the age his father had been when he died of a heart attack. Chuck's father had always expected Chuck to be mature and responsible. Chuck had not been allowed to go through that period of transitional rethinking as a prelude to adulthood that we call "adolescence."

When Chuck reached the age at which his father died, he had become depressed and panicked that he would die after having been a parent to both his family of origin and his own family.

The part of Chuck that was damaged and in need of restoring growth was his broken will, his ability to make free choices without a sense of obligation. When his father insisted on duty without choice, Chuck's will went into hiding, outside of awareness, outside of time, and away from access to the healing elements he needed to grow. There it stayed, in isolation, while the rest of him grew up without it.

Growing in Both Ways

We need both types of growth. We need to keep maturing into the image of God in those areas in which we are undamaged. That was the "pre-Fall" plan. But we also need to find and let God restore those aspects of our souls that are damaged, in a state of permanent immaturity, split off from relationship, and in need of restoring growth. Restoring growth is redemption. It is "buying back." It is God's reclaiming, by Jesus' death, what has been lost.

It isn't easy to know what parts of ourselves do need restoring growth. We will discuss this in more detail in later chapters. The prime place to start, however, is to notice what parts of our character begin malfunctioning under stress or in times of loss.

Have you ever seen a small child at play, trying desperately to keep up with an older sibling and her friends? She runs faster, tries harder, and talks louder to fit in, but she's just out of place. That's how our injured parts feel. They can't keep up. They're out of place.

Vivian, a working mother who entered our hospital treatment program, stated it this way: "I'm so adult in so many ways. I'm a professional person, a good parent and wife, and I love the Lord. But whenever my boss is angry with me, I immediately begin losing my grown-up feelings, and start feeling like a bad little girl, about three years old, who's being punished." Vivian was identifying a part of herself in need of restoring growth, one that became injured and paralyzed when she was the target of someone's anger.

HOLINESS VERSUS THE "SPLIT"

Many of us can identify with Vivian's experience. It's as if some of our different parts—perhaps our feelings, our actions, or our thoughts—don't mesh together well. There's a "jolt," like when your car's engine misfires every few seconds. We were meant to function with all aspects of our character working together in an integrated fashion, like the pistons of a finely tuned engine firing at precisely the right moment so the car moves smoothly along.

That's the goal of our growth process into Christlikeness: the integration of our character into a smoothly functioning whole. The term *holiness* in the Scriptures refers to believers being wholly devoted to and connected to God, and detached from evil. It is a positive attachment to Him and a refusal of whatever does not come from Him.

God wants us to have this sense of belonging to Him only: "You shall be holy, for I the LORD your God am holy" (Leviticus 19:2). That's why people who have injured parts never feel "right"— something is not attached to the rest of themselves, nor to God. People with compulsive disorders—for example, addiction to food, work, sex, or substances—often feel that they have a "split" in their hearts. Life's fine for a while; then periodically the "split" occurs and they operate in destructive ways, feeling very much out of control. Then life settles down again, almost as if the "split" had never happened. What remains for this person is only a guilty or shameful memory.

That "split" is the opposite of holiness. It is the evidence that part of us is struggling to be reconnected to God, self, or others. The split prevents us from growing. When the broken part is reconnected, God's growth plan resumes itself.

The term *splitting* needs a bit of explanation here. It can be somewhat confusing, as it can actually refer to more than one thing. Here is a brief explanation of the three main ways "splitting" is used in the book:

1. *Splitting as the alienation that occurred as a result of the Fall.* Sin broke our original closeness between God, others, and ourselves. Intimacy was "split" and a wall of enmity was formed instead, such as the one mentioned between Gentiles and Jews in Ephesians 2.

2. *Splitting as an inability to experience the good and bad of ourselves or others together.* This happens to the person who feels "all bad" when he experiences a minor failure. This type of splitting is largely due to a deficit in grace: that is, the person is afraid that his badness will overwhelm his, and God's, goodness. It's an emotional all-or-nothing struggle, and can be resolved only by experiencing the forgiveness of God and His people.

3. *Splitting as losing access to certain aspects of the soul*

because of some injury to those aspects. In other words, some people have "split off" their loving characteristics because love resulted in abandonment. Though these split-off parts still exist in the soul, they are injured, undeveloped, and lost to conscious awareness. These individuals can't "sense" certain feelings or aspects of themselves.

A concern that many Christians struggle with is the problem of identifying where they are in the growth process. Not everyone needs hospitalization, individual outpatient counseling, or group therapy. These are resources for those problems that have become sufficiently disruptive to cause moderate to severe difficulties in everyday functioning.

You may be able to identify your own hiding patterns. You may be aware of ways you have been injured, and ways you have stayed injured. Yet the level of severity of your hiding may not warrant professional help.

This is where the resources of God can clearly emerge in all their varied ways: closely knit relationships in local, growing churches; time in God's Word; thoughtful, fervent prayer for ourselves and others; reliance on God's Spirit; and exposure to helpful biblical teachers on areas of healing growth can make a great difference in helping us come out of hiding.

AN ARMY WITHOUT AN ENEMY

But let's go back to maturing growth—the original plan. We were created to be growers, learners, and students. We were meant to learn to receive and give love, and to be active and productive. A large part of that process is trial and error. It is experimentation, or practice: "But solid food is for the mature, who by constant use have trained themselves to distinguish good from evil" (Hebrews 5:14, NIV). As we make mistakes, we are to learn each time.

Hiding wasn't meant to be part of the practice process. Before the Fall, practice, mistakes, and "training errors" had no fear of condemnation or loss of attachment connected to them. Fig leafs were not standard issue for "subduing."

Instead of causing us shame, errors we make while practicing should draw others closer to us. Our learning curve should bring us love. Steve's case is an example.

Steve entered the hospital program with anxiety attacks and a deep defensive pattern. He was bent on feeling "great," "on top of it," and "other positive mental attitude experiences." With a permanent smile on his face, Steve was upbeat and cheerful.

Finally, Steve's group members in the program had enough. "Steve, we don't feel like you can weep with us when we need it," they told him. "Where are your own hurts?"

Gradually, Steve began seeing his lifelong pattern of being forever positive and keeping his depressed mother buoyed up. Finally, one day in group he said, "I just want to say that today I really feel sadness—I'm remembering my past, that it wasn't as great as I like to think it was, and there's a lot of pain there. I don't have much to give anybody today."

To Steve's surprise, the group verbally swarmed over him in affirmation and several said, "Now I feel like I know the rest of you—not just the 'up' part."

Steve had discovered that exposing problems to others in this particular group didn't bring him shame or condemnation, but increased attachment. That's how God meant it to be. Our humanness draws other loving humans to us. We all feel like we belong to each other when we're all telling the truth.

There was no need for hiding in Plan A. It's a little like having an army without an enemy. There's just no need for the army. That's why hiding is learned, rather than intrinsic. It's not an innate trait. Before the Fall, in a world with no danger, we didn't need protection.

Obviously, the situation has changed since then. In the next two chapters we'll be dealing with the needs we have that require protection. For now, let's recall how Jenny dealt with detachment and how she learned an important way to protect herself while in hiding:

In the weeks following her parents' arrest, fear and loneliness became Jenny's constant companions. She hated being alone, but she was more afraid of exposure, especially to the men in uniform.

During her worst moments, the little lost girl thought her heart would break from the sadness. She missed Mother and Father so much! During these sad times, Jenny learned to comfort and soothe herself with warm memories of the old days at home. She replayed favorite scenes, of love and safety, over and over, gathering as much warmth from them as she could.

In one of her favorite scenes, Jenny was sitting in her mother's lap by the fire on a quiet night. Her father read stories to her from his chair nearby, while her mother rocked her until drowsiness turned into sleep. Then she was gently carried off to bed and lovingly tucked in.

Jenny's memories of the safety of her family life helped her survive. She remembered a time in her life when there was no need for hiding. These memories weren't much, but they were all she had access to.

You and I also have a safe place in our heritage back in the Garden of Eden. There is a part of all of us that longs for that safety, when there was no need for hiding.

Our human nature was scarred terribly at the Fall. We became a depraved and sinful people. But the image of God in us was only scarred; it was not completely destroyed.

As bearers of the image of God we have an opportunity through the person of Jesus Christ to "reattach" to our Maker and experience the redemption of our souls and the reconstruction of our memories of Him. At the same time, once we have that reattachment through salvation, we have a new opportunity to review our own hiding patterns. We're now better able to evaluate why we detach from God and others, and how hiding actually protects us at times from further evil. In other words, we can learn when hiding is helpful and when it may harm us. Like Jenny, our memory of safety can help us survive.

NOTES   1. R. Laird Harris, Gleason L. Archer, and Bruce Waltke, *Theological Wordbook of the Old Testament* (Chicago: Moody Press, 1979), page 430.

2. Ryrie Study Bible (Chicago: Moody Press, 1987), text footnotes on 2 Corinthians 3:18.

CHAPTER FOUR

Our Need
for Attachment

✣

T HE FALL changed things for us. You and I now live in a world
that isn't as safe as when God first designed it. There are
dangers within us and dangers outside of us.[1] Those of us
who have been betrayed by another person, or even by our own
hearts, know this firsthand.

This is why the Bible warns, "Watch over your heart with all
diligence, for from it flow the springs of life" (Proverbs 4:23). Yet
it's not enough simply to understand that we need protection. *We
need to know what parts of our soul need protecting.*

God has created within us different, specific parts of the soul
that need safety as we continue the process of maturity. As we
understand these different parts, we become more able to pay
attention to the weaker, more immature aspects of the self that
need more help. To understand this better, let's take a deeper look
at the soul.

Imagine the soul as a castle ruled by a king. To protect and
secure the castle, the king has posted trained sentries in strategic
areas. In order to perform their job functions, these sentries need
to know the nature of the area they're protecting.

For instance, one group of guards may look after the food and supplies of the castle. Another might watch over the weapons and ammunition. A third group could guard the royal family's living quarters. Each protected area needs specific kinds of support to be safe.

Our souls are a remarkable creation of God, capable of great resiliency, yet at the same time extremely fragile. Let's look now at those vulnerable, fragile parts.

DEVELOPMENTAL NEEDS: OUR VULNERABLE PARTS

The best way to understand what parts of us we are to take care of is to look at our *developmental needs*, the foundational building blocks that make up who we are. These needs prepare us for living and working in the world in an adult fashion. God has arranged these needs in definable stages of maturity that we are to grow through.

Spiritual growth is a stage-specific process. In other words, the Bible speaks of growth in identifiable steps that build one upon the other. As one is completed, we move to the next, just as a plant grows from seedling to shoot to maturity. John refers to this when he writes to believers in three different stages (1 John 2:12-14). He addresses:

Little children—new believers, whose "sins are forgiven";
Young men—maturing believers, who "have overcome the
     evil one"; and
Fathers—mature believers, who "know Him."

We learn from John that each different stage has different tasks assigned to it. The young Christian is to experience the intense gratitude and freedom of forgiveness. The maturing believer is to be encountering and combatting evil. The mature Christian is to know God in a deeper way with a more eternal perspective.

Not only do we have different tasks for our differing stages, but also different ingredients to help us grow. The writer of Hebrews refers to it in this way:

You have come to need milk and not solid food. For everyone who partakes only of milk is not accustomed to the word of righteousness, for he is a babe. But solid food is for the mature. (Hebrews 5:12-14)

Have you ever known middle-aged people who can't seem to master the task of emotional intimacy? If so, then you can understand better that they haven't yet grown through the "milk stage." These individuals have a handicap in relating to others in a mature way.

The Scriptures paint a picture of our spiritual and emotional needs as a process of developmental stages. God didn't fashion us out of a cookie-cutter mold; we are much more complex than that. Our needs are built on each other in a logical order. Just like the mansion, the foundation must come before the roof, or both will suffer. As we work through the tasks required in each stage, we progress to a new and deeper level of maturity that prepares us for the next. (For a more in-depth perspective on this developmental stages model, see *When Your World Makes No Sense* by Dr. Henry Cloud.[2])

OUR FIRST NEED: ATTACHMENT

There it was again: Stuart's blank look every time Betsy would reach out and ask him for emotional support. We were in our third session of marital counseling, and the relational difficulties were beginning to surface. The couple had come largely due to Betsy's feeling of dissatisfaction with the level of intimacy in the marriage. When I'd asked her what she meant, her eyes filled with tears and she began talking about loneliness and emptiness in her life.

While she spoke, I noticed that Stuart seemed concerned, in a polite sort of way. He would pat her hand while she wept. He asked, "Anything I can do?" But there was no sense of empathy for the pain Betsy was feeling. It was like Stuart was tuned to a different channel than she was—or, perhaps, to no channel.

"What are you feeling right now, Stuart?" I asked.

"Well," he replied, "I hope Betsy gets better soon."

"Betsy's talking about a deep, lonely place in her heart," I continued. "Is that a feeling you're familiar with?"

He thought for a second. "I—don't think so. Being alone is sort of a relief for me. I get nervous around people. I thought everyone felt this way until I met Betsy."

Stuart was not a hostile or uncaring husband. He was kind and responsible, and he genuinely wanted to be good to Betsy. But her needs were confusing for him. Stuart had a deficit in his ability to connect emotionally. This deficit was limiting his marriage.

What is an attachment?

Almost everyone has heard of the adventuresome boy who, one winter, was dared by his pals to lick the sheet of ice covering the house. An hour later, with the help of a pail of warm water, he was able to stop "kissing the house." From his first tug after putting tongue to surface, he had learned something about attachment. Pieces of boy were attaching to the house, and vice versa.

An attachment between people, and between people and God, is like that. You know you're attached when you experience loss after someone you love leaves you. Their "pieces" stay in your heart. The sad feelings are a sign of how deeply the person got inside you. Individuals who can't feel that sadness have an incapacity to be close. That sadness is a mixed blessing.

Our ability to attach is our ability to relate our spiritual and emotional needs to others. The key word here is "relate." To relate our needs to others is to connect, or expose ourselves to them. Attachment means letting others inside the private, vulnerable parts of ourselves.

This isn't necessarily a description of friendship. Friendship can be an attachment. Then again, it can be an acquaintance. Not all friendships are bonds, though all bonds are friendships. Attachments occur when we take the risk to allow someone else to matter enough to us to hurt us if they choose to.

Attachment, or bondedness, is our deepest need. This is because it is also the deepest part of the character of God.

The Bible goes so far as to identify the very nature of God with love: "God is love" (1 John 4:8). Love, which comprises the deepest part of who God is, determines what He does: "For God so loved the world, that He gave His only begotten Son" (John 3:16).

We see this principle of attachment in other places besides the character of God. It's also the guiding law of God's universe. God is pro-relationship and anti-isolation. The world is constructed so that there's a ripple effect from one thing to another. Everything affects everything else.

We see this in the physical universe. The term *ecosystem* has become increasingly familiar in recent years. It refers to the idea that the earth is a delicate balance of millions of factors, from microbes to humankind. Remove one of these relationships, and the system is injured. The result is an increasingly worn-out planet, less and less able to sustain life.

Relationships are portrayed as crucial in the Bible. As I've said, Jesus pictured His attachment to us as a vine and branches: "As the branch cannot bear fruit of itself, unless it abides in the vine, so neither can you, unless you abide in Me" (John 15:4). Connection is necessary for survival.

Our need for connection extends not only to God. It also means we need each other. During the Creation, the only "not good" God mentioned in an otherwise perfect universe was that Adam was alone. God wasn't simply dealing with the benefits of marriage in this passage. He was addressing the deeper issue of our need for attachment and relationship, of which marriage is one important component.

Isolation has disastrous consequences. Solomon stated it this way:

> Two are better than one because they have a good return for their labor. For if either of them falls, the one will lift up his companion. But *woe to the one who falls when there is not another to lift him up.* Furthermore, if two lie down together they keep warm, but how can one be warm alone? (Ecclesiastes 4:9-11; emphasis added)

People who suffer from depression often have a deep sense of isolation in their lives. Individuals with an isolation-induced depression will report that their heart feels cold and lifeless. This coldness is the lack of warmth referred to by Solomon, which only relationship can bring.

We see perhaps the most explicit example of the "ripple effect" of relationship in the New Testament passages on the Church. Believers are inextricably and mysteriously entwined as part of the Body of Christ on earth, so much that "if one member suffers, all the members suffer with it; if one member is honored, all the members rejoice with it" (1 Corinthians 12:26).

ATTACHMENT AS A DEVELOPMENTAL NEED

It's easy to see why attachment would be our first, and primary, developmental task. Since the Fall, we come out of the womb empty, terrified, and isolated, part of the legacy of pain Adam and Eve bequeathed humanity. More than anything, we need to be drawn in to love, to be connected out of our aloneness.

For my wife, Barbi, and me, one of the more difficult things about the birth of our son Ricky was that for the first few minutes of his life he was being weighed, tested, and observed. Though it was only a brief interlude before the doctor handed him over to Barbi, it was gut-wrenching to see and hear Ricky's terror and disconnection. Then, just as quickly, as he was held and soothed, he began to quiet down and fall asleep.

The beginning of life should be a sense of welcome, transferred from parent to child, a feeling of "you belong with us . . . we're glad you're here . . . you're a part of this family." The concept of the Church is built on a sense of family: "So then you are no longer strangers and aliens, but you are fellow citizens with the saints, and are of God's household" (Ephesians 2:19). The Body of Christ is God's second "family" for us, after the biological one.

The entire first year of life is ideally built around helping the infant to take in, or internalize, this sense of belonging and safety. Internalization takes thousands of experiences of the parents' being there for the infant when he needs them. This is because we are creatures of memory.

God gives us memory to help us understand the world and avoid mistakes. The church of Ephesus was to "remember therefore from where you have fallen, and repent" (Revelation 2:5)—in other words, to learn humility from their past. Israel's struggles "happened as examples for us, that we should not crave evil things, as they also craved" (1 Corinthians 10:6).

It's particularly sad to see people in the later years of life who, for some reason, weren't able to learn the lessons God had placed in their path. Their lives become riddled not with thousands of bad decisions about love and work, but with the same bad decision thousands of times.

The infant builds an emotional picture of the world inside, based primarily on how he was treated in this first year. If his mother is responsive to his needs for holding, feeding, or changing when he cries, cuing in to his needs and not her own schedule, he learns over time that the world is a reasonably safe and predictable place.

Internalization means that the infant receives his mother inside him as his representation, or image, of the world.

The goal of good attachment is *emotional object constancy.* This term refers to a state of feeling connected even when one is alone, or "being rooted and grounded in love" (Ephesians 3:17). It's the result of responding to many experiences of constant reassurance by a primary caregiver.

As love is taken in, it forms an emotional memory that soothes and comforts us in times of stress. The infant who panics when her mother leaves the room has not yet attained emotional object constancy. The baby who looks for her mother and protests for a few seconds when she leaves, then occupies herself otherwise, is closer to the goal.

An extreme example of a lack of object constancy is the condition known as autism. A combination of genetic and environmental factors, autism is an almost-complete cutting off of the child's ability to connect emotionally. This is in no way an intellectual deficit. Autistic children are quite often extremely bright. Autism is an emotional deficit—a relational prison preventing the child from connecting to his world.

Attachment deficits occur in different forms. There's a common denominator, however: *a lack of connectedness in the person's significant relationships.* The detached person was not "met where he was" in some way.

At times, this lack is blatant, such as the emotionally cold or hostile family. It's clear that here the need for constancy was not met. Other times, it is more subtle, as in the superficially warm family that appears to be intimate. In this case, there's generally a withdrawal of the warmth when painful subjects are brought up. The developing child learns that she can be attached when she doesn't have needs or problems. But her hurts and fears go deep inside into an isolated place in the heart, where they may stay for a lifetime.

Just as connectedness is our most basic need, isolation is our most injurious state. The most severe punishment in prisons throughout history has always been solitary confinement. In fact, the whole message of the gospel is the restoration of connectedness between God and humanity.[3] Why is isolation so serious?

The reason is found in the law of entropy, or the second law of thermodynamics. This law of physics states that things that are isolated move toward deterioration. After a hundred years, a junk heap will turn into a rustier junk heap. Vegetables left too long in the refrigerator will tend toward something resembling penicillin. And people in their thirties begin noticing that staying in good physical shape takes more effort than it once did. During Sunday afternoon football, they don't get off the ground quite as quickly after a hard tackle.

Entropy operates in the spiritual world, too. Whatever is cut off tends toward deterioration. That's why the ultimate punishment, hell, is not defined by loss of consciousness or annihilation, but by its utter and complete separation from the love of God.[4] Jesus' sacrifice for us involved His own separation from the Father when He became sin on our behalf.[5] He suffered in that "He was cut off out of the land of the living" (Isaiah 53:8). In other words, there is no life without relationship.

It's quite common for believers to have active, purposeful lives in which they seem to have their "priorities right." These same Christians are often bewildered by painful psychological symptoms that don't appear to make sense until the quality of their personal attachments is investigated.

Sheila is an example of this dilemma. "But I'm doing everything right," she told me. "I'm a committed believer. Jesus really is Lord of my life. I work hard. I help people as much as I can. I try to stay away from unhelpful activities and influences. So why do I wake up in the morning not wanting to live?"

Sheila's schedule was full of helpful activities. Her commitment to God was authentic. But her life was devoid of relating to anyone on other than a "helper-helpee" basis, with her as the helper. *She was unable to ask for comfort for herself.* Though busy, Sheila's life was meaningless and empty.

When Jesus called us to be like little children,[6] He was referring to the openness that children have in asking for their needs to be met. Humbly acknowledging our need, rather than pretending to be self-sufficient, should characterize our lives. Sheila was lost in sincere but misguided self-sufficiency.

A lack of emotional object constancy always shows up in some form during adulthood. "I don't believe you," one patient said to me in the hospital program. "You're saying my eating disorder has to do with isolation. But I like being alone. I can spend my time more profitably that way."

"I don't doubt that," I replied. "I just noticed that what you *actually* do when you're under stress or in emotional pain is withdraw to your room and eat large quantities of cookies." The woman actually could not experience her lack of attachment—she had lost access to her need for connection. The only sign of it was the fact that when she hurt, she turned to food instead of relationship.

This brings us to another point about attachment. Since God created us for bonding, it's part of our very essence, just as it is in His essence. We cannot *not* bond. We are created to bond in either a growth-producing or a death-producing manner. If we cannot bond to loving relationships, we will bond to something else that is not so loving. This is the root of the addictive process. It's also the root of Satan's strategy to sabotage our maturity process.

Satan's plan is to help us get God-given, legitimate needs met in a way that will destroy us. He is a counterfeiter who hates being a creature and having needs himself. That's why the original sin was the pride of self-sufficiency: "I will make myself like the Most High" (Isaiah 14:14). He hated being in need of God.

The counterfeits for getting our needs met are explained by John: "For all that is in the world, the *lust of the flesh* and the *lust of the eyes* and the *boastful pride of life,* is not from the Father, but is from the world" (1 John 2:16; emphasis added). Sexual affairs, materialism, or professional success meet our needs for maturity in temporary but unsatisfying ways. They ultimately cause self-destruction.

As fallen beings, we are very susceptible to buying into this lie of what is satisfying. A part of our nature agrees with the deception that we can get needs met in ways other than those God has prescribed.

When people do realize that they've been emotionally cut off most of their lives, they often ask me what they've bonded to instead. At that point we usually discuss Luke 12:34: "For where your treasure is, there will your heart be also." Whatever is taking up emotional energy, money, and time is generally the bonding substitute. It tends to have an addictive nature to it. There's never really enough.

What's really confusing for most of us is that the list of attachment substitutes can include good things:

- Work
- Sports
- Hobbies
- Food
- Parenting
- Sexuality
- Shopping
- Religious activities

- Knowledge/information
- Rescuing or "one-way" relationships

Many committed Christians are unknowing "sanctified addicts" of otherwise good things that help keep them away from a black hole of loneliness in their hearts and the crucial necessity of close relationships.

Not-so-good substitutes include drugs and alcohol, which of course are physically dangerous. The long list of bonding subtitutes indicates the range of what an unbonded person might take in to fill up an attachment deficit.

The existence of emotional attachments in our lives is not an option; it is not a luxury. It is a spiritual and emotional necessity. God designed us for it! In fact, research now indicates that chronic, untreated isolation can result in physical problems and even contribute to shortened lifespans.

It's a sad fact that Christians who have never been able to be vulnerable with their needs for connection sometimes are then drawn to fellowships where true bonds are trivialized— or, even worse, dismissed as "trusting man too much." The fact is that having relationships with God and other persons is not an either-or proposition; it is a both-and necessity. The heart has a deep need for God, who placed eternity there. The same heart yearns for satisfying and safe human attachments in which we can be truly known and truly loved, that we may all be one.

HOW TO REPAIR ATTACHMENT DEFICITS

"I understand the problem," Jerry told me in session. "I know I can't get close to people. I know that's why I'm depressed. I know how I got this way. So what? Where do I go to buy this missing part?"

God's plan for repairing those unattached parts of ourselves is the story of redemption. The undeveloped, unloved heart is still lost in the past where the emotional object constancy process was prematurely ended for some reason. Just like the lost sheep in a hundred, God wants that isolated part to be brought out of darkness into the light of His love.[7]

Wherever the process was interrupted, it must be continued. The emotional memories made up of deep, loving experiences with safe people are to be continued until the person's heart is "caught up" with the rest of him.

Repairing bonding deficits involves two factors. First, *it requires finding safe, warm relationships in which emotional needs will be accepted and loved, not criticized and judged.* Sometimes this may involve changing friendships or locations in order to find the right relationships in which comfort, not denial, is the norm.

Second, *repair requires taking risks with our needs.* This means taking a step of humility. It means bringing our loneliness and abandoned feelings to other believers in the same way Jesus revealed in the Beatitudes: "Blessed are the poor in spirit, for theirs is the kingdom of heaven. Blessed are those who mourn, for they shall be comforted" (Matthew 5:3-4).

These are genuine risks. No matter how safe others appear, God allows each of us a choice to be unloving. Yet when those unattached parts of the self become connected to others, our ability to tolerate loss of love from others increases. The more we internalize, the less we need the world to approve of us constantly. This is a hallmark of maturity. Loved people can feel loved even when their circumstances are emotionally dry. This is the position of being rooted and grounded in love.

Christians who have experienced attachment deficits understand the fragility of this part of the soul. Though relationship is what the soul needs most, it was relationship that injured it. An unbonded person can be devastated by further emotional abandonment. Jesus' metaphor of the men who built their houses on rock and on sand is a picture of this dilemma: bonded people have a good foundation; they can withstand more difficult times.[8] The unbonded person doesn't have the emotional resources to tolerate the same suffering. It's easy to see why this part of our character needs to be carefully protected and nourished, as a nurse tends a sick infant.

Jenny provides a picture of our need for attachment and some of the consequences that occur when that need goes unfulfilled. In the next chapter we'll look at the flip side of the attachment need: our need for separateness. Meanwhile, recall Jenny's situation:

The Woods were her safety, but memories kept her going. She would cry herself to sleep each night and then wake up the next day and get on about the business of surviving. She found the best places in the stream to get fresh water; she learned where the best berries and food plants were. Once in a while she would sneak back to her old vegetable garden just after dark and take a few potatoes or turnips. She knew how to build a fire and where to find warm places in cold weather.

Jenny was making a place for herself in the forest. Food and shelter weren't problems anymore. She began to feel that she was out of danger—at least for now.

But something was different inside the little girl's heart. Her heart had been broken, and it did not mend while she was busy learning how to live in the forest. The part of Jenny that had trusted, had longed for caring, had reached out for a warm embrace or a kind word, became still and quiet. It was replaced by a dull, painful emptiness. She had felt it shriveling up inside, until now there was nothing. Jenny hadn't wanted that part of her to break. But it just did, anyway.

Your attachment need is like a muscle. Left alone, that part of your soul will atrophy and wither. Only with exercise will it grow and be properly reconstructed back toward the image of God that was defiled at the Fall.

Jenny experienced this atrophy in her aloneness. She felt brokenhearted, just as you and I do when we fall into hiding patterns within. We need to move toward relationship, toward attachment, to grow in Christlikeness. We need the emotional resources that God has provided: Relationship with Christ, and relationship with other image-bearers.

NOTES   1. See Psalm 139:23-24 and 2 John 10.
        2. For a more detailed treatment of these four needs, see *When Your World
           Makes No Sense,* by Dr. Henry Cloud (Nashville: Oliver-Nelson Pub-
           lishers, 1990).
        3. 2 Corinthians 5:18-19.
        4. Revelation 20:10.
        5. 2 Corinthians 5:21.
        6. Matthew 18:3-4.
        7. See Matthew 18:12-14.
        8. Matthew 7:24-27.

CHAPTER FIVE

Our Need
for Separateness

✛

"**M**AYBE there's such a thing as being too loving," Cathy told me one day. "I just care too much for the people around me, and that's why I'm always burned out. So I guess I've got to find out how to become a selfish person. The problem is, I *like* being caring."

Cathy's struggle came after a lifelong pattern of feeling overwhelmed, torn by her various responsibilities, and generally unable to control her life. She was a single parent with two out-of-control teenagers, an ex-husband who had been chronically unfaithful, and a nowhere job where she remained because of a sense of loyalty.

Cathy understood her symptoms, but not the problem. It wasn't that she was too loving. We can never have too much of that quality. It's part of who God is. Cathy didn't have too much love—*she had too few boundaries.*

Many Christians who are deeply attached to others find that the pages of their lives are often earmarked with a sense of being overwhelmed by the demands of life. They experience problems in "keeping up," or of feeling controlled by the needs and crises of others. They have difficulty filtering out others' needs from their own.

Our second developmental need involves the quality of being separate, maturing our will, and setting boundaries.

WHAT ARE BOUNDARIES?

Boundaries are another way to refer to ownership, or stewardship, or responsibility. Remember the cattle brands of the Old West? Successful ranchers burned a unique marking onto the hide of each cow. It was a good system. If a fence broke, and the animals from neighboring ranches mingled, the owners could easily sort out which animals were theirs and which weren't. Without brands, the confusion over who owned what would have been overwhelming.

Boundaries are our own personal "brand." They're a way for us to identify ownership. They tell us what is ours, and—just as importantly—what isn't. People with poor boundaries find themselves continually taking on problems that aren't theirs and neglecting their own. After taking on everyone else's problems, there's no time for their own.

Boundaries are foundational to a sense of identity. They give us a clear sense of where "who I am" begins and ends. This is essential for us to be able to love. People who aren't clear about their own thoughts, feelings, values, motivations, and behavior can never be sure if some sacrificial act they are performing for someone else was done freely, or out of a sense of obligation, fear, or guilt. (Those acts should be done freely, if they're motivated out of a sense of loving God or others.) Clear boundaries are a gateway to a loving heart.

BOUNDARIES AND GOD

Much of the Bible is a portrait of the character of God, a way to put Him into word pictures that we can carry in our heads. When God describes Himself, He does so in two ways: positively—what He is; and negatively—what He isn't.

If you've ever been with people who "like everything," you've probably had the experience of not feeling that you really knew who they were. Any restaurant, any movie, any opinion is fine with them. This trait may *appear* to be open-mindedness, but more often than not it's a sign that these individuals lack a clearly defined sense of self. It's been said that people who are too open-minded need to be careful—their brains might fall out.

This is one reason why both sides of God's self-descriptions are presented in the Scriptures.

First, God makes positive self-statements. He describes Himself as holy, loving, just, and compassionate, to name a few character traits.[1] These qualities cover a wide range of aspects of His personality.

God's self-description isn't only positive, however. He also tells us what He is *not,* so that we can judge if someone or something isn't from Him. For example: God has no part in evil. He hates lying tongues and lovers of violence. He isn't a man.[2] Without these "not" assertions, He would be the god of pantheism (or the "New Age"), which asserts that God exists as the creation as well as the creator.

These "nots" are the boundaries of God; they are His method of letting us know Him. In fact, God's essence in the Trinity also has boundaries. In some mysterious way, He exists in the Father, Son, and Spirit, united and yet uniquely distinct—one God in three persons.

There is a great deal of comfort for us in understanding God's boundaries. They help us trust Him, because we know where He stands on issues. Because God's yes is yes, and His no is no,[3] we don't have to worry that He'll tell us His opinions in indirect, passive-aggressive ways.

BOUNDARIES AND US

We don't have to stop with God's nature to see the evidence of boundaries—we simply have to observe His creation. Our own nature reflects the same principle. The Bible refers to that principle as "stewardship."

Many Christians struggle with constantly feeling "drawn and quartered" by the needs and demands of others. Some people feel as if they can't get to their own tasks because the crises of others keep getting in the way. This reflects a conflict in stewardship.

A steward is an administrator, or director, of people or property. He can be responsible for the care and maintenance of a Fortune 500 company, a garden, or a family. Stewardship is about responsibility. The buck stops with the steward.

God has made us all stewards of certain things in our lives for which no one else can take responsibility. How we conduct our lives on earth, for example, is one aspect of our stewardship. As Paul puts it, "For we must all appear before the judgment seat of Christ, that each one may be recompensed for his deeds in the body, according to what he has done, whether good or bad" (2 Corinthians 5:10).

The message here is that all of us will answer, in some fashion, for how we've lived. Ultimately there will be no one on whom we can blame the directions our lives took, whether toward or away from love.

More specifically, stewardship also means that we are responsible for several aspects of what goes on in our lives. Examples of things that have our "brand" on them include our time, money, feelings, opinions, thoughts, actions, values, and gifts and abilities.

We have been given these aspects of life to help us in surviving and to help others survive. Our task is to nurture and develop these aspects of ourselves and use them responsibly. The unwise servant's wasting of the master's talents is a picture of the life spent not utilizing the gifts of God.

But that's not all of stewardship. The second important aspect of this principle is that *the good steward knows what is not his responsibility.* He knows when a problem needs to be delegated, or isn't a high enough priority, or is simply someone else's. Good administrators have the ability to know what the most effective use of their time is. They know what to say no to. Poor administrators say yes to too much, and end up with missed deadlines, angry coworkers, and poor track records.

It's not easy to distinguish what's ours and what isn't. Dr. Howard Hendricks, a renowned speaker and seminary professor in the area of Christian leadership development, tells his classes, "For every invitation to speak that I accept, I have to turn down forty. These aren't forty bad invitations. They're generally places where there's a real need, where I'd love to speak."

Clear boundaries help us decide what is ours, and what isn't. They lead to good stewardship over our lives. Without an accurate sense of our limits, our lives will resemble a "double-minded man, unstable in all his ways" (James 1:8).

Next to bonding deficits, the problem of unclear boundaries is probably the most serious cause of emotional and spiritual struggles experienced by Christians today. Depression, anxiety, feelings of powerlessness and helplessness, a diffused sense of identity and direction, and codependency problems are all linked to boundary deficits.

THE KNAPSACK AND THE BOULDER

Let's look at a biblical principle of how to set responsible boundaries. The Apostle Paul gives us a key:

> Brethren, even if a man is caught in any trespass, you who are spiritual, restore such a one in a spirit of gentleness; each one looking to yourself, lest you too be tempted. Bear one another's burdens, and thus fulfill the law of Christ. For if anyone thinks he is something when he is nothing, he deceives himself. But let each one examine his own work, and then he will have reason for boasting in regard to himself alone, and not in regard to another. For each one shall bear his own load. (Galatians 6:1-5)

It's easy to be confused by this passage. Paul is discussing our responsibilities, and he seems to be saying, "Take care of each other" (verse 2) and "take care of yourself" (verse 5). I know many Christians whose lives are marked by fruitless attempts to take care of everyone in their lives as well as themselves. But that's not what the verses say.

The Greek word for *burden* in verse 2 means "overwhelming

load." It's a picture of a gigantic boulder crushing the back of a hurting person. Boulders represent deep, catastrophic losses in our lives—family and marital losses, financial devastation, physical illnesses, and so on. When a person has a boulder, he is rendered helpless, unable to pick himself up and move on. He stays in an injured state.

We are to look out for each other's boulders in the Body of Christ. When one of us is "crushed," those of us with something to offer are to swarm around the hurt individual and love, support, and encourage her. This is being responsible to each other.

The Greek word in verse 5 for *load* is different—it means "knapsack." What is a knapsack for? It carries whatever daily essentials the hiker needs to make it through the day. A knapsack is an individual affair. It's only for the carrier. And each person is to carry his own. No one can take my knapsack for me—and I can't take on anyone else's. This is being responsible for ourselves.

Look back at the aspects of what we're responsible for—our time, money, feelings, and the like. These are the "supplies" that go in the knapsack. We are to take full ownership of these things. And, just as importantly, we can't take ownership over anyone else's knapsack items—even if we want to. Even if we're asked to.

Boundary conflicts happen when Hiker A tires of his knapsack and wants a free ride. Hiker B, wanting to be caring, takes it on. After a few miles, two things happen. First, Hiker A learns it's a lot of fun not to have to be responsible to pay his own rent, find a job, or take responsibility for his own happiness. Second, Hiker B shifts from love to resentment to bitterness as he takes on the impossible task of being responsible for another person's life.

Many families are built on this conflict. One member of the family controls the other members by such messages as, "If you separate from me mentally or physically, I'll become depressed, lonely, or die—and it will be your fault." This member is making the others responsible for his or her inability to be alone, or to cultivate friendships.

Jesus' parable of the good Samaritan makes the "knapsack-boulder" issue clear. The Samaritan helped the victimized man with his boulder: stripped and half-dead, lying by the side of the road.[4] Yet he didn't take him to his home—he took him to an inn, a temporary residence. The idea is that when the victim had recovered, he was again on his own. With his own knapsack.

Taking responsibility for other people's feelings never works, because it deprives them of learning from the consequences of their behavior. Consequences are our teacher—they show us that driving too fast brings tickets, and that waiting too long to finish a project brings failure. It's what the writer of Hebrews refers to as "practice": "But solid food is for the mature, who because of practice have their senses trained to discern good and evil" (Hebrews 5:14).

The more we practice, make mistakes, and fail, the more we learn from the mistakes. But the irresponsible person who is chronically spared the consequences of his behavior by the "loving" friend is denied the gift of learning, and never matures.

I know a woman whose alcoholic husband had been a problem drinker for twenty years. She couldn't understand why her continuous nagging hadn't brought him to repentance. It wasn't until she realized that she was taking responsibility for him that she herself began repenting, and he began recovering. How had she been taking responsibility? She was budgeting for his liquor in the weekly grocery list!

She realized she was training him to put up with the nagging and hold on until she brought the groceries home. But when she began saying "no" to his use of family money for drinking, and began setting more limits on his irresponsibility, he came out of his denial and began getting help.

BOUNDARY DEFICITS

People with healthy boundaries can say yes to the good and no to the bad. They are just as free to say no to someone they love as they are to say yes. That's because love is impossible without freedom. The person who is saying yes to someone else's demands because of a fear of hurting their feelings, or a fear of emotional withdrawal, cannot be loving.

Love and fear cannot coexist, because fear removes the freedom not to love. That is, you can't love someone if you don't feel free not to love them. Love entails free choice, not forced compliance. That's why John says that "perfect love casts out fear" (1 John 4:18). Saying yes to someone else because of fear is compliance, or people-pleasing, but it's not love.

Jesus makes the same comparison between love and compliance. Quoting Hosea 6:6, He says, "I desire compassion and not sacrifice" (Matthew 9:13). God's not interested in external acts performed because we are afraid. He wants an authentic, grateful, abiding love from us, because we know we are loved.

People who have been injured in their ability to set clear boundaries tend to fall into two categories:

(1) those who take on others' knapsacks and ignore their own;
(2) those who need others to take their knapsacks.

The first type tends to be giving, caring, over-responsible, and always behind schedule with their over-commitments. The second type presents either a needy, dependent style or a seductive style. And, strangely enough, these types are strongly drawn to each other!

Many marriages are typical of this boundary confusion. Why does this occur? Primarily because each type is looking for someone to help repair the boundary injury. Over-responsible people find someone like their needy, dependent parents so that perhaps this time, "If I'm caring enough, my needs will be noticed." Under-responsible people seek out a caretaker with the deep wish that the caretaker will put some limits on them and help them mature.

As long as these reasons aren't understood, we don't have opportunity to take responsibility for them. This is the primary reason most marriages get "stuck." Whatever we aren't aware of, we can't repair.

Boundary deficits can be deeply disabling to anyone, including Christians. People with unclear boundaries can find themselves making commitments under pressure that they would never make with a clear head. They find themselves "caving in" to others. They have trouble speaking their mind. They are afraid to be honest and tell the truth. They often can't protect themselves in injurious situations, such as being wrongly criticized. They are unable to stand firm and separate with their values, as Joshua did when he declared, "as for me and my house, we will serve the LORD" (24:15).

Unclear boundaries can also lead to a lack of direction in life. Boundaries are the conveyors of our personal power. People whose boundaries are underdeveloped find themselves floating along in their careers or relationships with no sense of initiative or goals.

The psychological fruits of these boundary problems can be devastating. Depression, anxiety, substance abuse, eating disorders, panic attacks, and identity disorders are a few of the results of boundary conflicts.

HOW TO REPAIR SEPARATENESS DEFICITS

If you can identify a problem in separateness, or in having clear boundaries—being a good steward of your knapsack—you are not alone. No one has perfect boundaries. At times we all take on what's not ours, or don't take on what is ours.

God has provided help in repairing and developing our broken boundary-setting abilities. His resources involve skill-building. Just as we need to exercise and work with an atrophied leg after it comes out of its cast, setting appropriate boundaries is an ability we must learn. Here are some ways to develop boundaries:

1. *Ask God to help you become a truth-teller, even of negative truth.* Proverbs 10:18 tells us that "He who conceals hatred has lying lips." Often, people with shaky boundaries may feel resentful about the supposed power of others over them, not realizing that they have given their power to those others. If they begin to feel they don't have choices they will also feel angry and resentful. Often, the first step to reclaiming their "brand" is to admit the anger to themselves, God, and others.

2. *Find people who celebrate your separateness.* "As iron

sharpens iron, so one man sharpens another" (Proverbs 27:17). Separateness helps relationships.

It isn't possible to learn to develop boundaries in isolation with unsupportive people. When we try, we repeat our original boundary injury. That is, we find ourselves in a controlling relationship with an unsupportive person and attempt to set a limit on the relationship. The person rejects it, and we find ourselves alone.

Most of us would choose being in a bad relationship rather than no relationship. We need to find maturing, caring people who will love our boundaries just as much as they love our attachment.

Here is an important litmus test for the quality of your relationships. Ask yourself, "Do the people closest to me love my *no* as much as they love my *yes*?" If those closest to you affirm your compliance, but withdraw, throw tantrums, or attack when you set limits or have an opinion, there's a problem. Your *yes* is being loved, but your *no* is not. If your *no* isn't loved, then you aren't, either.

Even God loves our *no*. He knows that without it, what worship He'd get from us would be simply robotic compliance. He wants all to repent and be saved, but allows people to refuse Him: "The Lord is not slow about His promise, as some count slowness, but is patient toward you, not wishing for any to perish but for all to come to repentance" (2 Peter 3:9). His love for our boundaries is a model for our finding people who will have boundaries with others.

3. *Practice disagreement.* Truth telling always involves differing opinions. You can't find out who you really are without first knowing who you aren't. A sign that you're beginning to set boundaries is that you will rock some boats. There's most likely a problem if no one ever reacts negatively to you.

Jesus said, "Woe to you when all men speak well of you, for in the same way their fathers used to treat the false prophets" (Luke 6:26). It's a disconcerting thought that for us to recover spiritually, some people will probably get upset with us! Yet these are usually people who have a difficult time relating to adults with boundaries of their own.

4. *Take responsibility for your mistakes.* People with boundary

problems sometimes see themselves as out of control of their lives. They feel helpless to change their own problems and others' treatment of them. This can lead to a blaming or rationalizing attitude. "If I can't control my life, then my problems aren't my fault," might go the thinking.

Taking stewardship over your life means learning to admit when your problems are the result of your irresponsibility rather than finding excuses. People who "own" their problems tend to mature much faster than those who excuse or transfer blame. The excuser has nothing to fix.

A woman in the hospital was surprised to find in group therapy that she couldn't talk about her issues without mentioning her husband in every sentence. Another patient told her, "He's not in the room, so we can't help him." She hadn't realized how she had blamed most of her problems on him.

5. *Learn to respect others' separateness.* One indication of a boundary deficit is an inability to live with the *no* of another.

I once worked with a couple who experienced this problem. Every time the wife disagreed with the husband, he would head toward the door exclaiming, "That's it! — the marriage isn't going to work out." Panicked, she would chase after him and apologize for the "sin" of having an opinion. After some work, she was able to sit quietly in the living room when he made his dramatic exit statements. And he never made it to the car before he returned to resume the discussion.

When we learn to accept another's boundaries, we are saying, in effect, "If you don't give me what I want, God and I will find another way to get my need met." It keeps the other person out of a position of indispensability, which is actually a form of idolatry.

If our needs to be understood, listened to, or loved can't or won't be met by the person we'd like, we are to find someone else to help meet that need. That's why there is a multiplicity of believers in the Body of Christ: when one friend is busy, we are to call another. This allows us to support the boundary-setting freedom of others in the way we'd like to. If we want others to accept our freedom, we must respect theirs.

A FINAL NOTE

Cathy, the woman with insufficient boundaries, was worried that she'd have to become less caring to learn limits. Actually, the opposite is true.

People with fragile boundaries have a harder time loving because of their lack of freedom. Their *yes* is tinged with obligation, fear, or guilt. It can never be the "cheerful" *yes* of 2 Corinthians 9:7, which is the result of a free choice, or "purposing": "Let each one do just as he has purposed in his heart; not grudgingly or under compulsion; for God loves a cheerful giver."

The most loving people in the world have a clear sense of their separateness and stewardship of themselves. Their freedom to say *no* allows their *yes* to be an unqualified act of love to others.

Jenny had a very healthy separateness that was a direct result of the loving home life her parents had given her. When she was forced into hiding, she survived with aplomb and daring. Only a soul that had been cared for the way Jenny's had could have made the split-second decisions she had to make to escape the soldiers when her parents were captured. Only a healthy little girl could have survived the way she did when thrust into such a difficult situation.

Jenny had clear boundaries, and she knew when they were being violated. That's not to say she didn't have some clearly undeveloped abilities or emotional ups and downs during her hiding experience. Indeed, there were many times when she got "stuck" in the decision-making process. But she had a clear sense of her responsibilities and knew that she had to take stewardship of herself seriously.

Jenny's ability to experience separateness was generated by her past and her parents' having developed in her a sense of bonding and belonging. These two needs are different, yet clearly dependent on each other. Like Jenny, our soul needs both in order to build relationships and function in life. Most important, as we have seen, these two needs are part of our basic nature in being made in the image of God.

As you examine your own needs in these two related areas

of the soul, think carefully about how the Fall has affected your ability to experience separateness. How do you survive times of loneliness? Could you survive the sort of experience Jenny had with the same sort of responsible stewardship? If you're a parent, are you providing the same kind of bonding love and healthy attachment that will enable your children to separate from you when the time is right? Or if and when an emergency arises, as with Jenny?

Learning separateness, and when it's appropriate to set limits, begins early in childhood, but comes to full bloom in adolescence. People who have learned the lessons of this chapter regarding truth-telling, our separate identities, taking responsibility for mistakes, handling legitimate disagreement, and respecting the separateness of others, should take the time to develop these skills in their children as well. It will make the more difficult times of parenting later more fruitful, although not necessarily less painful.

Our ability to bond deeply with God and others, and our ability to take biblical responsibility for ourselves, determines much of the quality and meaningfulness of our adult lives. These two needs for attachment and separateness can become important pathways to growth. But along the way, as we'll see in chapter 6, a third developmental need emerges for the ability to accept the presence of good and bad in the world and in our lives. This is an important step toward understanding ourselves and others.

NOTES   1. Leviticus 11:44, 1 John 4:8, Deuteronomy 32:4, and Deuteronomy 4:31.
   2. Psalm 5:4, Proverbs 6:17, Psalm 11:5, and Numbers 23:19.
   3. James 5:12.
   4. Luke 10:30-37.

Chapter Six

Our Need for Resolving Good and Bad

✛

"I JUST KNOW he's out there waiting for me," Carol said hopefully. She was recovering from a depression that had led to a suicide attempt after the failure of her second marriage. The "he" Carol was referring to was her "prince," the ideal man who would be everything her first two husbands hadn't been.

Carol's ex-husbands had been "intolerable." The first husband had been "insensitive, cold, and uncaring." The second had been more emotionally connectable, but was "weak and needy." Both relationships had been extremely fast-paced and infatuational; Carol had married each man within months of meeting him.

In both marriages, however, Carol had experienced a sense of gradual letdown and disappointment: "They weren't who I thought they were." Time after time, they would show themselves to be flawed, inconsiderate, incompetent, and so on. And as their imperfections and shortcomings became clearer to her, all hope of the special marriage she'd longed for grew dimmer.

The same problem was happening in her work. Carol found herself changing careers every couple of years. At first each job promised success, fulfillment, and financial security. But

within a few months, the problems in each company would surface, leaving Carol feeling betrayed. She would quit the job in a
flurry and quickly reengage in a new position with the "perfect"
organization.

Carol's deep sense of disappointment in her husbands and
careers led to a sense of resentment toward God for "not being
fair" to her. All this was aggravated by the fact that now, in her
early forties, the hopes and dreams of the special family and job
were much more elusive than when she was in her twenties. She
was no closer to the ideal life than when she was younger. Carol's
hope moved to despair. As the Bible says, "Hope deferred makes
the heart sick" (Proverbs 13:12).

THE CLASH OF REAL AND IDEAL

Carol's conflict illustrates our third developmental need: *We must
learn to live with the tension of a fallen world, of knowing that the
universe, like us, is sinful, marred, and imperfect.* It is less than
ideal, sometimes hostile, and yet it's the only one we have to live
in. As Woody Allen said, it's not great, but it's still the best place
to get a good steak.

Why is the conflict between the real and the ideal a problem?
Actually, there would be no problem, had there been no Fall. We
weren't created to experience or handle evil. In fact, the plan for
you and me was just the opposite. We were to have a life of unbroken connection and purposeful activity. However, for a variety of
reasons, this ideal life for us was not to be.

If you've ever seen a child hurt by another child for the first
time, you get a picture of how jolting the experience of badness
is. I watched the face of a one-year-old girl as she was pushed
down by another child during a get-together of families. The first
emotion that registered was surprise—she didn't have a place
in her understanding for aggression by another. There was no
framework for it. The second emotion was a sense of betrayal and
withdrawal. The third was rage. At that point, the parents had to
separate them.

Of course, we experience evil inside as well as outside us. The ravages of the Fall, in the form of sin, loss, and injustice, are hard on us. Living with imperfection is destructive to us. Look at the skin of an infant, then put it up against the weathered hands of an eighty-year-old. The world takes its toll. That's why Paul's vivid picture of the world wrestling in the throes of childbirth has such impact on us: "For we know that the whole creation groans and suffers the pains of childbirth together until now" (Romans 8:22). This pain surrounds us all in one form or another.

But that isn't the only problem. Not only is living in a fallen world wearing on us, but it's worsened by the fact that we know good and evil—that is, we have an idea of what the ideal, perfect world would be. The contrast is brutally difficult to swallow.

Most of us have experienced serendipitous moments a few times in our lives—unexpected times of deep, tender, genuine joy in a loving relationship, or of satisfaction in a day's work, when "the day was good, dinner's on the barbeque, God's on His throne, and all's well with the world." Unanticipated pleasures or satisfaction don't seem to overcome the failures, losses, and pain of the real world, however. Comparing them is often a genuine letdown.

This comparison should never have been. That's why God was so concerned that in all the freedom Adam was to have, there should be only one limit:

> And the LORD God commanded the man, saying, "From any tree of the garden you may eat freely; but from the tree of the knowledge of good and evil you shall not eat, for in the day that you eat from it you shall surely die." (Genesis 2:16-17)

God never wanted us to be able to make moral judgments of good and evil. The reason seems to be simply because He wanted to spare us the experience of evil. It was for our benefit. It was to save us from something that would hurt us terribly, and it did.

The knowledge of evil is so contaminating that God alone can deal with it without becoming evil Himself. Our creatureliness makes us susceptible to its power. This is why I believe God's eviction of us from Eden was actually a blessing in disguise. Had Adam stayed, he might have eaten from the tree of life, become immortal, and been imprisoned in his isolation from God and others forever:

> Then the LORD God said, "Behold, the man has become like one of Us, knowing good and evil; and now, lest he stretch out his hand, and take also from the tree of life, and eat, and live forever"—therefore the LORD God sent him out from the garden of Eden, to cultivate the ground from which he was taken. (Genesis 3:22-23)

In a way, the Garden is always with us. Our memories of good moments, and our wishes for ourselves and others to be better, keep the image of the ideal in our hearts. At times this encourages us, and at others it torments us, such as when we have thoughts like, "I shouldn't have made that error—I knew better. Why did I let it happen again?"

So the jolting experience of imperfection and the knowledge of good and evil land a one-two punch on most of us, and a dilemma is born. It can be stated this way: *I'd like to be the ideal me—living in an ideal world. I can even imagine it. What then do I do with the badness in myself and in the world? How do I coexist with injustice? Failure? Imperfection? Disappointment?*

The reason this is such a monumental issue for some of us, such as the perfectionist or the frustrated idealist, is that the kernel of the problem is a fear that bad will overwhelm and contaminate good. The one bad apple spoils a lifetime, thinks the idealist. This is a sign of a developmental inability to trust that the good can coexist with the bad.

A friend of mine had one of the most beautiful weddings I've ever seen. From opening song to final dance at the reception, it was a testimony to God and a great party for the friends of the couple. Yet she confided that for several months afterward, she'd been unable to reflect on and enjoy the warm memories. The "culprit" was one isolated incident lodged permanently in her memory: a tense argument between her future mother-in-law and the church hostess over how quickly the bride was to walk down the aisle—an argument which no one but the bride noticed. She couldn't enjoy a great wedding because of her inability to see past one "bad" moment. Her perfectionism would not allow her to.

Carol, the woman who was chasing the "ideal" husband, family, and job, was in the middle of a similar dilemma. Unable to accept mediocrity and flaws in her life, she embarked on a lifelong journey to a sort of land of Oz, where she'd never have to be disappointed again in love or work. Good enough wasn't good enough for Carol's idealistic dream.

A DEVELOPMENTAL VIEW

The same difficulty occurs in early child development. After gaining a sense of attachment (the first stage), and a sense of separateness, (the second stage), the infant becomes aware of a new issue in life: the existence of good and bad. It's normal to see a cooing, satisfied baby feeding in his mother's arms switch instantly to rage when she puts him in his playpen—then right back to bliss when the anxious mother quickly retrieves him!

The mind of the infant isn't yet sophisticated enough to understand his mother's actions. He only knows that Mother was "good" when he was held. When he was put down, all the good left. He now had a "bad" mother who frustrated his wish. But that was okay, because "good mother" returned in a few seconds and rescued him. The infant hasn't yet developed the understanding that the loving mother who hugs him is the same one who sometimes withholds things from him.

Infants can't resolve the conflict of people whom they love being the same ones at whom they rage. This is because, since the Fall, we're born into the sinful state: without grace, unloved, and unloving. We have emptiness, terror, and anger in our hearts from the womb. At this point there is no antidote to "badness," because babies haven't yet received enough grace to forgive badness.

Solving the baby's state of gracelessness requires a great deal of time with Mother. Along with providing a sense of constancy and a framework of love for the infant, she also needs to give him enough that he doesn't lose his emotional memory of her goodness when he encounters delays of gratification. At some point, he is able to remember that the same "mean person" who gave him a bath is the wonderful woman who played with him that night. The good doesn't leave with the presence of the bad.

We see the same dilemma in the Apostle Paul, not turned toward his mother, but toward himself. He suffered greatly through the reality that sin lived within him:

> For that which I am doing, I do not understand; for I am not
> practicing what I would like to do, but I am doing the very
> thing I hate. But if I do the very thing I do not wish to do,
> I agree with the Law, confessing that it is good. So now, no
> longer am I the one doing it, but sin which indwells me. For
> I know that nothing good dwells in me, that is, in my flesh;
> for the wishing is present in me, but the doing of the good is
> not. For the good that I wish, I do not do; but I practice the
> very evil that I do not wish. (Romans 7:15-19)

Christians throughout the centuries have found comfort in the anguish of this passage, saying to themselves, "He knows what I live with." The passage could just as well be describing someone in the throes of a compulsive behavior problem, stuck in the cycle—wanting the goodness, yet lost in the badness. Paul felt the internal conflict—the alienation—the destructive splitting between his goodness and badness, knowing who he should have been, and yet also who he really was.

FALSE SOLUTIONS

People who have not received enough grace to solve the badness problem are terrified people. They are constantly on the run from the shame of their own sin, or the disappointment of seeing the badness of others—or both. If a person gets a 95 on an important test and yet feels like a failure, she may start believing the only way out is to live in a world of 100s. This temporary solution of the tension between real and ideal is always inadequate and involves some sort of splitting between good and bad, keeping the two apart rather than realistically resolving them through forgiveness from God and others.

A typical temporary solution is intolerance of our own badness. Jeff came to therapy after his wife discovered his involvement with pornography. The damage to his marriage was immense, as was his shame at his "badness" being found out. What emerged after some time in therapy helped clarify why he started.

Not only was Jeff's addiction a longstanding pattern beginning at puberty; it also served an important purpose for him. "I was always the star," he said. "There wasn't a place in my family for mediocrity." Jeff's parents had needed a "star" to fill up the voids in their own hearts, and his talents had been useful for that. Sports, leadership, and academics all came easily for him. He had the "perfect" background.

Yet Jeff had begun noticing at an early age that he often felt strangely unreal about himself. He would lead his church youth group's rallies brilliantly, but felt that "the real me wasn't there—it was just this actor who looked like me." Sometimes it felt as if he would watch himself from the sidelines, going through his performance paces. In fact, there were several years of his childhood and adolescence of which he had almost no memory. "How could I remember?" he asked. "I wasn't there—the actor was."

When Jeff had discovered pornography in his father's closet, he became hooked on something much deeper than the sexual stimulation. The pictures became an entrance to a fantasy world where he could be "bad"—meaning, in Jeff's case, impulsive, needy, or sensual. The material became a container for all the unloved, imperfect (in the eyes of his family) parts of himself.

Fixating on goodness—while ignoring badness—can lead to an addiction to self-admiration. It leads away from love. Love sees—and forgives—the bad: Love "does not rejoice in unrighteousness, but rejoices with the truth" (1 Corinthians 13:6). Love doesn't deny the truth, positive or negative.

Jeff learned that he was to experience only positive truths about himself. Feeling like a double agent, he was split down the middle. There was his idealized perfect self, with an adoring fan club of church friends and family. And there was his secret self, where he felt "bad"—but alive. Even so, he hated this aspect of himself. "All I ever thought about was all the people who looked up to me—how disappointed and hurt they'd be if it came out."

Jeff's solution to his badness had been to keep it in a secret compartment, away from the rest of his life. He was terribly frightened of the repercussions of humiliation and disappointment once others knew of his badness.

It was in a group situation that Jeff first opened up to several others about his sexual struggle. Instead of receiving truckloads of shame, Jeff found that several group members wept as they listened to the story of how hard he'd had to work to stay "special" instead of allowing himself to be ordinary. For the first time, he was able to bring his "bad self" to grace. "I thought that bad part of myself was supposed to be beat up, not loved." Over time, as Jeff gave up the demand to be perfect, his addiction was resolved.

Did Jeff have a sin problem? Certainly. But it's important not to confuse the fruit and the root. The addiction was the result, or symptom, of a deeper issue of not being able to integrate his good and bad parts. Jesus taught that the roots inside the heart are what we need to pay attention to; we should not be misled by the symptoms on the outside:

> And [Jesus] was saying, "That which proceeds out of the man, that is what defiles the man. For from within, out of the heart of men, proceed the evil thoughts, fornications, thefts, murders, adulteries, deeds of coveting and wickedness, as well as deceit, sensuality, envy, slander, pride and foolishness. All these evil things proceed from within and defile the man." (Mark 7:20-23)

Have you ever dealt with a well-meaning "sinbuster" Christian? These folks spend a lot of time confronting behavioral problems such as Jeff's without dealing with what Jesus called the "defilement-from-within." Jeff's struggle with his own defilement needed to be discovered, so that it could be brought to the light and resolved.

The "sinbuster's" sort of confrontation is helpful to us, because it brings us to a place where we can admit a problem to God and others. But to end the confrontation with a "don't be bad anymore" handslap is to repeat the mistake of the Pharisees — *cupwashing*:

> "Woe to you, scribes and Pharisees, hypocrites! For you clean the outside of the cup and of the dish, but inside they are full of robbery and self-indulgence. You blind Pharisee, first clean the inside of the cup and of the dish, so that the outside of it may become clean also." (Matthew 23:25-26)

Cupwashing, or painting over the bad, never works, because the source of the problem hasn't been dealt with. That source simply waits, festers, feels more unloved and unforgiven, and emerges again.

A second false or temporary solution is the problem of intolerance of the badness in others. Carol's need to deny badness in her search for the ideal began in a chaotic background in which her parents fought constantly, in private and public, and included the kids as targets in their wars. There was very little time for the kids' needs.

To escape from the craziness of her family, Carol constructed an "all-good" idealized fantasy world, where no one let her down, no one criticized her. Here she was surrounded by affirming, empathic people who understood without having to explain herself. Her fantasy job was fulfilling, exciting, meaningful, and never drudgery. Her fantasty marriage was to a perfect man with absolute love and caring for her every need — no warts!

It makes sense that Carol wound up in middle age with a string of relational and career disappointments. Encountering the blemishes and wrinkles of those around her threw Carol back into the dark, graceless state of her childhood. Even little reminders, such as a friend's clumsy attempt to be encouraging, would backfire.

One day, one of Carol's closest middle-aged friends tried to compliment her. "You're really moving into middle age gracefully;

you're an inspiration to me," she said. Carol was crushed. At forty-four she'd never considered herself "middle-aged." Her constant state of gracelessness, or her feelings of unlovableness and bad-ness, made her hypersensitive. The hypersensitivity would then make Carol feel wounded and misunderstood if her friends' state-ments weren't exactly mirroring her feelings.

Often, denial is the only way people learn how to deal with these unpleasant aspects of the soul. Splitting off the feelings, thoughts, or memories from awareness helps ease the unloved feelings and shame that seem to be part of that aspect. The only problem is that *denial doesn't work*. Feelings that are buried are always buried alive.

THE BIBLICAL SOLUTION

Since none of us is as "graced" and secure as we could be, all of us need help in solving the tension of what to do with our bad parts. God's solution is not perfectionism, or splitting off our badness. It is quite the opposite. It's called *forgiveness*.

Love Versus Law

Biblically, the antidote to the badness in our hearts and in the world isn't our goodness. That would be legalism, or self-salvation: "But if [the love of God] is by grace, it is no longer on the basis of works, otherwise grace is no longer grace" (Romans 11:6). The antidote is love.

The uniqueness of the Cross is this: Jesus' death took moral-ity problems out of the arena of *law*, and into the arena of *love*. We no longer need fear that our imperfections will rip us away from attachment to Him and others because we're "too bad." That is a given—we are "too bad" to reach a perfect standard of lovability: All of us have sinned and fallen short of the glory of God. We have been sought out and bought out of isolation by a Father who will never break His promise of unconditional love for us.

People who have a hard time understanding this find them-selves either (1) making up for their imperfections or (2) being in denial about them. Their flaws are like a sword hanging over their heads by a thread. They are terrified of an inevitability. It's a foregone conclusion to them that at some point the thread will finally snap and their exposed weaknesses will heap shame, rejection, and isolation from God and people upon their uncovered heads.

The message of the Bible, though, is that our sanctification includes having these imperfect parts exposed to relationship. It means our problem will be revealed to others who can care for, forgive, and support us. This happens through the process that the Bible calls *confession.*

Confession

To confess means *to agree with the truth about ourselves.* If that truth is a secret compulsion, a shameful memory, or an unloved self, we are to agree about it with God and other people: "Therefore, confess your sins to one another, and pray for one another, so that you may be healed" (James 5:16). Rather than being a path to condemnation, confession to God and others is a gateway to solving the problem. Being realistic and vulnerable leads to healing.

Christians struggle with a great deal of confusion about the role of confession. It is not, as some believe, so that we will no longer be guilty. We simply *are* guilty. But the guilt problem under the Law was abolished on the cross: "by the appearing of our Savior Christ Jesus, who abolished death, and brought life and immortality to light through the gospel" (2 Timothy 1:10). Our former legal guilt is an irrelevant issue, in terms of our being attached to God. There is no condemnation for the believer. There is no need, therefore, to confess in order to be forgiven. It is a finished issue.

The purpose of confession, instead, is to bring the unloved, hated, bad parts of ourselves into both the light of God's grace and the clear direction and instruction of His truth. It brings the parts that need forgiveness into relationship. The toxic nature of the badness is disinfected. Therefore, it can't contaminate the rest of us. In fact, love reduces it to its essence: our bad part is simply a problem in getting our needs met biblically.

When Jeff was able to talk freely about his addiction to his group, an interesting thing happened. His tone changed. At first, there was a deep hesitation, embarrassment, and a great deal of tension in him when he described his habitual patterns of acting out his addiction. Then the group's growing attachment to him, and the honest confessions of the members, began seeping into him. After a while, there was a matter-of-factness — not indifference — about his sharing. It was just another problem — a bad one, but something that needed to be solved — just like issues of trust or boundary conflicts in the group.

We could almost visibly see Jeff's "bad" aspects becoming integrated into the rest of his character, where he could take responsibility for them, and be accountable to have them loved and understood by others.

HOW TO ATTACH THE BAD TO RELATIONSHIP

For a minute, think of a person with whom you feel very free in your life. This person may be undisciplined. He or she may have a lot of problems. But there is one sure thing: you know this person loves you, good and bad. You feel forgiven; your badness doesn't make your friend nervous, critical, or withdrawing. It's just part of the attachment. For all that person's weaknesses, he or she has chosen the "good part" that Mary did: to love you. (If we have to err on one side or another, God grant us grace to err on the side of love.)

I'll never forget the clearest example in my life of this principle. I went through college in the South in the early seventies. Like some of my friends, I'd grown a pretty lengthy head of hair, for various reasons: peer relationships, rebelliousness, experimenting with adult decision-making, and so forth.

Back then, the South wasn't particularly fond of long-haired kids. Though I'm sure I asked for it, I was hurt by the reactions of some people.

One weekend home from college I paid a visit to my grandmother, who lived in a tiny rural town. Granny was petite, not much over five feet tall and in her seventies. She wasn't well-educated by today's standards. She'd farmed all her life. She'd raised six children. Granny was culturally the opposite of the open-minded, issue-sensitive adult.

After a few minutes in her home, Granny motioned to me. "Come outside, come outside," she commanded. Perplexed, I followed her into the front yard, where she had me stand still. Then, looking up at me, she smiled and said, "I just wanted to see your hair in the sunlight. The color comes out so pretty in the sunlight."

I can remember crying all the way back on my drive to the campus. A part of me that had brought me a lot of pain had been cherished by someone. Something that had been broken in me began healing.

That's what grace is about: not being afraid of imperfect things in ourselves or others, because of the relationship of grace to imperfection: there is always more grace than badness. As the Bible says, grace can — if we let it — always triumph over sin or evil: "And the Law came in that the transgression might increase; but where sin increased, grace abounded all the more" (Romans 5:20). If imperfection is a large landmass in our lives, grace is an ocean that can swallow it up. Badness will never compete with grace. It's not in the same league.

The acceptance that comes from grace removes the fear of loss of love, so that we can work on our problems without the threat of isolation. As for me, I eventually got a haircut for the right reason: I needed a job. Consequences and responsibility were the motivators, not fear of abandonment. No one can learn love in that atmosphere. There's too much at stake.

As the negative parts of the soul are confessed and attached to loving, accepting relationships, we learn to deal with them honestly and without fear. The reason for this is that in these accepting relationships there's no threat of impending rejection, so we can feel safe discussing, exploring, and confessing these bad parts.

Do you need help in resolving your good/bad split? You can start by learning several skills:

1. *Confess your lacks to God and people.* The more you admit your imperfections to yourself, God, and others, the less

frightening they become. Secrecy is the power of badness. That's why John says "the darkness did not comprehend [the light]" (John 1:5). When secret badness is revealed, it can be healed.

2. *Receive forgiveness.* You can become a loving person only by putting yourself in a position of allowing someone else to accept and forgive your weaknesses. As Jesus said, "He who is forgiven little, loves little" (Luke 7:47). Find a support group of forgiven people. Forgiven people understand living with imperfection.

3. *Let go of the demand for the ideal.* Having ideals is good. It gives you goals to accomplish that help you grow. But when the goal becomes a demand, it is no longer a help, but a taskmaster. Relinquish your need for perfection.

4. *Accept "good enough" in yourself and others.* "Good enough" means that you are aware of problems, but the attachment is worth it. When you're able to hold onto the good traits of a relationship, in full awareness of the imperfections with it, or when you can enjoy a project even with its flaws, you enter a position of gratitude instead of envy and emptiness.

5. *Make sadness your ally instead of your enemy.* God's solution for resolving your loss of relationships, dreams, ideals, and opportunities is sadness. Rather than something to be avoided, this sadness, or grief, allows you to let go of what you *cannot* have in order to make room in your heart for what you *can* have.

Those who don't feel safe enough to grieve find themselves holding on to lost hopes and relationships. Then it's difficult for them to seek out new attachments, since the ghosts of the past still occupy their emotional life. Solomon understood the value of grieving: "The mind of the wise is in the house of mourning, while the mind of fools is in the house of pleasure" (Ecclesiastes 7:4).

So it can be good to be sad, but we must not confuse sadness with depression. The two are quite different. Depression is *the inability to process loss or rage.* It's a heavy paralysis of the soul that won't allow it to finish resolving a problem. Sadness is actually the antidote to depression.

Depression is static and unmoving, but *sadness moves toward resolving loss.* That's why David declared, "Weeping may last for the night, but a shout of joy comes in the morning" (Psalm 30:5).

We see the functional, temporary nature of sadness here. It does a job: *Grieving prepares us for love.* When we're ready, sadness ends. Its "season" is over, as Solomon says: "a time to weep, and a time to laugh; a time to mourn, and a time to dance" (Ecclesiastes 3:4). People who try to "get through" times of loss often find that the unprocessed feelings emerge in some form later in life.

TWO BADNESSES: A FINAL NOTE

It's important here to recognize that there are really two types of badness. The first refers to the actual sinful, depraved part of our souls:

> All have turned aside, together they have become use-
> less; there is none who does good, there is not even one.
> Their throat is an open grave, with their tongues they keep
> deceiving, the poison of asps is under their lips; whose
> mouth is full of cursing and bitterness; their feet are swift to
> shed blood, destruction and misery are in their paths, and
> the path of peace have they not known. (Romans 3:12-17)

This type of "badness" is that aspect of our character that refuses our creatureliness and demands to be like God, as Satan did. It is a movement *away from* meeting our needs in God's way, and *toward* meeting them in Satan's counterfeit way.

Let's call the second type of badness "perceived badness." In other words, it may or may not be an actually sinful aspect of the self. It is, however, *experienced* as bad.

The isolated person experiences herself as a "bad" person. Whatever is disconnected from relationship can't feel "good," because life comes from attachment. When others withdraw from us because of certain traits we have, we see those parts of ourselves as bad. Again, such withdrawal has nothing to do with the actual sinfulness of that trait, but we begin to see that trait as "bad."

Examples include our needs, our anger, our will, our anxiety, our sadness, and even our exhilaration. Terri came from a family in which self-sufficiency was the norm. Asking for help or comfort was cause for a cold isolation. In adulthood, whenever Terri would feel empty and lonely, this feeling would be instantly followed by an internal tape saying something like, *You're too demanding—don't drain everyone with your problems.* And she would resort to her ministry, until her depression and burnout necessitated counseling. "Needs"—real emotional needs, not wants or desires—became Terri's "badness."

Whatever is unloved by us and by significant others will be seen as "bad"—and we will begin to believe that until it becomes a *part* of us.

The resolution of both badnesses is similar, however. Both our actual and perceived bad aspects of the personality need confession and relationship. Both need to be accepted as part of the self. The only essential difference is that we need to take responsibility for our actual badness, and learn from its consequences. Our perceived badness needs to be seen as a character trait that has been perceived by others in *unbiblical* ways.

Jenny was forced to deal with good and bad in her experience with two different kinds of men in uniform. The invading soldiers appropriately terrified her, and she learned to hide from them. She had learned a particularly difficult lesson the first time she encountered the enemy in the woods, and only the old oak tree saved her. In her terror, she spontaneously ran from the soldiers, the tree marking the spot where she had to make the sharp turn into the protective brier patch.

Later, however, when she ran from the soldiers the second time, she was well-prepared to hide—she'd marked all kinds of escape routes. The problem was, *Jenny had not resolved the difference between the two kinds of soldiers.*

The first soldiers were indeed "bad" and would have captured Jenny. If she had only taken the time to discern the difference between theirs and the other uniforms, she would have realized that it was her *perception* of the soldiers that caused her to run away the second time. The second group wanted to take her back to her recovering parents. It would be some time before Jenny resolved the difference between the good and bad soldiers.

Like Jenny, we sometimes go into hiding because we have not resolved what's good and bad in our lives. Is this the case with you? Are there incidents in your past that haunt you and cause you to perceive others as "bad" when they aren't necessarily so? Or do you have certain personal traits that you have decided are "bad"—but this impression has been formed largely because of unpleasant experiences with others? Or, more foundationally, perhaps you've never come to grips with your own nature—in which case it may be helpful to seriously consider the claims of Christ and His offer of forgiveness through the cross.

In any of these cases, serious reflection on your goodness and badness is necessary. Your humanness possesses both—goodness because you are created in the image of God, badness because you're a descendant of Adam and Eve and you have a sinful nature. Resolving this split is one of your most important tasks in maturing.

The last chapter in our exploration of "the hiding dilemma" focuses on our fourth developmental need, for authority and adulthood. We'll see how this emerging need is the culmination of our needs attachment, separateness, and the resolution of our good and bad selves.

CHAPTER SEVEN

Our Need for Authority and Adulthood

✤

W HILE consulting with a corporation on the relational patterns of their top employees, I encountered a problem: a
vice president named Phil who seemed to be two people.
I'd never met Phil before. His name, however, came up in my conversations with several different executives.

Opinions on Phil were radically inconsistent. The views were
divided into two categories. First, I heard that "he's a conscientious, cooperative worker who goes out of his way to please."
Then I heard the second opinion: "He's tyrannical, critical, and
demanding." Maybe there's a typo, I thought.

Perplexed, I took a look at a flowchart of the job positions of
the company. That solved the mystery. All those in positions above
Phil in rank loved his compliance. All those below him felt beat
up by his control. All of Phil's work relationships were uneven:
either one-up or one-down. There was an absence of eye-to-eye
connections.

Phil's situation introduces our fourth developmental need
in restoring the image of God in us: *coming into adulthood,
and taking on appropriate authority roles*. Authority has to do
with the following issues: personal power, expertise, responsi-

bility, appropriate submission, sexuality, and the ability to think independently.

People who have difficulties in authority issues will generally have struggles in one or more of those areas. Properly developed, those aspects make up the characteristics of the mature adult.

A BIBLICAL VIEW

To understand the proper place and importance of authority, we need to look at God. God is a king. He rules over the universe:

> Both riches and honor come from Thee, and Thou dost rule
> over all, and in Thy hand is power and might; and it lies
> in Thy hand to make great, and to strengthen everyone.
> (1 Chronicles 29:12)

> Thou, O LORD, dost rule forever; Thy throne is from genera-
> tion to generation. (Lamentations 5:19)

A king, or ruler, is in charge. He leads, guides, instructs, and corrects.

Wise leaders throughout the world bow to the kingship of God. One unwise king learned this lesson in a unique way. To teach him about pride, God temporarily lowered Babylonian King Nebuchadnezzar's position below that of his lowest subject: He gave him the mind of a beast. In fact, part of the evidence of Nebuchadnezzar's sanity was his humble homage to the King in power above him:

> But at the end of that period I, Nebuchadnezzar, raised my
> eyes toward heaven, and my reason returned to me, and I
> blessed the Most High and praised and honored Him who
> lives forever; for His dominion is an everlasting dominion,
> and His kingdom endures from generation to generation.
> And all the inhabitants of the earth are accounted as noth-
> ing, but He does according to His will in the host of heaven

and among the inhabitants of earth; and no one can ward off His hand or say to Him, "What hast Thou done?" (Daniel 4:34-5)

These words convey the essence of God's ultimate authority: His unchallengeable dominion over the universe. God rules.

Yet like any good chief executive, God is a delegator. He confers power on others to carry out His plans. Adam and Eve were delegated this authority in ruling the earth:

And God blessed them; and God said to them, "Be fruitful and multiply, and fill the earth, and subdue it; and rule over the fish of the sea and over the birds of the sky, and over every living thing that moves on the earth." (Genesis 1:28)

Adam and Eve had an awesome responsibility. They represented God on earth, the way ambassadors in foreign countries represent their president. Adam and Eve were give the job to rule the earth the way God would have.

Had there been no Fall, perhaps you and I would still be ruled by Adam and Eve on earth. Rebellion against God, however, ripped rulership from their hands. They were disqualified. The result was that the dominion of God was lost. Though God was the rightful ruler, His creation began moving away from His rule.

Since that time, God has instituted other leaders to govern: the patriarchs—Abraham, Isaac, and Jacob; the judges and prophets; and kings. They have been allowed by Him to govern: "The Most High God is ruler over the realm of mankind, and . . . He sets over it whomever he wishes" (Daniel 5:21).

But it hasn't gone well. Like a progressive disease, each ruler, though allowed by God, has, for the most part, moved further away from the ideal of pre-Fall Adam and Eve.

Instead of authorities over earth in God's image, we became the opposite: slaves to sin. Instead of reigning over the planet, we experienced sin's reign over us.[1]

This is a tragic turn of events. The representatives of the King became prisoners. And this is the motivation behind the coming of Christ. His death freed us from bondage to eternal isolation and darkness: "having been freed from sin, you became slaves of righteousness" (Romans 6:18). The Son, under the authority of the Father, gave us the freedom to be reestablished as image-bearers, to work again in the role of subduing and ruling.

This is what the concept of the Kingdom of God, or Kingdom of heaven, is about: God reestablishing His rightful role as king over a universe careening out of control and toward destruction. He is reclaiming His territory through redeemed lives. And the day will come when His rule is again complete.

This is where our own abilities to deal appropriately with authority are so important. Knowing how to respond to—and become—an authority helps us with the task of discharging our responsibilities. The centurion whose servant was sick understood his position in authority when he requested Jesus' intervention:

> Lord, I am not worthy for you to come under my roof, but just say the word, and my servant will be healed. For I, too, am a man under authority, with soldiers under me; and I say to this one, "Go!" and he goes, and to another, "Come!" and he comes, and to my slave, "Do this!" and he does it. (Matthew 8:8-9)

The centurion knew how to be under authority, and how to give it. Jesus called him more faithful than anyone in Israel.

As believers, we'll one day be in positions of evaluation and authority that right now are hard for us to understand: "Do you not know that the saints will judge the world? . . . Do you not know that we shall judge angels? How much more, matters of this life?" (1 Corinthians 6:2-3). In some way, we'll be called on to exercise the authority originally delegated to us: "Thou dost make [man] to rule over the works of thy hands; thou has put all things under his feet" (Psalm 8:6).

We're born to rule wisely, under our Wise Ruler. That's why learning to exercise the authority we have over our lives today is so important.

A DEVELOPMENTAL VIEW

"He's out of control," said an anxious Robert while Cheryl, his wife, nodded. Billy, their sixteen-year-old son, had just been arrested by the juvenile authorities for the third time for drug use and disorderly conduct. Since turning thirteen, Billy had seemed to lose all respect for his parents' words. He would talk back, curse them to their faces, and openly defy them.

Robert was the most perplexed by the change in his son. "My own father was a military type," he told me. "I always felt harshly treated, with much stricter punishment than my friends had to endure. It seemed like my dad was never pleased with me. That's why I swore to myself that if I ever had a son, I wouldn't be his dad . . . I'd be his friend. But Billy won't talk to me now."

Robert's own reaction to his background was the soil from which much of Billy's problem grew. Thinking to spare Billy from the authoritarianism he'd suffered from, Robert had stayed away from being "in charge" of the family. Rules and standards of conduct were seen as "legalistic"; when Billy had a childhood tantrum his parents would apologize to him for being "too strict."

Billy had no authority model to internalize. He had no one in control who could teach him how to love healthy authority. His situation was like the old days in Israel: "In those days there was no king in Israel; every man did what was right in his own eyes" (Judges 17:6). The result was that Billy could not submit appropriately to authority.

The family, as a creation of God, has a central purpose: *to develop adults who can continue the subordinating of the earth to the Kingdom of God*. The successful family moves its children gradually to the place where they can take charge of their lives. This means they learn to function as independent adults and to use their gifts and talents in a productive way. They will be able to deal with their sexuality maturely and know when to lead and when to follow.

This process involves taking a child who feels very small and inadequate and helping him develop until he feels on an equal level with the other adults in his life. It's hard being on eye level with other people's kneecaps. You can't negotiate or disagree on an adult level when you feel three years old.

Ideally, preparing the child for adulthood terminates at about age eighteen, the age of emancipation in most families. In some, that age seems to be around thirty-seven! But if all goes well, the child learns to have his own moral and religious values, career dreams, tastes, interests, and the social structures in place to help him go it alone in the adult world.

This emerging independence generally takes place in two phases: the preteen and the teen years. From birth till puberty, parenting is a matter of love and limits, as the child learns that "I can't do everything I want—other people are in charge. Maybe I better listen to them." The internalization of family values and rules becomes a part of the child's character.

At around ages four to six, the child learns to identify with the same-sex parent. This prepares the child for his or her gender role. A little later, competition for the opposite-sex parent's love enters the picture. Here, urges to replace the same-sex parent threaten the child with guilt, as the connection to the same-sex parent is still quite important. These desires are then repressed, and the identification with the same-sex parent is strengthened. The idea is that we'll choose a mate and a lifestyle of our own one day in much the same fashion that Mom or Dad did.

After this, the second major phase of parenting is more of a "de-parenting" time. From puberty until leaving home, the job changes *from controlling the child's behavior to helping him stand on his own.* This still involves rules and limits, but now they must be more flexible and negotiated. The goal is for the teenager to "own" the values he's developing and live with their natural consequences.

Some parents are better with the first style, and some with the second. I remember one family in a church I attended who had seven children under eleven years old. All seven were perfectly well-behaved. All the other parents felt woefully inadequate next to them, until one wise parent among them said, "Don't condemn yourselves until the kids are adolescents." He knew that was the acid test of parenting.

This shift in parenting styles is very difficult for many mothers and fathers. They wonder why the child wants to be with friends more than them. Why their advice isn't sought out as much. Why the idealization of the parents is gone. That's because these are necessary preparations for adulthood, when the child must be able to live with his own internal view of the world—a mixture of parental values and his own. If these "pushes away" don't occur, the child is easy prey for authoritarian leaders, cultists, parental bosses, controlling spouses, and manipulative friends.

The best thing parents can do during this time is to permit children to go through questioning, challenging periods. However, we must be careful to enter into these as consultants, helping children see the consequences of the values they're thinking about. How much better off are children who question compared to those whose questioning was suppressed, only to rebel in their thirties. The suppressed children lost so much more.

This fourth developmental stage, then, is the culmination of the first three. The family teaches the child to attach. Next, it trains her to be separate—to set boundaries and respect the boundaries of others. It provides a place where she can deal with good and bad in herself and the world, without having to split them off. And it reinforces the abilities and strengths of the maturing person as it helps her take her place in the world.

THE MEANING OF AUTHORITY

Authority also means "expertise." We always pay more attention to an "authoritative source" quoted on the news, because they know more than we do about a subject. God's plan for our maturity is that we become an expert in something. It may be in management, or parenting, or music. But the expertise entailed by authority is God's way for the Body of Christ to operate in an interdependent way.

This interdependence is much like the structure of an old small town or village. The blacksmith shod the horses. The livery stable took care of them. The grocer fed the people. Each one was necessary, but each one needed the others.

Authority means looking at the meaning behind rules, not simply at the rules themselves. I saw a bumper sticker one day that said "Because I'm the Mommy." Obviously it had been written as the exasperated reply of the parent to a child who had a severe case of "But why can't I?" And for young children, that answer is sometimes enough. Children don't learn logic and reason until around eighteen months. After that, though, reasonable "whys" need to be addressed. They help the child make sense of her world. To have to tell a teenager "Because I said so" generally is an admission of the parent's failure to lead by guidance and therefore having to resort to control.

The Pharisees were rule-bound individuals. They were unable to see the law of love behind the traditions (loving God and others). The traditions, and rules, are the servants of love, not the opposite. When a tradition prevents love, or hurts the innocent, it needs to be broken in the name of love.

That's why Jesus told the Pharisees that they had condemned the innocent. He allowed His hungry disciples to pick grain on a sabbath; He healed on a sabbath; and He criticized anyone who would not rescue an animal out of a pit on a sabbath, saying that people are much more valuable than animals.[2] The Pharisees would have let the rules cause people to suffer needlessly.

Rule-bound people who have a controlling edge to them can be identified by the same trait as the Pharisees: they would rather be right than loving. For them, correctness is a matter of action, not of relationship. When these people are in positions of authority, they attract hurting, self-condemning people who are unconsciously looking for someone who will agree with their critical internal parent. The relationship becomes typified by the "parent" criticizing, then the "child" feeling guilty and trying harder to please. It becomes a cycle, since the pharisaical "parent" is fundamentally unpleasable.

SEPARATENESS VERSUS AUTHORITY

It's easy to mistake the stage of authority and adulthood for the stage of separateness and boundaries. Both involve the development of more aggressive functions in us, more confrontation, and more "pushing." But these stages are fundamentally different: *boundaries result in the existence of a separate person; authority results in our introduction into the world as a functioning, mature adult.*

Many people with solid boundaries have no clue about career goals, special abilities, how to handle sexuality, or how to take their place of authority in the world. They still feel like a child in a grown-up world. These people have not felt permission to become an adult.

HOW TO REPAIR ADULTHOOD

Resolving the problem of feeling like a frightened or enraged child in a grown-up world is a crucial developmental task. We must move from feeling one-down or one-up to others, to taking responsibility for developing our own position in the world as an adult. Accomplishing this task requires developing the following skills:

1. *Question authority.* People who learn to ask questions learn not to idealize others, but to accept the good and the bad.

Find a spiritual, financial, relational, or career leader and ask yourself, "What do I disagree with here?" If there is nothing, you're moving toward a form of cultism. Ask questions of this person. Mature authorities aren't threatened by questions. They welcome the presence of other adults. They don't need children agreeing with everything they say, because they know that questions are a source of growth for them, also.

2. *Submit to authority.* The Bible says that God has delegated offices of leadership, which we are to follow:

Let every person be in subjection to the governing authorities. For there is no authority except from God, and those which exist are established by God. (Romans 13:1)

Obey your leaders, and submit to them; for they keep watch over your souls, as those who will give an account. Let them do this with joy and not with grief, for this would be unprofitable for you. (Hebrews 13:17)

Two points need to be clarified here:

a. *We are to see authority as a positional, not a personal, issue.* God has delegated people over us for His own reasons. We do not pick which supervisor is over us at work. But that supervisor's authority does not rest in his fairness, or whether or not we respect him. It rests in the authority of the corporation. And the authority of the corporation rests in God.

We are to respect the position that some people have over us, as well as the fact that God has chosen them to be in our lives at that point in time, even if there is nothing to respect in the character of the person. This is why we are to honor our parents.[3] To honor is to respect the position, or to give weight to what is weighty. If the character of our parents is not weighty, or full of integrity, that's not honorable, and we shouldn't pretend it is. But their position is from God.

b. *Authority has parameters.* When we're children, our parents are a temporary model for God, to help us learn what God is like. When we're adults, our authorities are more limited in their areas of authority. This is to give the "bottom line" to our relationship with God.

For example, I would listen to my surgeon about an upcoming operation. His opinion on how to fix my leaky water heater, however, wouldn't carry a lot of weight.

People who make one person or group their unlimited authority for making all decisions involving spiritual life, money, career, and love relationships run the risk of making someone on earth their "Father."

3. *Take an inventory of your values and convictions.* Ask yourself, "What do I believe about God? Jesus Christ? Salvation? The Bible?" Then find out why you believe what you believe. This is a good "faith evaluation."

Do you have to run to a certain commentary or author to find out what you believe? A lot of people are afraid of this exercise, but God isn't. He applauded the Bereans for "examining the Scriptures daily, to see whether these things were so" (Acts 17:11). If our views about the Scriptures and the Christian faith are true, they will stand up to scrutiny. If not, they should be exposed.

4. *Address adults as adults, not parents.* Begin relating away from the one-down position. Some people have a hard time maintaining eye contact with parental figures, or using their normal vocabulary. Instead, they sound much younger than they actually are. Use the parental figure's first name, for example.

This also applies to our given parents. They leave the position of parent when we become adults, and at that point we should relate to them as friends. Jesus' statement that "whoever does the will of My Father who is in heaven, he is My brother and sister and mother" (Matthew 12:50) reflects this same principle. Good parenting should culminate in equality, not continued control.

5. *Develop your talents.* Adulthood involves finding out what your passion is, what you really want to accomplish in your lifespan, and what gifts you have to do it. They may be very different from your family's expectations. But the Bible says parenting is not deciding the role of the child. It's *discovering* his role: "Train up a child in the way he should go, even when he is old he will not depart from it" (Proverbs 22:6). "The way he should go" in the Hebrew text refers to God's blueprint for the child, not the parents' wishes.

6. *Make sexuality a good thing.* Christians who are still fused with their parents can't feel like adult sexual beings. They still feel like a child, and children aren't sexual. There can be severe internal prohibitions about sex. One woman reported to me that she couldn't enjoy sex with her husband, because a large picture of her parents hung on the wall facing the bed! Every time she and her husband got sexual, all she could see was her parents looking at her disapprovingly. She found another place for the picture.

Often, these inhibitions require a relationship in which sexually frank discussions can take place among mature adults, to normalize that sex is "something adults do." In time, a person can cherish sex for the gift that it is, and feel more spontaneous.

7. *See guilt as a sign of growth.* This may sound odd, but it refers to the fact that for us to become adults, we have to disobey the "traditions of the elders" (Mark 7:3), rethinking them in order to obey God's direction.

This process often means challenging and questioning, which

can lead to an angry, critical "internal parent." Sometimes this produces intense feelings of guilt: "I'm bad for thinking or saying that"; or "If they knew, they'd be so disappointed in me." With enough adult practice, that critical voice can be tamed from judgmentalism to ideals.

People who never feel guilt have generally avoided taking risks to grow up because of a fear of being a disappointing or bad child. Guilt can be helpful to us. It often shows us that we are attempting to become adults.

SUMMARY

In these last four chapters, we've looked at the building blocks of character in the image of God:

- the ability to be attached and to attach,
- the ability to set boundaries and be separate,
- the ability to live with the good and bad of ourselves and others,
- the ability to establish oneself as an adult with appropriate adult authority.

These four aspects are the foundation of personality. God's plan is for us to develop them all fully. *The more we develop these traits, the more we become like Him.* The problem is that we are all injured, at some level, in the development of all of these aspects.

This is where hiding comes in. When our growth is arrested in the development of these parts, we remove ourselves from further growth. By hiding, we try to protect ourselves from further pain. And sometimes we bury certain aspects of our soul—perhaps our trusting feelings, or our adulthood—so deeply that we lose awareness of its existence.

It's the redemption of these parts of the self that we are afraid of—and need—the most. These frozen aspects of our souls desperately need the light of grace and the instruction of truth. But we're terrified at the same time that we'll experience even more isolation, hate, or criticism than we've already felt.

This doesn't make all hiding bad. Some self-protections, in fact, are necessary for spiritual and emotional growth.

Remember that Jenny struggled with the adult decisions thrust on her by her hideout in the Woods:

> *Jenny felt too small to confront these questions all by herself. Yet they had to be answered in some way for her to make a life for herself in the Deep Woods.*
>
> *Whenever Jenny felt inadequate to solve a problem or make a decision, she would think back to Officer Josef's kind face. He had helped her with so many grown-up questions when she was back home. He'd helped her get to her friend's house. He told her the best way to catch crickets and had taught her to ride a bicycle.*
>
> Now what would Officer Josef say I should do about this? *Jenny would ask herself. On many occasions this would help her come up with solutions to her problems. And sometimes she'd remember her mother's or father's wise advice about things.*
>
> *But at other times, Jenny would sit on the ground and weep. She just felt too little and too overwhelmed for all these questions and decisions. Her aloneness had become deeply painful.*

Jenny's authority need was great, but she was developmentally incapable of such maturity. So she developed a helpful inner hiding pattern of recalling Officer Josef's wisdom to help her deal with the challenges of her external environment. Jenny's recollection of Officer Josef protected her from moving prematurely toward adulthood by helping her make adult decisions before she was able to do so alone.

When Jenny began having conversations with Big Jenny and Little Jenny, however, she had developed a harmful hiding pattern when trying to make adult decisions.

Have you ever considered your own struggle for adulthood? Are there painful memories that have hindered your ability to function as an adult? Jenny wasn't ready to function with adult authority because of her age and developmental process—helpful hiding enabled her to survive anyway. But your adult maturing process requires that you develop the skills listed earlier. Take time now to look back over these skills. Ask yourself some tough questions about your abilities in each area. You'll be helping yourself to further growth.

In part 2, we'll look at how hiding can sometimes be helpful and other times be harmful. It's important that we recognize these patterns in order to become healthy and fully functioning adults.

NOTES   1. See Romans 6:17 and 6:12.
            2. Matthew 12:1-7 and 12:10-13.
            3. See Exodus 20:12 and Ephesians 6:2-3.

Helpful and Harmful Hiding

✠

CHAPTER EIGHT

Helpful Hiding: Dealing with Suffering

CONNIE, a bright, middle-aged Bible college graduate, came to me with deep theological questions—and depression. "I'm having problems accepting life the way God's dealt it to me," she said. "Do you help people adjust to unchangeable situations—situations that are our 'lot' in life?"

"If that's the case, sure," I responded. "But why don't you tell me about the situation?"

Connie told me the story of her twenty-year marriage in which she'd served time as a doormat for a critical and unpleasable husband. "It's nothing obvious," she told me. "Hal isn't abusive or anything like that. He never raises his voice. But no matter how clean the house is, or how much time I spend making a special dinner for him, there's always a comment about something I missed. Or forgot. Or burned. I always wait, and it always comes along in a few minutes."

"What happens when you tell him how this hurts you?" I asked.

"Nothing," Connie replied. "I don't tell him."

"Doesn't it hurt your feelings?"

"That's the point," she said. "It shouldn't hurt. I must be too unspiritual to take his comments in love and grow from them. I'm trying to bloom where I'm planted. I need help with my pride problem."

Connie's dilemma involved a common misunderstanding of hiding: Even though it's a "post-Fall" concept, *some hiding is necessary.* Many Christians feel that they should not only *endure* whatever is thrown their way, but even *volunteer* for more pain, because they view that as "suffering for Christ."

This is not a biblical view. Much suffering we experience is neither for God's glory nor for our good. Without some types of self-protection, we suffer in destructive ways. There are good and bad reasons to withdraw from pain. Connie was unfamiliar with good or helpful hiding. To understand this distinction, let's look at what the Bible tells us about suffering.

A BIBLICAL VIEW OF SUFFERING

We experience two kinds of pain in our lifetime. The first is physical pain, such as cuts, bruises, broken limbs. Obviously, this type generally comes from physical injuries, such as fingers being under the window sill at the wrong time.

Second, there is emotional and spiritual pain, which hurts on a far deeper level. Depression, anxiety, sadness, anger, shame, and guilt are a few of the negative emotions we feel rather regularly. *Primarily, emotional pain comes from problems in our relatedness to God, self, or others.* When someone we love leaves us, we feel a loss in our hearts. This is a "good pain," because it's a sign that the person mattered to us. There's also "bad pain," which is often the result of ignoring "good pain."

For example, when we become angry at someone's lack of love for us, that anger (good pain) tells us there's a problem to solve in the relationship. If we ignore the anger, it gets internalized in the heart as a "root of bitterness" (Hebrews 12:15)—that is "bad pain."

Physical and emotional pain interact constantly. Think of a single parent with too many daily burdens who develops migraines several times a week. Or a construction worker with a debilitating back injury that leads to severe depression.

These types of suffering are part of the labor pains of creation. They remind us that the universe is still in the process of redemption. It's beyond the scope of this book to deal extensively with the question of why suffering exists in the first place. At the same time, it's important to understand what suffering is, so we can know how to respond to it.

Let's define *suffering* as *what we experience when a need or wish goes unmet.* It is a consequence of the Fall that we experience loss of love, emptiness, and other deprivations. Suffering can be a friend or an enemy. The jogger who hates every second of his running suffers, but for a purpose: to be able to get into that favorite suit. The parents who lose a child also suffer, but it doesn't make as much sense to them.

TYPES OF SUFFERING

What we do with the suffering we encounter has to do with the meaning of the pain we're in. There are some suffering experiences we are to embrace joyfully, and some we are to resist with all our strength. The types of suffering in the chart below help us understand how to respond.

RESPONDING TO SUFFERING

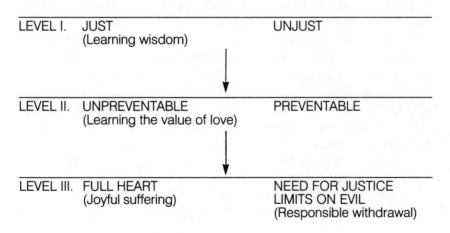

LEVEL I.	JUST (Learning wisdom)	UNJUST
LEVEL II.	UNPREVENTABLE (Learning the value of love)	PREVENTABLE
LEVEL III.	FULL HEART (Joyful suffering)	NEED FOR JUSTICE LIMITS ON EVIL (Responsible withdrawal)

The chart is a decision tree with three levels to help explain the various types of pain and what to do with them.

Level I: Just and Unjust Suffering

Just suffering is our teacher. When we experience some sort of danger signal that pain is ahead, the first question to ask is, "Do I deserve it?"

Some of the things you and I feel distress about are the natural consequence of our actions. These aren't punishments from God as much as they are teachers and friends to us. Suffering can help us train for life.

The highway speedster who gets a ticket and cries foul isn't learning from his teacher. The ticket is a somewhat painful incentive to slow down before having a wreck. The worker who's fired because of chronic lateness has been done a favor. If he learns from his lesson, he'll go to bed earlier and become more responsible. Painful consequences teach us to be accountable for what God has given us. That's why Paul told one of the young churches, "If anyone will not work, neither let him eat" (2 Thessalonians 3:10) – that consequence has a tendency to get attention!

Psychological symptoms have a "just" and an "unjust" component to them. Depression, eating disorders, addictions, and compulsive behaviors are generally the fruit of a combination of two types of sin: sin done *by* us, and sin done *to* us.

Diane came from a family where her anger brought on hurt feelings and withdrawal by her parents. Her ability to be angry, and yet not sin was stunted (sin done to her). Diane learned to conceal her anger by sarcastic, biting humor, which she could justify by saying, "I was just kidding" (sin done by her).

Finally, Diane sought help with her struggles in intimacy. Whenever people tried to come close to her, sooner or later she ran them off with her stinging words. Her symptom was an intense feeling of isolation.

We need to understand this sort of emotional suffering. Our suffering is inevitable when we don't pay attention to our psychological symptoms, or deal with the hurt part of the heart. In other words, these sorts of troublesome emotions and behaviors are friends saying to us, "Here's a problem—start working on it." When we don't pay attention to emotional pain—and treat it appropriately—then, as in the effects of physical pain, we will suffer the consequences.

Unjust suffering brings on pain that we don't deserve to experience. Sometimes we can be like the innocent passerby who is hit by a car. Before we embrace or refuse this type of suffering, we need to ask a second question: "Is my suffering preventable?" In other words, is it beyond my control?

Level II: Preventable and Unpreventable Suffering

Unpreventable, unjust suffering is a product of the Fall.

Christine was sexually abused by her father between the ages of six and ten. One day, against his order never to tell "their" secret, she told her mother, in the best terms a ten-year-old could find, what was happening. Her mother's response was, "If it's happening, you must be encouraging it." Shamed and confused, Christine never told anyone about the molestation again until intense panic attacks in her adult life brought her to treatment.

Christine's story is an example of unpreventable suffering, contrary to what her mother thought. She wasn't able to stop her father's physical and emotional violations. Children are in an especially vulnerable position for this type of suffering. They are undeveloped, afraid, and unprepared to know how to protect themselves, especially from those they love.

Of all the types of suffering out there, most of us find unjust and unpreventable suffering the hardest to take. There seems something fundamentally "wrong" with those forms of pain that we haven't caused ourselves.

Some Bible teachers explain this kind of pain as something God sends us to teach us a lesson. Though God does allow this kind of suffering, it's not always true that it's a "blessing" or "lesson."

This type of suffering seems to be the result of the very high value God places on our freedom to choose love or evil. He did this because He knew that love without freedom is slavery, compliance, and performance. It is worthless, because it isn't obedience from the heart. *The cost of people's choices to love Him or others is this: we are as free to move away from love as we are to move toward love.*

It's only when we can say no to love that our yes means anything. Consider Jesus' parable of the two sons in the vineyard:[1] needing workers in his vineyard, a father asked his two sons for help. Their responses were quite different. One son, unable to say no in his words, did say it in his action—he never made it to work that day. The other son was openly rebellious. His honesty allowed him to repent—and he eventually made it to the vineyard.

God wanted Christine's father to love her and treat her as the precious gift from Him that she was. Instead, he chose evil. Christine suffered because of her dad's freedom to be unloving.

The Bible does teach us the value of discipline from God: "My son, do not reject the discipline of the LORD, or loathe His reproof, for whom the Lord loves He reproves, even as a father, the son in whom he delights" (Proverbs 3:11-12).

This kind of pain is "training pain." To strengthen his runners, a good track coach will often tell them to go an extra lap. This pain has meaning and direction. A responsible coach, however, won't let his runners drop from dehydration. There's no benefit to them or him.

God is a good parent. He disciplines with reasons. But He allows the freedom of others to do evil, because of the high value He places on love.

Unpreventable and unjust pain is all around us. It's there in our physical limitations. It's present in times when we're let down by someone we trust, or when we are the object of someone's unjustified anger. Handling this type of suffering usually entails one of two responses from us: denial or grieving, or both.

Many of us demand justice on earth. Some of us constantly fight against unjust treatment of ourselves by others. We may evaluate our day by how often we are able to confront others' sins against us. Sometimes, too, we project victimized feelings onto others. Or, those of us suffering from this malady may become a "crusader" for several different causes. This is often a denial of our impotence to bring absolute justice to others or the world, which is in God's domain: "Vengeance is Mine, and retribution" (Deuteronomy 32:35).

For some of us, "righteous rage" is less painful than *the sadness of knowing how much suffering we really are helpless to prevent.* The illusion of control keeps us away from accepting our powerlessness in some situations. "At least I'm doing something about the wrongs of the world," we rationalize. But just as often, we desperately fight the sad acceptance of the fundamental "unfairness" of living in a fallen world. Just as Paul "kicked against the goads" (Acts 26:14), we resist what we can't control.

One symptom of this kind of orientation is chronic restlessness and dissatisfaction. There's always another wrong to right. For this person, *anything* is preferable to sadness.

God chose to limit Himself by allowing us freedom, and in doing so He also experienced that sadness:

> "O Jerusalem, Jerusalem, who kills the prophets and stones those who are sent to her! How often I wanted to gather your children together, the way a hen gathers her chicks under her wings, and you were unwilling." (Matthew 23:37)

Jesus felt the self-induced helplessness of watching people destroy themselves.

Although we are certainly to be agents of justice on earth, we also need to enter the "house of mourning" over the injustices we can't control. Grief is God's solution for accepting what we cannot change. Sadness allows our heart to let go of what it can't have and prepare for what it can. God values mourning so much that Israel had professional mourning women who were to teach that skill.[2] Our grief allows us to accept our creatureliness and look to God as the final Judge.

Preventable, unjust suffering raises the question of love versus justice. Think of Connie's situation with a critical husband. She wasn't helpless. She could have confronted Hal about his critical tongue. Yet for what she thought were biblical reasons, Connie chose to allow him to criticize her for years. Before we embrace or refuse this type of suffering, we see that this problem leads to the third question we must ask about our suffering: "Is it a question of love, or justice?"

Level III: Joyful Suffering and Helpful Hiding
Think about your daily encounters in which you have an opportunity to suffer or not to suffer:

- When your friend wants to eat Italian food, which you aren't partial to, you can go along.
- When the boss yells, you can be silent and take it.
- When your spouse overdraws against the checking account for the fifth time in three months, you can quietly cover the drafts.

These and countless other situations provide us with the choice to allow ourselves to experience some sort of distress. A second "distress" is determining whether to keep quiet or confront; to allow irresponsibility or to prevent it; to suffer pain or avoid it.

Some people say, "Christians should just 'take it.'" Others say, "We must always confront injustice." Actually, it's not that simple, no matter which side you take. God says a great deal about suffering voluntarily, and yet also a great deal about refusing evil.

The pivotal point between these two worlds has to do with two aspects of God's character: *love* and *justice*. The principle here is this: *When our ability to love is greater than our need for justice, we joyfully suffer. When our need for justice exceeds our ability to love, we responsibly withdraw.*

This "responsible withdrawal" is helpful hiding.

The Bible speaks often about *joyful suffering* when referring to Christians submitting to hard times. Jesus taught that there are times when we should turn the other cheek to whoever slaps us, to give our cloak to the one who wants our shirt, and to go the second mile with the one who forces us to travel one. He said that we all have a burden to carry as believers.[3] The entire book of 1 Peter speaks of enduring or bearing up under injustice, particularly the following passage:

> For this finds favor, if for the sake of conscience toward God a man bears up under sorrows when suffering unjustly. For what credit is there if, when you sin and are harshly treated, you endure it with patience? But if when you do what is right and suffer for it you patiently endure it, this finds favor with God.
>
> For you have been called for this purpose, since Christ also suffered for you, leaving you an example for you to follow in His steps. (1 Peter 2:19-21)

These are difficult words. Yet these same words also give us a glimpse into the heart of God. The principle here is that *suffering is the pricetag of love*. When someone is important to us, we willingly suffer for that person's benefit.

In Peter's understanding, suffering unfairness joyfully is an act of deep gratitude to God for what He has done for us. This passage is set against the backdrop of the ultimate act of voluntary, unjust suffering: the crucifixion. The message of the cross is that Christ endured the fatal pain of the world for no other reason than because of God's desire to heal our estrangement from Him. An innocent suffering for the guilty doesn't fit our concept of fairness, but it does show the supremacy of God's love.

There are times when the heart is empty or injured and has nothing to give. In these times we need justice, in the form of support away from suffering, in order to become reconnected to God and others.

This reconnection lifts us out of deprivation and need and into a position of gratitude. When the heart is full, it indicates that we have received love. At this point, allowing another to inconvenience us would not damage our heart. Our ability to love is enhanced beyond our need for justice. The following example illustrates this point.

After regularly reminding Alan for several months about his habit of leaving clothes all around the house, Margie had noticed improvement. Alan was starting to pick up socks off the floor, take jackets off the sofa, keep shirts off the table. Neatness didn't come naturally for him, as it did for her. Alan was proud of himself the day he rounded up clothes from around the house and did the wash.

A few days later, Alan left the house in a hurry, with more clothes on the floor in his wake than he'd been wearing. As Margie surveyed the damage she kept seeing Alan's big grin when he'd shown her the clean laundry. She felt a glow of love for him as she thought, "He's really trying." She bent down and began to pick up after him.

You may have had an experience similar to Margie's, in which your ability to love was greater than your need for justice. Margie had felt loving and close to Alan. Her heart was full. At that point, her ability to love became greater than her need for justice. She didn't need to confront Alan at that time, though she probably would have to continue the process later—he wasn't well yet!

Be warned, however, that it's easy to misunderstand the "love versus justice" principle. Someone like Connie might say, "I don't feel the love that Margie feels. I need an attitude adjustment." Some people may think they need to "make" themselves feel gratitude in order to suffer joyfully. But this is backwards thinking.

Love, joy, and gratitude are the fruit of God's Spirit of grace. They are the results of being loved; they're not something we can choose at will. That would be like attempting to choose a normal temperature when we're running a fever! Just as we need to diagnose the infection that's causing the fever, so we need to understand spiritual and emotional isolation as a cause of our lack of love, joy, and gratitude during times when we're not experiencing the fruit of the Spirit.

If we're allowing ourselves to suffer because of fear, obligation, or guilt, we can't respond from a loving position: as John says in his first epistle, perfect love casts out fear. Connie couldn't suffer joyfully because she wasn't in a loved position. She couldn't give what she didn't have. Her heart was still in a wounded state, injured by Hal's sharp criticisms.

I once heard someone tell his wife that the only reason he

was loving toward her was because God commands it. I'm sure his fear of God's disapproval didn't translate well into tenderness inside her.

To feel unloving in situations like Connie's is not a sign of pride or being unspiritual. It's the heart's way of saying that we're disconnected from relationship in some way. There's been a break in our need to be rooted and grounded in love.

Helpful hiding is the opposite of forcing ourselves to suffer resentfully. It takes wisdom to know how much deprivation we can take in a relationship before real damage occurs. *The biblical solution is to withdraw in order to protect the soul.* This means knowing when our need for justice is greater than our ability to love.

In this context, withdrawal is not selfishness, but responsible stewardship: "The prudent sees the evil and hides himself, but the naive go on, and are punished for it" (Proverbs 22:3). Some suffering is not "for Jesus' sake." We can find ourselves in situations that are too difficult, too painful, too destructive, or too injurious. This is when we need to set limits.

The ability to set limits requires knowledge of the state of our heart. We need to know which parts of ourselves are more tender and in need of more grace. Sometimes we're particularly fragile, such as when we suffer despair: "For the despairing man there should be kindness from his friend; lest he forsake the fear of the Almighty" (Job 6:14). Many people whose hearts are weak and sick listen to poorly timed and insensitive criticisms – and distance themselves further from God.

It's significant that God tells how to handle people in different spiritual and emotional states. We are to "admonish the unruly, encourage the fainthearted, help the weak, be patient with all men" (1 Thessalonians 5:14). We admonish when people are unruly (rulebreakers). The unruly need the structure they don't have. On the other hand, we all need encouragement when we feel fainthearted.

To reverse these is tragic. Encouraging the unruly is like a watchdog making friends with the burglar! It increases license. But even worse, to admonish the fainthearted is to cause a great deal of damage to an already-injured part of the soul.

God hides Himself from closeness with unloving people:

> "But I will surely hide My face in that day because of all
> the evil which they will do, for they will turn to other gods."
> (Deuteronomy 31:18)

> "In an outburst of anger I hid My face from you for a moment;
> but with everlasting lovingkindness I will have compassion
> on you," says the LORD your Redeemer. (Isaiah 54:8)

You can almost feel the Lord's tuggings toward and away from His wayward people.

The Old Testament tells us that David, one of Israel's wisest kings, withdrew from relationships with people who weren't loving: "He who walks in a blameless way is the one who will minister to me" (Psalm 101:6). Jesus told the disciples to get out of town if they weren't well received. He knew that suffering had limits.

We saw that Connie's need for justice was greater than her ability to love. She was not able to suffer biblically, but the solution was not for her to "white-knuckle" her way through it. The solution she needed was to confront the damage that her husband, Hal, was doing, which he may not even have been aware of.

Limiting evil is a second reason for refusing to suffer wrongdoing. To ignore a friend's continual irresponsibility or evil is to deny him the lesson of learning from the consequences of his actions. "Better is open rebuke than love that is concealed," declares the writer of Proverbs (27:5). The parents who continually excuse their child's bad grades as the school's fault set up the child for even more failure later.

Nowhere is the "love versus justice" principle more graphically found than in the missionary population. Christian missionaries have some of the most demanding careers possible, with long hours, low pay, hardship, and often few earthly rewards. Yet the differences between individual missionaries can be striking.

I knew one man, Lee, who worked for twenty years with a small tribal nation under very adverse conditions—and flourished.

Another missionary I knew, Raymond, worked in a civilized country with a much easier job—and suffered a nervous breakdown and a marital breakdown within eighteen months.

Why the contrasting results? It wasn't a matter of faith or spirituality. Lee had come from a warm, accepting family and church background. He had internalized many years of unconditional love—he had a full heart. Once on the missionary field, he had the influence of past loving relationships to support him. And because Lee had been connected in healthy ways all his life, he was able to build a good support system even in the sparse country where he lived. Love multiplies love.

Raymond, on the other hand, came from a much different family background. His emotionally detached parents had been divorced while he was growing up. Becoming a Christian in his teens had helped him separate from his environment, but Raymond had never been able to connect well with others. The missionary field seemed a way for him to feel productive, yet still keep some distance from people.

When Raymond began his position, he was unprepared for the isolation and stress of the job. Because he had no memories of support, he had no ability to ask for it. The fallout was inevitable.

The more loved we are, the more we're able to withstand suffering from a loved position. We can endure more deprivation in the present if we've had enough consistent, warm, accepting attachment in the past. Jesus was fully connected to His "support system," the Trinity. Therefore, He was able to endure unimaginable suffering willingly, as the writer to the Hebrews tells us in his instruction to fix our eyes on "Jesus, the author and perfecter of faith, who for the joy set before Him endured the cross, despising the shame, and has sat down at the right hand of the throne of God" (Hebrews 12:2).

Jenny endured an incredible amount of deep suffering in a short, condensed period of time. In effect, she took a crash course in pain. Within a few hours she went from loving, warm attachment to terror and complete alienation. Yet she survived. Why?

Jenny had a history of years of consistent bonding with her parents. She'd been fully connected to them, and they had given her an excellent picture of love and faithfulness in relationship.

Perhaps you've never had such a picture. Or, if you have enjoyed this kind of family history, perhaps you've rejected it for some false substitute for appropriate bonding—perhaps an addictive behavior. Maybe you're simply struggling with the more philosophical question of justice. In any of these cases, you have an important decision to make: *to balance the love-justice principle.*

If you can recognize and accept the fact that both love and justice exist, and that God has provided some clear provisions for dealing with these co-existing realities, perhaps you'll come to a decision to endure suffering in a Christlike way. Seeking out loving relationships that will move you toward that ability will do a lot to help you prepare for suffering when it comes. Withdrawing from injustice when you recognize it will protect you from unnecessary suffering.

PRINCIPLES VERSUS RULES

The "love versus justice" principle may be frustrating for some Christians who would like more defined "rules of conduct" about suffering. They may feel anxious without specific guidelines for the particular kinds of situations in which they should or shouldn't allow themselves to suffer.

Rules certainly make some aspects of life easier. But allegiance to them indicates a fear of error, not a mark of love. People who love know they'll make mistakes. But they also know they'll learn from them and mature through them.

Jesus taught in principles. Principles require a degree of maturity in discerning how to apply them. Jesus' summation of the entire Law in loving God and people was a slap in the face of religious tradition. Tradition had taken the place of a relationship with God.

HELPFUL HIDING

We've looked at when we should endure—or resist—suffering. I hope it's clear that there are many situations in which we need to withdraw from dangerous or hurtful situations.

Hurtful situations can arise from two sources of emotional pain: *internal* and *external.* Internal sources include our thoughts, feelings, and memories. They tells us there's injury inside, generally from dealing with past relationships. Quite often, individuals grieving a loss will, for no obvious reason, suddenly begin thinking about the face of the loved one who is gone. This is a sign that the grieving process is continuing. External sources occur primarily in our present relationships. Someone we're close to can fill us with joy one day and make us miserable the next.

To learn how to deal with both internal and external sources of pain, let's take a closer look at *helpful hiding.*

NOTES   1. Matthew 21:28-32.
2. See Jeremiah 9:17-20.
3. Matthew 5:38-45, 10:38, and 16:24.

CHAPTER NINE

Helpful Hiding:
Preparing for Relationship

❖

D WIGHT couldn't make Martha understand it, so he stopped
trying to explain.

Every day when Dwight came home from work, he
kissed Martha, picked up the kids for a few seconds, and
then headed straight for his workbench in the garage. For
twenty or thirty minutes he puttered with home repair projects,
in total silence. Then, finding a good stopping point, he cleaned
his tools and returned to the house to help her with dinner and
the kids for the rest of the evening.

"It used to really hurt Martha's feelings," Dwight told me. "She
would say that I must not want to be with her if I preferred building birdhouses. So I stopped going to the workbench after work,
and stayed with her and the kids. For three weeks. It was the most
miserable time any of us have ever had. I felt overwhelmed by the
kids' needs. I couldn't get work pressures out of my mind. I either
grouched at everyone or just withdrew.

"Finally, Martha sent me back out to the garage, and we began
trading off 'alone times' for each other to be able to get away from
the kids for a few minutes. Things have been fine ever since."

Dwight's puttering illustrates the purpose of helpful hiding:

It's not to isolate, but to withdraw. Isolation and withdrawal are not the same thing. To isolate is to remove oneself from relationship—to move into emotional and spiritual emptiness. It has a permanent component. *Withdrawal, however, is a temporary distancing so that the heart can regroup itself to reattach.*

When we withdraw, we remove ourselves from the pain or injury or distractions that keep us from love. When we feel safe again, we can move back into connection. When we're under stress, or have been hurt in a relationship, we need a time of boundary repair before our soul is ready to reattach. Once our boundaries are reestablished, we are prepared for love.

Misunderstanding this principle has done a great deal of damage to many people. Many folks see withdrawal as selfish, insensitive, or unloving. And sometimes we place tremendous pressure on those who have been hurt or wounded to be open and vulnerable before they are ready. This generally leads to reinjury of some kind.

To reenter relationship doesn't always mean we reattach with the person who hurt us. Some relationships need permanent limits put on them, because the person doesn't have God's values. The point is, we do need to reattach somewhere, but it must be with the right people.

Jesus used withdrawal when He needed it. When He began to bring the synagogue official's daughter back to life, the jeering crowd was in "noisy disorder." He had a job to do with no distractions, so He had the crowd removed from the area.[1] And when He needed time alone with God, He took action: "After He had sent the multitudes away, He went up to the mountain by Himself to pray; and when it was evening, He was there alone" (Matthew 14:23).

Quite often, people in a relationship need time apart, especially if there's been injury on either side from elements such as hostility, chronic irresponsibility, hypercriticism, or betrayals of trust. To attempt closeness too soon is to risk reinjuring an already-damaged heart. The Bible warns us: "Do not lay hands upon anyone too hastily and thus share responsibility for the sins of others; keep yourself free from sin" (1 Timothy 5:22). We are to be discerning and careful before rushing into vulnerability in relationships too quickly.

HELPFUL HIDING REQUIRES RESPONSIBILITY

Michelle's husband had left six months before our meeting, and his absence had been devastating for her.

Michelle and her husband had shared many mutual friendships as a couple. One of Michelle's most difficult adjustments was with the small segment of her friends she knew were still socializing with him. Though she cared for these friends, being with them brought up so many overwhelming feelings that she stopped seeing them for a few months. Writing each a letter, she told them why she was bowing out of the relationship for a while—and that she would call when she was ready.

This is a good example of how withdrawal from pain could be seen as selfish by some, but is actually the right thing to do. Michelle knew her emotional limits. She knew that her first priority was to recover emotional stability for herself and the kids. So she withdrew from these few relationships to prevent any handicaps to that priority.

Helpful hiding involves deliberation, prayerful awareness, and conscious choice. It is a component of wisdom: "be sober in all things" (2 Timothy 4:5). It is *not* reactive, automatic, or impulsive. Helpful hiding isn't a knee-jerk response. Had Michelle cut off her relationships without thinking or planning, she could have done more damage to herself.

Helpful hiding is also truthful. It never involves lying to God, ourselves, or others. Had Michelle been afraid to tell her friends about her conflict, she might have told them how busy she was getting these days. A wedge of falseness would have risen between her and her friends from that moment on.

BARRIERS TO HELPFUL HIDING

It's not the easiest thing in the world to protect ourselves from pain. Though it is our responsibility as stewards of our souls, several forces are at work to undermine our attempts to withdraw responsibly:

Fear of isolation. It's common for people who are afraid of being separate to have great difficulty being able to set limits, withdraw, or avoid destructive relationships. This is a "codependent" problem, and involves a fear that "if I am separate, I am isolated." One woman told me, "It's more important for me that everyone around me be happy than that I tell the truth."

Fear of injury or attack. Many of us learn early in life that going along with others helps us survive. We may have intense fears of confronting others. We want to avoid the risk of hostility or criticism. Most of the time, people with this barrier have come out of relational settings in which they've been the recipients of hostile outbursts. The terror they experienced then keeps them paralyzed in fear in the present when they encounter the anger of others.

Naivete. An inability to sense danger in relationships characterizes people with this orientation. They find themselves constantly in a "trust-injury" cycle. They become attached quickly, idealize the relationship, put all their eggs in the basket, then suffer severe disappointment when their hopes are shattered.

This has to do with a conflict in being wise about our own and others' badness. Sometimes we may fear that some badness in the other person means all badness. That is, if things aren't ideal, they can't be good. Jesus was wise about this sort of naivete: "But Jesus, on His part, was not entrusting Himself to them, for He knew all men, and because He did not need anyone to bear witness concerning man for He Himself knew what was in man" (John 2:24-25). We are to trust the trustworthy.

Giving up naivete doesn't mean becoming cynical or jaded. That's why Jesus said, "Behold, I send you out as sheep in the midst of wolves; therefore be shrewd as serpents, and innocent as doves" (Matthew 10:16). We can be aware of evil without being participants.

Repetition compulsion. Some people stay in emotionally damaging relationships because it's what they're used to. They are drawn to the same sorts of injurious situations that they grew up with.

Along with this cycle, however, is a childlike wish that they will be able to repair the lack of love they experienced the first time around. The hurt child within them takes responsibility for the injury, rather than understanding that the lack of love had to do with the other person, not themselves. These people work hard at fixing others, generally to no avail.

TYPES OF HELPFUL HIDING

God has provided many ways to deal with spiritual, emotional, and relational pain. These methods can help us stay in relationship, not in denial.

Do you remember the "castle" metaphor we used in chapter 4? We said that different parts of the castle need different sentries to guard and protect them from attack or misfortune. These "sentries" are our helpful hiding tools.

The good sentry knows two things: *who to keep out of the castle, and who to allow in.* Our helpful patterns are like that, too. They help keep us from injury, debilitating pain, or mistreatment by others. Yet they bow to love. These hiding patterns never keep the soul out of connection. They allow us to stay in contact with God and caring people.

Emotional Helpful Hiding

We all have a storehouse of painful memories, feelings, and thoughts inside. Some are lonely, some terrified, some guilty or shameful. If we were to feel the impact of all of these emotions simultaneously, we would run the risk of losing touch with reality.

This is what some panic attacks and psychotic episodes are about. Our ability to be in charge of what and when we'll remember has been damaged, and we become emotionally flooded.

That's why children split off and lose access with periods of their past. Otherwise, they run the risk of being overwhelmed or chronically depressed with the pain inside.

Our ability to experience emotional pain is measured by the amount and quality of love we've received over the years. David's prayer for God to "search and know" him was an indication that he was ready for more knowledge about himself.

Here are some examples of emotional hiding that help us:

1. *Anticipation.* Looking forward to realistic good things such as spending time with a loving relationship provides hope when we are in pain.

2. *Forgiveness.* Letting go of the demand for others to repair us can eventually free us from the pain of isolation, helplessness, and bitterness. We must remember, though, that this letting go — forgiveness — is a process and not just a one-time event.

3. *Perspective.* This is getting the "big picture" on our pain. Perspective helps us see our situation from a broader view, and closer to the true reality, which is God's viewpoint.

When Jack began experiencing some symptoms of a mid-life burnout crisis, he read several books on the subject and talked to professionals. His situation was still very difficult, but greater understanding — a new perspective — helped calm his fears.

4. *Humor.* Similar to perspective, humor can be a helpful way to live with a painful situation. A friend of mine who suffers from severe memory losses told me, "It's got its advantages . . . I keep meeting new people." She was not denying her pain, but her humor eased its intensity.

5. *Patience.* The ability to delay gratification is helpful to the person who faces a chronically difficult situation. Patience, an important aspect of self-control, involves living responsibly in the present while waiting for the future. The Scriptures recommend it, "You too be patient; strengthen your hearts, for the coming of the Lord is at hand" (James 5:8).

6. *Adjusting* (compensation). Quite often, when we're aware of a deficit in a relationship, we can make adjustments to compensate for that deficit. For example, one woman who was unable to confront a friend face to face who had hurt her communicated to her by letter until she felt safe enough to talk to her in person. She adjusted for her fragility.

7. *Confession.* Confession is a healthy defense because it takes our injured and isolated parts from their destructive aloneness, and brings them into connection with other forgiven and forgiving people.

8. *Making restitution.* When our actions have hurt another person, we need to do as much as possible to repair the damage. Rather than being merely an exercise in assuaging a guilty conscience, genuine restitution is motivated by compassion for another's suffering.

9. *Putting it on hold* (mature sublimation). If we were to remain aware of all our emotionally painful feelings constantly, in most cases we couldn't function. When we deliberately decide to focus temporarily on another task, relationship, or subject, it's not denial. It's waiting until there is a safe enough relational connection, and until we are in an appropriate state of mind, to bring painful issues to light.

Relational Helpful Hiding

Not only do we experience painful memories and feelings *inside*, but we also encounter destructive situations *outside*: that is, in our present relationships. Much of the work we need to do here involves learning to set appropriate limits on the irresponsibility or selfishness of others.

Here are some ways to deal responsibly with the evil done against us:

1. *Verbal limits.* Setting a verbal boundary is a clear way to take ownership of our souls. The word *no* is a good example. Children who grow up in homes where their *no* isn't nurtured often suffer in needless ways in adult life.

2. *Physical limits.* There are times when our *no* is not heard or respected. This is often the case when others are defensive, uncaring, out of control, have lost their temper, or are under the influence of alcohol or drugs.

The limits we need here are more geographical in nature, such as leaving the room, leaving the house, or calling for help. Jesus gives us a program for limiting evil against us in Matthew 18:15-17:

> "And if your brother sins, go and reprove him in private; if he listens to you, you have won your brother. But if he does not listen to you, take one or two more with you, so that

by the mouth of two or three witnesses every fact may be confirmed. And if he refuses to listen to them, tell it to the church; and if he refuses to listen even to the church, let him be to you as a Gentile and a tax-gatherer."

Jesus gives four "levels" of the intensity of our physical limits: one-on-one, three-on-one, an intervention with the church, and expulsion. We are to match the resistance of the one doing the evil with the appropriate level of confrontation.

JENNY'S SUFFERING

God never intended that we embrace all forms of suffering. Like Jenny, we must learn when to accept pain and when to resist evil. Hiding can be the most caring and responsible thing to do in many situations, as long as its ultimate aim is for us to reenter a loving relationship.

Remember when the ancient oak tree saved Jenny from the soldiers?

> One day during one of her long walks, Jenny was surprised to hear a man shouting. Looking back over her shoulder, she was horrified to see four uniformed soldiers—the same ones who had broken into her home and taken her parents! It was obvious that they also recognized Jenny. Breaking into a run, they spread out to catch her.
> For a split-second, Jenny was paralyzed with fear. Then her brain told her feet to move and she was off. She quickly scanned the pathway through the brush, trying to remember where she had been on her walk.
> The ancient oak tree saved her. Hundreds of years old, with a massive trunk that even her father had never been able to get his arms around, the ancient tree had always been Jenny's marker for a small fork in the path that she headed for now. The turnoff was almost invisible, but she knew the mark well and veered sharply to her left.
> Darting behind the oak, Jenny plunged into deep, almost

impenetrable brush along the narrow pathway toward a little tunnel that ran through the briers. It was barely big enough even for her to get through. She knew the foxes and badgers used this path often. She ran silently, although she could hear her heart pounding.

The soldiers ran right past the hidden path and rushed down the larger one. Perplexed and confused, their voices echoed off the surrounding oaks, sounding like bloodhounds losing a scent. Then their sounds died off in the distance.

Jenny waited for a while before she returned to her friendly cave, just in case they might have found it. She thanked the oak tree for being just where he was supposed to be.

Jenny had used her months in the Deep Woods well. Her understanding had helped her escape the soldiers. Silently, she began to thread her way back through the trees to her shelter.

Jenny did the responsible thing when she hid from the enemy soldiers the first time they tried to catch her. She was careful not to come out of hiding and expose herself to more terror and the same sort of suffering her parents had endured after capture.

Jenny did something very interesting after she escaped and waited patiently until the coast was clear—she actually thanked the old oak for being in the path and marking her escape route. Jenny used the skills she had learned in her isolation to keep her from further evil. Then she showed a respectable humility and thanksgiving when safe.

Does Jenny set an appropriate example for you in this part of her story? Think through the appropriate hiding skills you've learned and how certain relationships, primarily with God and with significant other people in your life, have contributed to your relational skills. It's often helpful to thank God for placing those ancient oaks in your path that He designed as markers for escaping evil. In addition, you may want to thank friends and family for their parts in helping you shape certain skills—even at times when it was painful (remember, iron sharpens iron) for you.

God places people in our paths for a reason—His own reason. Yet they act as instruments that help us prepare for relationship. Jenny might never have seen her parents again had she not learned how to hide responsibly from the evil that confronted her in the enemy soldiers. We also face such obstacles, yet in the long run they can prove to be instruments that help us learn appropriate hiding skills.

Now let's turn to the next chapter to look at harmful ways of hiding that God never intended for us.

NOTE   1. Matthew 9:23-25.

CHAPTER TEN

Harmful Hiding:
Six Critical Stages

✤

OUG AND I walked back to the car from the cemetary, the winter leaves crunching under our shoes. It had been a difficult day. Doug had just buried his elderly mother.

Doug and I had been friends for a long time. When he'd asked me to accompany him to the funeral after her lingering illness, I was glad to help out. During the proceeding, however, something had begun to bother me. At first I couldn't figure out what it was.

As the day wore on, the problem became apparent. It wasn't anything obvious. Just the opposite—it was something that *should* have been present that was conspicuous by its absence: Doug's sadness. There was no sense of loss or grief coming from him before, during, or after the proceedings. Just a matter-of-fact, let's-get-this-over-with purposefulness.

Curious, I told him what I had been thinking and asked him about his feelings. "That's true," he said. "I've been trying to feel my mourning for Mother's passing for the last several days, and I don't think there's anything there."

"Any idea why?" I asked.

"You had to understand Mother," Doug replied. "She was a

fine, moral, pleasant woman. But I never knew her. I don't think anyone did. I never saw her angry—never saw a tear, either. I think she must have decided a long, long time ago never to let anyone inside. Maybe she'd been hurt badly—I don't know. But there was a certain inaccessibility to her. I was never able to get past it.

"I guess that's why I don't have the sadness I'm supposed to have," he went on. "There's really no relationship to mourn. Now *that* . . . that's sad." And Doug began to weep.

For her own reasons, Doug's mother had made a lifestyle out of hiding from relationship and risk. She had lived an emotionally cautious life and had, as the saying goes, slid safely into death. The real tragedy here, as Doug now understood, was the consequences. She wasn't missed.

There's an old story about a proud man learning significance from a wise man. The wise man made the proud one put his finger into a bucket of water. Telling him to remove his finger, the wise man said, "See that hole in the water where your finger was? That is how significant you are."

Although we are actually much more significant than that in God's eyes (even the hairs of our heads are numbered, according to the Bible), the story is a good illustration for the lesson of Doug's mother. The extent to which we attach deeply to God and others is the extent to which we leave something behind in people's hearts. If we allow ourselves to matter to others, and they to us, we'll miss them and they'll miss us. The feelings of loss are like a signpost: "Love was here."

Hiding moves in two directions. It helps when it means withdrawing from injury of some sort, but it harms when it means avoiding the good things God has for us.

WHAT IS HARMFUL HIDING?

You may remember that helpful hiding is appropriate self-protection. Its design is to help us withdraw responsibly and prepare for loving reattachment. Harmful hiding is also self-protection, but with a very different result: *harmful hiding protects us from the very grace and truth we need.* It keeps us from the same ingredients of spiritual growth and repair that would mature us into the image of God.

Both kinds of defenses are similar in several ways, as we'll see later. At times, it may be difficult to distinguish between the two in a given situation. The one distinctive that always points to harmful hiding, though, is its fruit: *isolation.*

The irony of the situation is that the more we hide, the more grace we need. For example, people generally don't go through life as self-protectively as Doug's mother without having experienced some serious emotional injury. Most likely, she had been in some destructive relationships that had taught her it's not safe to be open and vulnerable.

Yet the only way Doug's mother could have been restored would have been to begin allowing herself to be slowly and gently connected to safe relationships. And relationships were the one thing she was most frightened of. She lived a dilemma.

A DEVELOPMENTAL VIEW OF THE SELF

Where do harmful hiding patterns come from? We need to look at early child development to answer that question. Basically, we are born literally "defenseless," in a helpless and terrified state. We can do nothing to stop the onslaught of sights, sounds, and feelings that rush at us in a bewildering array of sensations.

The only organizer of all this chaos is the mother. In her arms, the baby finds a place to rest, be soothed and comforted, and sort things out. Infants spend the first few months of life establishing the security of having a "home base" that they will later be able to internalize and take with them when they leave home on their own.

From the safety of the mother, the baby begins experimenting with her world through three important emotional processes called *introjection, projection,* and *splitting.* These processes are the building blocks on which the self is formed.

In the process of *introjection,* the infant receives an emotional picture of mother inside her heart. This eventually leads to the ability to love others maturely, from a position of empathy. Paul talks about this position of empathy as springing from our experience of comfort from "the Father of all mercies and God of all comfort, who comforts us in all our affliction so that we may be able to comfort those who are in any affliction with the comfort with which we ourselves are comforted by God" (2 Corinthians 1:3-4).

The process through which the infant not only learns to receive love but also to expel pain or badness from herself is called *projection*. The baby's rage at delays in gratification is too strong for her to handle at this age. There isn't enough grace in her heart yet to assure her that her rage won't rip mother away from her.

Projection allows the infant to place her rage into the mother. Though she then sees her mother as the angry one, rather than herself, she can learn to manage that much more easily than if the feeling were inside. Early projection prepares us for our adult aggressive tasks such as initiative, boundaries, and limit-setting. This responsibility to move away from badness is similar to God's commands to Israel to "purge the evil from among you" (Deuteronomy 13:5).

The third developmental process in building the self is called *splitting*. Splitting is the ability to make distinctions between unlikes. The baby senses a difference between the comfort of being held by her mother and the discomfort of being alone, hungry, or wet. She begins to see that she and her mother are two distinct individuals. Splitting helps the infant prepare for making distinctions, forming value judgments, discerning good and bad or right and wrong, and experiencing love and hate in adult life.

While necessary for the formation of the soul, these three processes can also be used in defensive ways, which we'll explore in later chapters. First, let's look at the series of events that lead to the development of harmful hiding patterns.

HOW WE FORM HARMFUL HIDING PATTERNS

We do not invent destructive hiding styles out of thin air. It's like the man who said to his wife during marital counseling, "Honey, contrary to what you think, I don't wake up in the morning planning how to ruin our marriage." Harmful hiding begins instead with our needs. That's the first stage.

Stage One: Our Needs Go Unmet

Our emotional and spiritual developmental needs are the starting point for understanding how we develop harmful hiding patterns. Let's review our four basic needs from chapters 4 through 7:

- Attachment
- Separateness
- Resolving Our Good and Bad Selves
- Authority and Adulthood

These are the foundations of building, over time, a loving, functional adult from a helpless, frightened infant. As we have these needs met in appropriate amounts and kinds at appropriate times, they become the basic tools or abilities for us to be able to create our own spiritual and emotional family, succeed in tasks, and further the kingdom of God.

It is the wise parent who is somewhat anxious about the tremendous responsibility of providing these needs in the right way. Parents are teachers of their children, but they're also sinners who have been sinned against. They aren't going to meet their children's needs correctly at all times.

Stage Two: We Experience Injury to Our Soul

Nowhere is the evidence of the Fall more apparent than in the universal experience of emotional injury in childhood. Things go wrong in everyone's childhood, and for four primary reasons:

- A lack of love in the parents (their own sinfulness).
- A lack of ability in the parents (the sins of *their* parents).
- The child's contributions (his own sinfulness).
- Circumstantial consequences of the Fall (accidental trauma, death of a parent, socioeconomic factors, physical limitations, and so on).

When any combination of these factors takes place, the child suffers an injury to the part of the self that is in need. The growth process stops, and that part of the soul begins to atrophy. It stays behind, out of time, while the rest of the person continues developing.

Angela's story can help us understand this process. Angela was age twenty-eight, married, and a Christian when she sought individual treatment to get help with feelings that were troubling her. Although she had been a believer for many years, in recent months she'd been feeling quite distant from God and Christian friends.

Once Angela and I clarified the symptoms that had caused her to seek counsel, we began to look at the events that had led to her symptoms.

Angela had come from a family that needed her strength. Her mother was constantly depressed, in crisis, and perceived herself to be inadequate. She always needed Angela's support to help her get along. "If it weren't for you, I don't know what I'd do," she would tell Angela while they both fixed meals or worked in the house. Angela's father was a very responsible businessman, but he was somewhat distant and perfectionistic.

Her parents' marriage conflicts revolved around her father's frustration with her mother's constant feelings of being over-whelmed. Mother, in turn, resented Father's over-controlling nature and would become more passive as a result.

Enter Angela: firstborn, bright, and emotionally responsive. She filled a place in both parents' lives. She was the comforting friend to Mother, always there to cheer her up. She was also the perfect antidote to Father's frustrations: she followed through with responsibilities and tasks, and made him "mighty proud."

As Angela talked about her life, it was apparent that several needs had been left unfinished in her past.

First, Angela's need for attachment was unfulfilled. She was a genuinely caring and sociable person. However, she had a very difficult time discussing her own needs for support or comfort. Once, as a little girl, she had cried over losing a girlfriend who had moved away. Her mother told her, "Honey, don't be sad. When you're sad, Mommy gets sad." Her father said, "Big girls don't cry."

Second, Angela's need for separateness had been denied. "No" wasn't a part of Angela's adult vocabulary. Her sense of responsibility for keeping the fragile family peace intact was too strong. The few times she could remember telling her mom she didn't have time to talk with her right then, her mom's feelings would be terribly hurt. Her lips would tremble, and she would silently withdraw. It was a horrible memory for Angela. Having her own boundaries would have upset things too much.

Third, Angela's needs for resolving good and bad were skewed and underdeveloped. Angela felt an intense pressure to keep her folks proud of her. They seemed to need an ideal daughter in order to survive. When she brought home poor grades one day, her dad was so upset that from then on, she forged their signatures for school records.

Angela had become a Christian in college. Before that, however, she had gotten involved with a boyfriend and had had an abortion. She and the boyfriend made all the arrangements. Her parents never knew.

Fourth, Angela's needs for adulthood were under attack. Being ideal was difficult, but staying a little girl was even harder. Angela could remember all the times she'd been lectured by her father on her decisions and values: what major to take, what college to attend, which sorority to join, and what kind of man to marry. Father had good ideas. The only problem was that it seemed to be all his way.

Whenever she questioned his values about issues, he would become critical and belittle her. She felt much more "one-down" than "eye-to-eye."

Obviously, to be as caring and high-functioning a person as Angela was, her upbringing must have had many good components. This vignette, however, helps us understand the kinds of things that can go wrong in our backgrounds and contribute to the harmful hiding process.

When a legitimate, God-given need goes unmet because of neglect or attack, that part of us goes into shock, just as we do when we're injured in a car accident. It begins to withdraw. If the injured part is brought back into relationship by the parent, the hurt can be processed through forgiveness.

This is an important point: *Injury doesn't necessarily lead to harmful hiding patterns.* When we are in relationship with people who love, who take responsibility, and who admit when they are wrong, the results of injury are much less destructive.

Take, for example, an angry fight between yourself and someone important to you. Your feelings may have been hurt by their attacking words. If nothing is ever said or done about the hurt, the pain may remain as a bitter memory, sometimes for years.

Now think about those fights that have been just as hurtful, but were resolved before the sun went down on your anger. Most likely you returned to a sense of equilibrium in the relationship and put the incident behind you.

Injuries heal much more quickly when we keep short accounts, take mutual responsibility, and express love. This is because *the injured part of the soul is quickly brought back into relationship, and not left in isolation.* The longer and deeper the isolation, the greater the injury—and the greater the chances for hurtful hiding patterns. The longer that part of the self is in isolation, the more it becomes a "bad" part. We lose the growth process when we are removed from grace and truth.

For example, suppose Angela's mom had a normal capacity to handle her daughter's needy, lonely, sad feelings. She would meet that part of Angela with open arms, warmth, comfort, listening, and identification. In that context, if every so often Mother had a bad day, and wasn't patient with Angela's needs, most likely it would have been dealt with, with little negative effect. Angela would have been able to forgive her mom and move on.

This would be even more true if Mother "owned" the bad day, took responsibility for her impatience with Angela, apologized, and asked for forgiveness. Angela would have learned a great deal about being loved and about how adults should act.

That's why it's so important for parents to be constantly evaluating their own spiritual and emotional issues. The parents who can deal with the logs in their own eyes, and who can then admit errors to their children, will minimize the effects of their parenting errors. Then there's no confusion inside the child's heart about why they hurt. The child of the confessing parent doesn't have to bear the burden of the errors all by herself.

We need to remember that not only do others injure us, but we also injure ourselves by our own sinful nature. Our spiritual and emotional state is always the result of a combination of both factors. For example, when Angela became pregnant, she had several friends to whom she could have gone and been loved and supported with no condemnation. Her shameful feelings, however, caused her to choose against those sources of help.

Stage Three: We Make Legitimate Needs Bad

So far, we've seen that when a pervasive, sinful, and unrepentant pattern of relating in the family persists, it affects the child in a very negative way. The part of the child's soul that has been hurt doesn't bounce back easily. There isn't enough grace and truth in the relationship for repair to take place. In this context, a destructive process occurs.

When there are chronic dysfunctional patterns of relating, a different mechanism takes over: *the legitimate emotional need is made bad.*

We learn from our experiences. If legitimate needs for comfort and safety are met with harshness or emptiness from parents, children learn not to ask for what they need. They come to believe that asking gets them into trouble and that part of them will be hurt again. It soon becomes much more preferable to make the need the culprit than to risk again.

You might be asking yourself, "But why do we make the need the bad guy? Why not the ones who hurt us?" The answer is developmental in nature: *children can't tolerate the idea that parents could be failing them.* Their helplessness and need for their parents' help is too great. To realize that Mom and Dad are fallible would make the universe much too frightening a place.

With enough time in the maturing process, children can accept the humanness of their parents. This is helpful for them, because it lets them understand that their needs are legitimate, and that they were let down in some way. They are then able to accept their own imperfections, move into forgiveness and being forgiven, and establish adulthood.

This is one of the reasons Jesus validated our neediness. He was overthrowing a pharisaical system that had no toleration for weakness or failure: "Blessed are the poor in spirit, for theirs is the kingdom of heaven" (Matthew 5:3). When Jesus taught that "It is not those who are healthy who need a physician, but those who are sick" (9:12), He reaffirmed that the needy, not the self-sufficient, are the ones who connect with Him. Therefore, *when we express our needs, we move toward connecting with Him and others.*

A second reason we blame our needs is *the perceived omnipotence of children.* One of the Fall's consequences is that children believe they are the center of the world. Often, young children will think that the sun shines when they are good, and that it rains when they are naughty. Jesus clarified this type of thinking when He said that God "causes His sun to rise on the evil and the good, and sends rain on the righteous and the unrighteous" (Matthew 5:45). We're part of the universe, not the core of it.

This self-centeredness generally works itself out as the child learns to grieve this idealized view of herself, learns to get her needs met without demanding that her wishes be gratified, and learns to share with others. But until that point, *perceived omnipotence can cause the child to take responsibility for her injuries.*

Angela felt sad and lonely when her friend moved away. Mother's response was, in effect, to tell her daughter that Angela's sadness made her depressed. Angela's childhood omnipotence helped her believe that she really was that powerful, and really that responsible for her mother's feelings.

Over time, Angela learned to dislike her own sadness. She became impatient with her lonely feelings, and she was self-critical when she needed support. Asking for help felt "demanding and immature" to her. While helping others was permissible, even desirable, reaching out for herself was wrong. Angela had learned to take an unbiblical view of her needs for attachment.

We see, then, that the following two factors lead to our blaming our needs for our souls' hurts:

(1) *injury to those needs;*
(2) *isolation of those needs,* caused by denial, lack of confession, or lack of forgiveness.

These factors plow fertile ground for the next step in developing harmful hiding patterns.

Stage Four: We Deny Our Own Needs

When our heart is injured and isolated, it doesn't stop with blaming our needs. It moves beyond that to a *denial* of our needs. Our injured soul demands to forget that this "troublesome" part of us ever existed.

Denial is behaving, thinking, or feeling as if some reality about us is not true. The forty-five-year-old party-goer who spends most of his social life with people twenty years younger is in denial of his aging process. The Bible study teacher who feels intensely ashamed when she's asked a question she can't answer is denying her finite knowledge. The businessman who can't tell the boss when he's being unreasonable is in denial of his power as an adult. Angela learned how to deny that she had any emotional needs at all.

Why is denial the next stage? It has to do with the development of reality perception in children. We don't necessarily learn reality the way God sees it. We learn it predominantly through our important relationships. If our significant relationships have God's values and perceptions at heart, we're that much closer to reality. But if those who are closest to our heart have unbiblical values in some places, children will accept those distorted values as true.

In other words, *reality perception is primarily relational.* That's why Jesus said, "I am the way, and the truth, and the life; no one comes to the Father, but through Me" (John 14:6). He was showing us that truth is more than an amassing of facts; it is enclosed in a connection to Him.

We learn reality primarily from our attachments. Learning it from books and propositional statements is a secondary process that occurs after our fundamental relational abilities are established inside. This is why good Bible teachers use examples of life as Jesus did in the parables: truth is made more meaningful when it's presented in the context of real life.

A good example of the relational aspect of perceiving reality happened to me several months ago. A woman in our hospital counseling program was shocked one day in our therapy group when she found Christians who admitted and talked about their angry feelings toward each other. In her family, anger was to be hidden, confessed in secret to God, and forgotten. Her surprise turned to relief when she experienced being able to discuss her rage safely with people in a biblical context.

We learn reality from relationship, especially in the impressionable and formative years of childhood. *Here we learn to affirm those parts of ourselves that keep us in relationship, and to deny the existence of those parts that isolate us.* It becomes a matter of emotional survival. It's "going along to get along," but on a much deeper level.

Angela learned over time to forget that she had needs for holding and comfort. It was nothing she consciously attempted. It was more like she grew out of that "childish" part. As her needs became more split off deep inside her, they were less and less apparent to her.

It's common for people who have been injured and isolated to grow up prematurely, becoming "small adults" at a very early age. Some people deny their needs and longings for closeness. Some deny their separateness and freedom. Some deny their badness. Some deny their adult parts. All of us, at some level, have been injured in all these aspects of our character and so there is within us some denial of their legitimacy or even their existence.

Denial can extend to not only our needs, but even to the actual *memories* surrounding those needs. This is why physical and sexual abuse victims sometimes lose memory of great segments of time: keeping the memories would be too catastrophic to the individual.

Beyond that, people who have had to develop a "false self"

often have the same type of memory denial. Those who find themselves "performing" or "on stage" for others often lose years of their lives. They are so attuned to the needs of others that they lose their own feelings. As one man told me, "I'm sorry, but I can't remember my childhood. I wasn't there at the time."

Denial of our need puts us on the road to developing harmful hiding patterns. It is the lie that gives rise to false answers in meeting our real needs.

Stage Five: We Develop False Solutions

When we deny the existence of our spiritual and emotional needs, we develop coping patterns that help us adapt to the loss of a part of our soul. These patterns protect us from further injury, and help us survive, but what emerges are actually *harmful hiding patterns*.

Some patterns help us avoid the risk of closeness; some assist us in staying away from aloneness. Some hide our imperfections from ourselves and others. Other patterns conceal our need for authority. We will look at specific hiding patterns in all these areas in the next chapter.

For now, it's important to realize that the defenses we develop as children emerge for a good reason. We experience genuine danger in the form of loss of relationship at some level. Otherwise, we would have no need for the hiding pattern.

This is significant because many well-meaning counselors assume that when our hiding patterns are confronted, we should automatically and instantly give them up. They will say things like, "Now that you know you intellectualize your feelings, stop doing it." This is a little like "admonishing the fainthearted," the misapplication of 1 Thessalonians 5:14 we looked at earlier. It crushes those who are already disheartened.

People can be deeply reinjured with this approach, since the hurt part is still tender. We hide for a reason. Awareness is certainly an important part of the growth and repair process. Sanctification takes a great deal of truth, but people also need time to grow up. Removing a cast from a broken arm too soon only leads to more injury.

The "sentries," or hiding patterns that guard the parts of our "castle," keep us from further injury to ourselves. As long as they can conceal our needs from danger, they've done their job. And various forms of denial are often their tools.

Angela learned several hiding styles to help her stay relatively safe. For example, she became proficient at *substitution*: exchanging her relational needs for food needs. She developed an eating disorder. She also learned *projection*: how to place her own needs into others who were hurting, and take care of them the way she would have wanted to be taken care of. In both these examples, Angela denied her own aloneness.

The problem with denial is that we can't fix what we deny. In other words, *denial leads to the inability to take responsibility for some aspect of our lives*. Anyone who's ever tried to confront a substance abuser in denial about his addiction understands the problem. His life, and the lives of those he loves, are being destroyed, but nothing can be done about it until the abuser "owns" his problem.

This failure to take responsibility is made into a teaching metaphor by Solomon. He describes a character type called a fool: "The way of a fool is right in his own eyes, but a wise man is he who listens to counsel" (Proverbs 12:15); "A rebuke goes deeper into one who has understanding than a hundred blows into a fool" (Proverbs 17:10); and "The wise man's eyes are in his head, but the fool walks in darkness" (Ecclesiastes 2:14).

The fool does not listen, does not learn, and walks in darkness. This is a picture of denial leading to irresponsibility—and ultimately, destruction. Not all denial is the same sort as that of the fool, but the result is usually the same. What needs attention or repair in our hearts goes neglected.

Finally, *denial usually leads to fear of others*. Generally, if our defenses are well-developed, the only way we can become aware of them is how we react in certain relationships. The part of the self that we bury alive is often far out of awareness. That's why many people are surprised by their "irrational" reactions to certain people in certain situations.

For example, Angela found herself drawn toward needy people.

She knew how to relate to them and how to help them feel cared about. But for some reason, she avoided "rescuers" like herself. It wasn't that she didn't trust them. It was more of a vague discomfort around them.

As she began looking at her needs and her hiding patterns, Angela began realizing that she was deeply afraid that a caring person might get too close and see her loneliness. That would activate the need again. And Angela needed to avoid activating her closeness needs at all costs.

The kinds of people we shy away from can be a clue to what our unloved, undeveloped, and denied needs could be. We are hiding destructively when we hate what we need.

Stage Six: We Produce Bad Fruit

For all their efforts, our "internal soldiers" can't guard their posts perfectly. There is always some failure to maintain the denial of our needs. This is generally experienced in the form of symptoms, or what Jesus called "bad fruit": "A good tree cannot produce bad fruit, nor can a bad tree produce good fruit" (Matthew 7:18).

Some examples of symptoms are depression, anxiety, panic attacks, addictive and compulsive behaviors, marital tensions, job difficulties, and physiological disorders. Though they are often quite painful, they exist to keep us aware of the state of our soul.

The reason that symptoms always occur is because of God's law of consequences, or *sowing and reaping*. Evil done to us by others or by ourselves has a consequence. Psychological and emotional symptoms are the heart's way of reminding us that we need to pay attention to a problem.

Many Christians are confused about their symptoms, thinking that their depression or compulsive behavior is the problem. Many more are also confused because it's sometimes difficult to understand how the "fruit" and the "root" are connected at first. As one patient told me, "Forget my past. Forget my relationships. Just help me get my life under control!"

This confusion is generally the result of a lack of safe relationships. It's impossible to look at the hurt aspects of the soul in isolation, or in critical relationships. Darkness always needs the light of unconditional love to give up its secrets. Once people become connected to a "grace and truth" relationship, their symptoms begin making more sense to them.

Lila, a lovely European grandmother, came to the hospital with a mysterious symptom: body tremors. Every waking moment of her day her hands and head shook gently. Distressed, she had undergone extensive neurological testing, with negative results. At the advice of her family doctor, she tried psychiatric help.

As Lila began working in the program, it emerged that she was unable to grieve loss. Her family and culture prohibited mourning, saying it was a "private matter." So Lila denied her need to be sad about her lost attachments.

One day in a therapy group, some of the members asked about her family. She began talking about "the most terrible day in my life": the day her young daughter had died in her arms after a short but tragic illness. As she told her story about that day, several group members began quietly weeping in their empathy for her. Somehow the safety affected Lila. Within a few minutes, she too began crying while she talked.

"When did this happen?" she was asked.

"Four years ago," she replied. Then her face changed as she realized what she had said. "That's when my shaking started."

"What did you do to mourn your daughter's passing?" I asked.

"Nothing," she replied. "We don't discuss death. We move on."

Obviously, Lila had not "moved on." Her grief was frozen, outside of time and outside of healing.

Then one of the members told her, "Lila, look at your hands. You aren't shaking." She held up her hand, and it was steady. Lila's entrance to the "house of mourning" allowed her to express her love for her lost daughter in grief.

For the rest of her stay, Lila's assignment was to learn to feel her sadness. She had a small silk handkerchief that she would carry with her all day. And whenever her grief for her daughter would well up, she would find someone caring to talk to and cry with. The shaking left. The symptom had done its job. It was no longer needed.

SUMMARY

The six stages of developing hiding patterns aren't a one-time event. Though they generally begin in the early years, they continue throughout life. Defenses have a cyclical nature: what is denied tends to be more split off as time goes by. This, too, is the result of entropy without an influx of help from outside. What is broken gets more broken over time.

How do we recognize our harmful hiding patterns? How can we tell when we're being wisely careful and when we're being resistant to love?

Let's go back to Jenny's story. Do you remember Jenny's two imaginary friends, Big Jenny and Little Jenny?

Jenny repeated one particular conversation over and over again. It was a discussion about a very important question: Why am I here? Jenny would sort out all the reasons why she had ended up in the Deep Woods all by herself. Then Big Jenny and Little Jenny would try to make sense of the sad situation.

As the weeks dragged on, the conversation began taking an unpleasant turn. It would sound like this:

BIG JENNY: Why are you here?

LITTLE JENNY: Because the bad soldiers took my parents and they were coming to get me!

BIG JENNY: You're sure of that?

LITTLE JENNY: Yes, I'm sure. But what do you mean?

BIG JENNY: Could there possibly be another reason?

LITTLE JENNY: No—well, could there be?

BIG JENNY: Of course! Remember the time you were sick and had to stay in bed for a week?

LITTLE JENNY: I remember. It was awful! I felt terrible.

BIG JENNY: That's not all. Do you remember what your parents did when you were sick?

LITTLE JENNY: Mother took care of me during the day and Father stayed with me in the evening when she was tired.

BIG JENNY: Yes, they took care of you. And did you notice how tired they both were? After all they had to do, then they had to play nursemaid to you!

LITTLE JENNY: They did look pretty worn out.

BIG JENNY: You bet they did. And that's really why you're here.

LITTLE JENNY: I don't understand.

BIG JENNY: Of course you do. Your selfishness was too much of a drain on them. You exhausted them. Your demands kept them from being able to prepare a getaway plan for when the soldiers came. If you hadn't asked for so much, you'd be safe with them today.

LITTLE JENNY: I did complain about my tummyache—maybe more than I should have. . . .

Jenny's isolation caused her to see her needs as demanding, self-ish, and destructive. What God had created good, Jenny's disconnected heart began to call bad. Her spirit was broken now. The lengthy separation from attachment to familiar relationships and a healthy emotional environment was taking its toll. This disconnected state was indeed devastating. Jenny was labeling "bad" something God had called good.

How about you? Are you in such a disconnected state? Do you isolate yourself from God and the very relationships that He has put in your path to help you? Are you hiding from love?

Search your own heart and begin exploring which legitimate spiritual and emotional needs have been called bad by yourself or others. After that, try to see if you have been denying what has had a "bad" label on it. Have you denied your own legitimate emotional needs?

Pretending that we have no needs often makes life easier than admitting we have "bad" needs. But this is a clear contrast to the value that God places on us, even in our immaturity: all of us are those for whom Christ died.

Learn the six critical stages of harmful hiding, and reflect carefully on your own condition. Rest in God's grace as you evaluate your life to find the harmful ways you may be hiding from legitimate needs and loving relationships.

CHAPTER ELEVEN

Harmful Hiding: The Results

MARSHALL and Judy came to therapy to save a floundering marriage. After eight years of coping with unhappiness, their arguments were reaching critical mass.

Actually, it seemed to me that Marshall and Judy had perfected their arguments into masterpieces of point-counterpoint debate, mostly about Marshall's personality.

Judy would generally lead off: "His lack of emotion keeps me away from him."

Marshall would then counter, "Maybe I just don't have as *many* as you do."

"Plus," Judy would add, "he doesn't pay enough attention to my emotional needs."

"I need time alone," would be the comeback.

Then Judy again: "He has a problem being affectionate, too."

Then Marshall again: "I work a twelve-hour day and I'm supposed to be Romeo!"

I finally asked, "Maybe it would help if you could tell me what things you *do* agree on."

There are two perspectives in this dialogue: Marshall's viewpoint on Marshall, and Judy's viewpoint on Marshall. While their debate is somewhat humorous, it raises an important point: *It's difficult to know when our self-protective behaviors, thoughts, or feelings are helpful or harmful.*

For instance, Judy was convinced that her frustration with Marshall was due to a lack of emotional warmth and accessibility in him. In other words, her diagnosis of the problem was harmful hiding: Marshall was hiding from intimacy.

At the same time, Marshall believed the problem was Judy's unrealistic expectations for intimacy. He thought his periods of withdrawal weren't at all defensive, but normal. Marshall thought his hiding was helpful, not destructive.

The previous chapter dealt with how harmful hiding begins in our early years. We switch in this chapter from "then" to "now" to look at the most important characteristics of destructive self-protection that affect us in the present. The question we'll be answering is, *How can we decipher our own patterns of relating?*

ISOLATION

The most telling aspect of our harmful hiding patterns is that they never stop with simply protecting us from evil or danger; *they isolate us from what we need to grow.* We saw in chapters 8 and 9 how helpful hiding protects us from injury and prepares us for reattachment to relationship. Harmful hiding keeps us safe from more danger but cuts us off.

One of the results of isolation is that *we lose grace and truth.* Generally, harmful hiding cuts us off from some combination of healing: unconditional relationship (grace) and some types of information that we need (truth). These two dynamics are the main ingredients of spiritual and emotional growth and repair. They work together like sunlight and soil to bring about the fruit of maturity in our lives. Without them, we wilt.

While traveling, I met Ron, a motel manager who told me his "success story." "I've saved up two hundred thousand dollars in this job," he said. "In another few years, I'll be able to buy my own motel."

Marveling at Ron's achievement, I said, "That's pretty impressive. If you don't mind my asking, how did you do that?"

"Well, I make about $25,000 as manager here. The job takes care of room and board. So I've spent $5,000 and saved $20,000, every year, for ten straight years." He was now thirty-three years old. He'd been saving since graduating from college.

To appreciate this feat of frugality even more, it might help to know that this motel was in southern California. There, even with room and board, living expenses aren't low. "How do you make it on that budget?" I asked Ron.

"The last ten years I've lived alone. I don't have friends; friends want to do social things that cost money. I work here during the day. I watch television at night. It's not that hard."

Obviously, Ron had mastered the art of saving money. He would say that he was hiding his needs for relationship for a worthwhile purpose: a good start in business. But Ron had lost his twenties along the way, a stage of life in which we make some of the most meaningful and long-lasting relationships of our lives. Ron had lost a decade of attachment-building.

Ron's withdrawing of his attachment needs was obvious. But when we hide our needs for separateness, honesty, and boundaries in relationships, it's a different situation. We don't seem to be hiding ourselves. In fact, we tend to be quite vulnerable and open people. What we conceal, however, is our freedom.

Mary was quite surprised in her therapy group when members told her one day that they felt distant from her. She had always seen herself as a loving, supportive person. "That's not the problem," said a member. "Your caring is easy to see; your honesty isn't. Sometimes it would be nice to see you disagree, get angry, or have a different opinion from one of us."

Without being aware of it, Mary was hiding an aspect of the image of God from herself and her relationships. Her choice-making mechanisms had been split off in an enmeshed family situation where "different" or "angry" meant "bad." She was much more comfortable in closeness encounters than she was in confrontations.

Reflecting on the experience, Mary noticed something: "I've always shied away from biblical passages about God's justice and righteousness. They seemed so harsh and uncaring to me. I've spent much more time learning about His love." This was an important revelation for Mary. Because she had hidden from her separateness, she also had to hide from essential truths about conflict and justice. Having avoided such teaching and experiences, she had compromised herself throughout her life "to keep the peace."

Mary had thus denied the very truths that would have supported her boundary-setting abilities. Her needs for separateness were wounded and isolated.

This point is important because so many of us Christians feel that our emotional, spiritual, and relational problems are "out there." We externalize them. The solution, then, becomes, "If I could just get away from this marriage/job/church/location, then my problem would be solved."

Believers are certainly intended to be initiators, not passive responders. And sometimes, as we've seen, withdrawal is strategically important. But Jesus said that "the kingdom of heaven suffers violence, and violent men take it by force" (Matthew 11:12), referring to the conflict that comes from telling the truth to people.

Often, when we place the responsibility onto others for our loneliness, for our feeling misunderstood, or for our feeling controlled, we miss seeing our complicity in the problem. Then it's only solvable by completely remodeling everything but ourselves.

A second result of the harmful hiding pattern of isolation is that *we resent or fear what we need*. As a good sentry, our defense pattern's job is to keep the castle of our soul secured. Suppose a particular sentry's job is to protect the ailing king of the castle. If there are no intrusions of relationship, we face less chance for reinjury to our damaged needs for closeness, boundaries, forgiveness, or authority.

The disadvantage to this, however, is that quite often the sentry cannot distinguish the enemy troops from the Red Cross. All visitors, not simply the dangerous ones, are prevented from entry to the king's chambers. This sort of exclusiveness is a product of the soul's fear of injury.

Harmful hiding blinds us to the good things we need that God may already have provided. It's a little like a hungry man wearing a blindfold and sitting at a loaded banquet table. He feels his hunger pangs, but remains unaware that what he needs is right in front of him.

Wayne had come from a family with an indulgent mother and a harsh father. Whenever Wayne needed to finish a homework assignment at the last minute, Dad would yell at him for not being more prompt. Wayne would retreat to Mom, who would lovingly write the assignment for him so he could get to sleep.

The result of this sort of imbalance between grace and truth was that Wayne had an extremely difficult time setting limits on himself in his professional life. Although he sincerely wanted to do a good job in his work, he constantly missed project deadlines and was always frantically playing catch-up. Internally, his lack of discipline was a dependence on Mom's permissiveness and rebellion against Dad's judgmentalism.

This condition made his life miserable. Then Wayne started a new job with a boss who was strict but loving. Glenn had high expectations for Wayne, but he cared for him as a person.

Glenn couldn't have been a better pick for someone to help Wayne work through his rebellion at harsh limits. He could teach Wayne discipline, yet in a loving environment, so that Wayne could get more control over his own life.

The problem was, harmful hiding was already in place in Wayne's heart. He resented Glenn's involvement, saw his suggestions as being "controlling," and was deeply hurt whenever Glenn criticized his work performance. "He's just like Dad, always on my back," Wayne would say.

The truth was, Glenn was just like Dad *should* have been: loving and limiting. But Wayne's own past injuries kept him from recognizing how Glenn cared for him. *Harmful hiding made Wayne hate what he really needed the most.*

LOSS OF FREEDOM AND RESPONSIBILITY

While helpful hiding patterns are generally the well-thought-out products of choices, harmful hiding patterns are just the opposite. Destructive self-protection is reactive, automatic, and often unconscious. This is because of the lack of grace that the defensive person feels inside. A knee-jerk reaction is far preferable to taking the time to deliberate over a problem when one's sense of rootedness and groundedness is at stake.

The net result is that *we lose our precious freedom.*

Faye was almost "too good to be true." She was beautiful, had the model family, was married to a dentist, and had led a women's Bible study in her home for years. Yet she complained of what she believed to be a biological depression that she wanted to get treated with medication.

When a psychiatric examination ruled out the biological aspect, she tentatively entered therapy. Her family didn't believe in counselors, Christian or otherwise. It would have been an affront to their "victorious" image.

What emerged with Faye was a subtle, unconscious avoidance of bringing her imperfections into the open. For example, Faye resented her husband's passivity. She was jealous of her friends who had more "family time" than she did. And she had stopped enjoying teaching her Bible study years ago. No one in the world knew about these feelings.

Talking about these subjects seemed to be taboo, however. Whenever we would touch on one, very quickly and adroitly Faye would shrug off the feeling, laugh quietly, and change the subject to one less painful.

Finally, I said to her one day, "It seems like you're scared of some land mines. There are certain subjects that you avoid so well and so quickly that I don't even know what's happened until I think about it later."

As I described her defense of switching subjects, Faye was genuinely shocked that it was even occurring. The phenomenon was a completely automatic response to her negative feelings. Like a security alarm, the defense kicked in whenever the "bad" part of her came into relationship, and quickly whisked that part out of connection.

As she began to understand the isolation she felt whenever these negative feelings arose, she began taking risks in her relationships to include these parts of herself in conversations, along with the pleasantries. When she was met with warmth and acceptance, her friendships deepened. The subject-changing defense passed from her life as the real need was met.

It was replaced, however, with a sense of discernment about who was safe to be "real" with and who wasn't. Faye learned how to accept her imperfect "bad parts," and to protect them from parental, critical, or pharisaical people who would send her back into isolation. When in the presence of those kinds of people, she learned not to bring up those thoughts at all. But she knew the thoughts, was aware of them, and *chose* to be discreet.

God places a high premium on our being able to autonomously choose to protect ourselves, rather than to react angrily or violently: "Do not envy a man of violence, and do not choose any of his ways" (Proverbs 3:31); "choose for yourselves today whom you will serve" (Joshua 24:15). Choice is a product of being attached to God and others, and of being responsible for what God has entrusted to us. Reactivity is a product of fear. It only furthers our isolation.

Mitch, a Christian businessman friend of mine, is very entrepreneurial. He's a dreamer, always coming up with projects and ideas and embarking on them. Some work, and some don't. Enough have panned out that Mitch has become quite successful.

One day Mitch told me, "When I have a new idea, I don't go to accountants. I go to marketing people." I asked him why.

"Accountants always say no. Marketers always say yes." My friend was wary of the constricting, automatic reactivity that some accounting professionals have—as if they simply whipped out a rubber stamp that says *No.* Those reactions slowed down Mitch's freedom to imagine and brainstorm. He knew that the day of the accountants would come—but after the dream had been worked around for a while.

In addition to isolation, a second major result of harmful hiding is denial. Let's look at the results of this kind of defense.

DENIAL

In the last chapter, we saw how in early years our needs for attachment, separateness, forgiveness, and authority can be perceived as bad. That perception moves on to denying that these needs even exist, which is our way to keep them protected from reinjury.

We see the fruit of this in our adult lives as spiritual and emotional handicaps — defective parts. It's like sending a plumber out to fix a leaky faucet with defective tools. There's a limit on what we can do when our "tools" are broken.

These four basic needs affect every part of our lives: our relationships, careers, ministries, and so on. When one or more of these needs is damaged, split off, and hidden, the ripple effect shows at some level in our lives. This makes sense: If it didn't show, we probably wouldn't have needed it in the first place.

Howard saw himself as a team player in his corporation. He was cooperative and always deferred to his superiors. He was well-liked in the job, but every time he was up for a promotion, he would sabotage himself by a lower production schedule, or a poor performance evaluation.

As he began working on his self-sabotage, Howard realized that his "cooperativeness" was a defense against his true leadership skills. Had they come out, he would have been terrified of being seen by his bosses as oppositional and pushy. The sabotaging kept him away from that frightening prospect, and the over-compliance cut him off from his true need to develop his God-given authority skills.

How can we tell that we're hiding in denial? One important indicator is shame. *Shame is a sense of "badness" about ourselves that urges us to withdraw further from relationship.* It tells us the lie that something about us is beyond grace and beyond relationship. Shame is a tool of Satan to keep us from reestablishing relationship to God and each other.

In taking our sins upon Him, Jesus Himself temporarily moved beyond grace: "He made Him who knew no sin to be sin on our behalf, that we might become the righteousness of God in Him" (2 Corinthians 5:21). He voluntarily lost fellowship with the Father and moved into isolation: "My God, My God, why hast Thou forsaken Me?" (Matthew 27:46). This is the shame of the ross that Jesus endured and also despised (Hebrews 12:2). He understood shame.

Shame is a prime motivator for harmful hiding. When we're ashamed of our needs, we can't feel safe about bringing them to the Cross or anywhere else. People who suffer from intense feelings of shame often use quite elaborate hiding mechanisms to avoid the experience.

It was Adam's shame that kept him from seeking God out when he sinned: "And he [Adam] said, 'I heard the sound of Thee in the garden, and I was afraid because I was naked; so I hid myself'" (Genesis 3:10). This compounded the spiritual dilemma from one problem (sin and the resultant loss of relationship) to two (hiding in shame).

As anxious new parents, my wife and I baby-proofed our home when our son was born. One of the tools of baby-proofing is a little rubber cornerguard that fits on all sharp corners of furniture. It protects the child from hitting his head on coffee tables, end tables, and the like.

At one year, Ricky had become agile enough to peel off the cornerguards. They were more fun for him than expensive trucks and toys. To counteract Ricky's interest, we would say a firm "No, no" and remove the cornerguard from his hand whenever he made contact with one. He seemed to respond to our limit.

One day, we heard Ricky's voice behind us in the family room. Turning around, we watched him toddle toward us, two cornerguards in hand, shouting, "No, no! No, no! No, no!" After we recovered from our laughter, I realized that Ricky had done Adam one better. After the transgression, Ricky brought himself *toward* relationship, instead of *away* from it. He brought his "no, no" to love. He hadn't had time to learn shame yet. Unfortunately, we all grow out of this shameless state as life goes on.

Annette came to therapy with a sexual addiction that had caused her unrelenting mortification. As an active Christian, a day never passed without her suffering from intense fears of being too "bad" for God and others.

After some time in therapy, Annette reflected one day, "I've noticed a difference in direction in my emphasis the last few months. For a long time, my sense of shame was greater than my sense of injury. Recently, it's shifted to the other way around.

Now, my injury is more felt than my shame." Annette had begun working on the spiritual and emotional problems that had given rise to the addiction in the first place. Shame, the false issue, had finally bowed to restoration, the real issue.

Think about the part of yourself you feel most ashamed of. It may be your neediness. It may be the look of your body. It may be a sexual or substance abuse problem. It may be something in your past. There is only one biblical response to shame: *disobey it*. Shame commands, "Conceal the badness." God commands, "Confess the badness to God and others" (see James 5:16, 1 John 1:9).

This is the difference between *humiliation* and *humility*. When we feel humilation, we are at that point living in the emotional corollary of hell, which is isolation. *Humiliation is the result of experiencing our badness outside of relationship.* Many of our worst nightmares are that some shameful secret will be exposed to the world.

Humility, on the other hand, is *experiencing our badness within the confines of love.* Humility brings us back to our need for God and His resources. It draws us to Him. It's always our responsibility to humble ourselves—that is, to bring our needs to God and His people. It's the first step toward sanctification.

Salvation itself is impossible without realizing the humbling fact that we are all in desperate need of "so great a salvation" (Hebrews 2:3). I believe this is why the Bible never places the responsibility for developing humility in God's lap. It's always presented as our job: "Humble yourselves in the presence of the Lord, and He will exalt you" (James 4:10).

Humility, then, leads to confession of our sin and brokenness to God and others, and helps us live and grow effectively in an evil, fallen world. But humiliation is the evidence of shameful hiding.

LIVING IN THE PAST

Pam, a graduate student in her early twenties, sought help because of changes in her relationships that had distressed and frightened her. "I'm afraid I've 'lost my first love,'" she reported.

"I used to care a lot about God and people. Now there's nothing inside. I resent my friends, my boyfriend, and my church ministry. It's like my heart has become a stone."

Pam's background included a family that idealized closeness as the only component of a "good family." Individual differences, boundaries issues, and disagreements tended to threaten the feeling of security and caring that permeated the home. The underlying assumption for the kids was that when they grew up, they would live within a few minutes' driving time from the homestead, or at least visit several times a week.

This was love at the expense of separateness. The result in Pam's life was that she valued family closeness above developing her own individual stewardship with God. Graduate school, where she specialized in the helping professions, was an extension of her attempt to keep people close and happy.

But being a graduate student had a different effect on Pam. She was thrust into an environment of bright, curious people who questioned everything under the sun. She experienced massive conflict with this change—feeling drawn to the exciting new information, yet sensing betrayal toward her family.

Pam's "cold heart" toward others was actually a hidden separation conflict. She didn't feel resentful of everyone, only a certain group of people. Pam tended to direct resentment toward people who *needed* closeness from her: her boyfriend, her church ministry, and those friends who habitually used her as a listening ear.

The problem then became clearer: Pam had not become an unloving person. Instead, spurred on by her school environment, she had begun developing desires to separate. She had never gone through the process of emotionally leaving home.

Pam hadn't realized how much she had resented the passive control the family had exercised on her all her life. She began remembering their various statements that she had thought were almost biblical in their truthfulness: "No matter how old you are, we'll always be your parents"; "You can't trust anyone if they're not family"; and "Let's keep the peace here—arguing rocks the boat." These family "commandments" reflected an unbiblical emphasis on connection that ignored the legitimate need for boundaries. It was a philosophy that had shaped Pam's life.

Realizing that she had an injured "*no* muscle" helped Pam understand her resentment problem. It wasn't the people in her present life she was angry at. Her suppressed anger, which she had never acknowledged or confessed, was directed at her family's lack of boundary development. When Pam encountered someone asking for support, she felt what she couldn't feel while growing up.

Pam's "cold heart" problem illustrates another aspect of harmful hiding: *the past becomes the present.* When we confuse the past and present with each other, it can unleash a destructive force in our closest attachments.

It's important to understand the relationship of the past to the present here. When we're injured in some area of the heart, that part isolates itself out of time. It stays in an emotional limbo, broken and immature. This isolation of the heart can last for an indefinite period of time. It only reconnects with the rest of the soul when it is brought back into relationship.

Since those injured parts of ourselves remain fixed and unfinished, they can function no better than their maturity level. These immature aspects of the soul can't function any better in the present than they could in the past. They haven't "grown up" enough yet, and that will take time. That's why telling people to do things with parts of themselves that are immature is futile. *It will always lead to failure.*

When I was in seminary, a faculty member who was a psychologist asked me to lead a growth group for students. A little anxious, I agreed to begin meeting with them.

After several sessions, I came away confused and somewhat frustrated with myself because of the lack of intimacy among the students. I found it impossible to bring the discussion away from intellectual abstractions to more personal issues.

Not knowing what to do, I asked my advisor what was wrong with the way I was handling the group. I wanted him to tell me how to open up the group emotionally so that we could operate as a group. I'll never forget what he told me.

"You don't realize something," he said. "They *can't* be intimate—that's why they're in the group." That one statement opened up the concept of injury versus choice for me: *We can't "do" something with what we don't have.* That's why we need patience, time, and work to repair.

In fact, *to demand that people be more mature than they are is to place them under condemnation.* Jesus said, "Woe to you lawyers as well! For you weigh men down with burdens hard to bear, while you yourselves will not even touch the burdens with one of your fingers" (Luke 11:46). These "burdens hard to bear" were the unreachable requirements of the law.

In Matthew 12:7, Jesus made a similar point: "But if you had known what this means, 'I desire compassion, and not a sacrifice,' you would not have condemned the innocent." Demanding that someone function on an adult level with capabilities that aren't developed yet is a judgment on an innocent person.

That's why someone whose independent functions such as judgment, decision-making, and autonomy are undeveloped appears to be a thirty- or forty-year-old infant. We say that these people have *dependent personalities*. Actually, they're adults whose independent parts have been frozen in the past and are emerging in the present at their state of injury.

A thirty-year-old dependent personality won't grow up overnight. He will have to move his injured autonomous functions into grace and truth. He'll have to take risks, learn about consequences, and then *practice, practice, practice.* In time, with the right support and enough sincere motivation, the autonomous parts will "catch up" with the rest of the functioning adult. That's what maturity is: all the parts working together.

Quite often, however, well-meaning Christians will tell their friends to "forget the past," citing Paul's description of his spiritual growth process:

Brethren, I do not regard myself has having laid hold of it yet; but one thing I do: forgetting what lies behind and reaching forward to what lies ahead, I press on toward the goal for the prize of the upward call of God in Christ Jesus. (Philippians 3:13-14)

To interpret this passage as license to ignore our background is to misunderstand Paul's meaning. "What lies behind" is not simply Paul's past. It's Paul's *redeemed* past. The passage assumes that what lies behind is actually "behind" him. In other words, Paul has worked through his past so that it does not keep intruding on and confusing his present.

In fact, Paul gives us the actual list of "what lies behind" him. Just before this passage, he presents the aspects of his past that had been stumbling blocks for him. This list had kept him trusting in his own righteousness instead of Christ's death. It is an impressive résumé:

> Circumcised the eighth day, of the nation of Israel, of the tribe of Benjamin, a Hebrew of Hebrews; as to zeal, a persecutor of the church; as to the righteousness which is in the Law, found blameless.
> But whatever things were gains to me, those things I have counted as loss for the sake of Christ. (Philippians 3:5-7)

In other words, Paul is showing us a past filled with deficits in the area of resolving good and bad. Before becoming a Christian, he had thought his "goodness list" outweighed any badness and guaranteed him access to God. Actually, it had denied him access.

A broken heart that can't trust isn't "what lies behind." Instead, a trust deficit will continue to bring up its past injury in all sorts of ways in the present — *to remind us to enter the healing process.*

Forgetting the past isn't a prescribed formula for spiritual amnesia. God frequently told the Israelites to remember their past. Remembering the importance of the past is what the Lord's Supper and baptism are all about.

Instead of going into denial about our past, we are to heal the parts of the soul that are still locked in the past in their injured state. In a very real sense, as long as those injured parts remain unhealed *we are living in the past.* When those parts have been brought into the recovery process, their immature perspective can be left behind. And *that* is the point at which we can "press on toward the goal" of a deeper maturity with God, self, and others.

Another term for this confusion of past and present is *transference*. Transference occurs when our feelings toward someone in the *past* affect our *present* relationships. Like a colored filter over our vision, past feelings distort present reality.

For example, a familiar battle cry among couples during arguments is, *You're just like my mother/father*. Even though that may be true, it's common for feelings about the parent to be coloring the actual person's characteristics.

Transference signals that an injury is making itself known. It indicates that sad, angry, hurt, frightened, or loving feelings from the past are struggling to be brought out of isolation. The more our past aspects are redeemed in the present, the less distortion of reality there will be.

The Bible refers to this principle operating in the lives of believers:

> If you have died with Christ to the elementary principles
> of the world, why, as if you were living in the world, do
> you submit yourself to decrees, such as, "Do not handle,
> do not taste, do not touch!" (which all refer to things des-
> tined to perish with the using) — in accordance with the
> commandments and teachings of men? These are matters
> which have, to be sure, the appearance of wisdom in self-
> made religion and self-abasement and severe treatment
> of the body, but are of no value against fleshly indulgence.
> (Colossians 2:20-23)

Paul deals here with believers struggling between the old system of law and Christ's system of grace. It was difficult for them to shrug off the shackles of rules and instead turn toward relationship. These believers were looking at their unconditional acceptance through a "transference filter" of their past bondage.

All Christians struggle with a tendency to submit to the old way of relating to God by "sacrifice instead of compassion." The Bible encourages us to move beyond a form of life that is in the past: "It was for freedom that Christ set us free; therefore keep standing firm and do not be subject again to a yoke of slavery" (Galatians 5:1).

Transference tells us that an injured part of our soul is still disconnected and therefore in hiding. It's still living in the past. Here are some examples of how transference may affect our character traits:

- The person with attachment injuries may see others as too needy, intrusive, or demanding.
- The person with separation injuries may see others as withholding, unloving, and controlling.
- The person with good/bad injuries may see others either as idealized or as constantly letting him down.
- The person with authority injuries may see others as critical and parental.

Certainly there may be a great deal of truth in our perceptions of others. Paul counsels to use sound judgment in our dealings with others.

However, it's important to examine and learn from consistent patterns of relating styles that we find ourselves in. The more we can separate out transference (seeing life through the filter of our past reality) from sound judgment (seeing life in its present reality), the better our relationships become.

Often, this is the first breakthrough in working with couples. The marriage relationship is, by design, a highly emotionally charged arrangement. When both members can see how they may be experiencing their spouse through the eyes of their past injuries, they can then take responsibility for the deficits that caused the distortions. That frees them to be responsible only for how they handle their end of the marriage in the present, instead of feeling responsible for cleaning up the injured part of their spouse.

JENNY'S TRANSFERENCE AND OURS

The second time Jenny spied the soldiers in the woods she immediately transferred her feelings about the past. With greater speed and skill this time, she again eluded them. She never took the time to consider that the men in uniform might not be the enemy:

> *One afternoon Jenny's reverie was shattered when the sound of shouting again broke into her seclusion. Less than a hundred yards away was another group of several uniformed soldiers. Just as she spotted them, they noticed her and began shouting and running toward her.*
>
> *The last frightening experience with soldiers had taught Jenny a lesson. Even during her meditation by the babbling brook, she had kept one eye on her possible escape routes. This time, though, her reactions were much faster.*
>
> *Without stopping to deliberate, the little girl moved into a dodge-and-weave pattern, running away from the soldiers and straight for the thickest part of the brush. Stooping over, she disappeared into the dense foliage.*
>
> *As she scurried through the brambles, Jenny stopped every few seconds to listen for the men's voices. Once again, they grew fainter and eventually died off.*

Jenny's act was harmful to her even though she had no idea that she was acting against her own interests. She feared the uniforms even though she needed those particular soldiers more than anything—they would have saved her. Her lengthy isolation led to a subtle denial that she needed any further companions. Eventually, her denial led to her disconnected state and feelings of shame that came out in the conversations between her imaginary companions. Finally, she lost her freedom—imprisoned ultimately by her own doing.

Consider carefully how Jenny transferred her feelings about the enemy soldiers to the friendly ones. Do you find the past infiltrating the present, protecting—or harming—your present

relationships? As we've seen, such harmful hiding can have terrible results.

Once we understand our own patterns of relating through the
signals that tell us we're in harmful hiding patterns, we're on the
road to positive change. Before we move into the final part of this
book, which will focus on moving out of harmful hiding patterns,
it's important that we understand the *cost* of harmful hiding – the
subject of chapter 12.

CHAPTER TWELVE

The Cost of Harmful Hiding

❖

E DWARD'S cocaine problem had brought him to the hospital for treatment. He wasn't a stereotypical drug addict with images of alley scenes and poverty-level living styles. He had an MBA, a family, and a promising career—and his habit was threatening to destroy all of them.

Edward's addiction manifested itself in binges rather than chronic use. He'd go for weeks at a time without using, then spend most of his paycheck doing coke for several days on end. He had no clue as to why or when he would use. "It just happens," he confided.

One day in a group, someone pointed out to Edward that he seemed to be a "nervous talker"—he would start conversations or ask questions with others apparently for no reason. Silent periods in the group were extremely uncomfortable for him. Edward would feel anxious, shift his body, and begin addressing others on one subject or another.

Noticing this pattern, Edward realized that it had been a habit all his life. During his dating years, he would always think of at least three interesting topics to discuss with the girl before going out to dinner. The topics were useful for those times when the conversation became quiet or he felt uncomfortable.

Thinking farther back, Edward remembered that growing up, his parents had been locked in a perpetually polite-but-simmering war with each other. To ease the tension, he had become a master at inventing bright, interesting topics. His light, distracting patter helped prevent hostility from flaring into open combat.

Popular at parties and church functions, Edward was always good for keeping things fun and conversational. He wasn't a "downer" who might upset or sadden people with his problems.

Edward's drug problem had developed in college. When faced with a dating breakup or poor performance in school, he would binge for a weekend, then return to life as though nothing had happened. He kept his symptom a careful secret because it could upset or disappoint his friends. He'd simply reenter the scene with his cheery repartee.

Edward had developed a harmful hiding pattern of distracting verbalization. Its function was to protect him from deep or uncomfortable intimacy. Every time he felt silence around him, he became frightened that someone would get too close, or that anger would erupt. Talking became Edward's way of controlling closeness at a manageable level.

The drug problem, however, signalled that his verbalization wasn't doing a perfect job. Cocaine was the place he went to be able to deal with his losses and failures.

"I've never talked to anyone about this," Edward said to the group. "I've always been convinced that these feelings were pretty distasteful to folks." The group listened with empathy. This time Edward's conversation wasn't a defensive "filler" or self-protective strategy. There was meaning in his pain.

I asked him to evaluate his closest relationships. He thought for a minute or so (an eternity for Edward!). Then he shook his head. "I'll be honest. Nobody on earth knows this part of me. I've spent twenty-seven years keeping people just close enough. It's taken so much time and energy that I haven't had anything left over to try to be close." Edward had connected his drug problem to his real problem: *hiding from closeness.*

Even though they perform as the good soldiers we originally

intend them to be, harmful hiding patterns exact a terrible price. We expend massive amounts of energy to create and keep up the walls we construct against bringing our hurt parts into relationship. *When we hide, the time and energy that we need to spend in loving and being loved is diverted—it's channeled instead into maintaining our isolation.*

Being human means having built-in limits as creatures. We have a limited life span, with only a certain amount of energy and resources available to us. We are to focus on a few important tasks of life: "He has told you, O man, what is good; and what does the LORD require of you but to do justice, to love kindness, and to walk humbly with your God?" (Micah 6:8).

God places limited energy, time, and resources into our stewardship for us to invest. The person who spends a lifetime trying to stay perfectly safe misses out on the healing and relationships that God has provided. We don't have time to do both.

"For whoever has, to him shall more be given, and he shall have an abundance," said Jesus; "but whoever does not have, even what he has shall be taken away from him" (Matthew 13:12). When we risk bringing part of ourselves into the light, we are "owning," or taking responsibility for, our lives. We "have." When we own or "have" ourselves, Jesus says, our heart is enlarged.

But when we keep part of ourselves in darkness, we deny the existence of that part. The denial prevents us from taking responsibility for ourselves. We "don't have." When we can't own, our heart is less accessible to growth. This is why extremely defensive people often feel very isolated. There isn't enough of them accessible to be loved. It creates a vicious cycle of isolation/defense/isolation. The cost of harmful hiding is a lack of love, and an increase in bad fruit.

THE COST IN REINJURY

We've seen that harmful hiding doesn't work. Destructive defenses don't *really* protect us from being hurt again. In fact, they contribute to our developmental deficits getting worse.

We got to know Angela a little in chapter 10. She was the

young woman who had learned to say "no" only to her own "no," and "yes" to anyone else. Caretaking her overwhelmed mother had trained her to hide her injured "separate" parts.

As she began to work on her emotional issues, Angela became very aware of a pattern that would happen any time she needed to set a limit for herself. Whenever she felt pressure to comply with someone else's need, an emotional memory of her mother would appear inside her head.

This wasn't a hallucination. It was a consistent constellation of actual memories. Every time Angela prepared to say no to someone, Mother's face would show up, sad and hurt, with trembling lips. Then her face would turn away, head down, and she would slowly withdraw to the living room chair. Silently she would sit, a single tear trickling down her face.

It's easy to see why Angela had such a difficult time setting biblical limits for her life. She would unintentionally project that picture of Mother onto anyone she might "let down." To refuse to comply with anyone brought on a memory much too painful to bear—breaking a parent's heart. It was intolerable, and Angela caved in every time.

Angela's conflict illustrates an important fact. When we hide in harmful ways that isolate us (Angela's way was codependent behavior), we don't actually keep ourselves from harm. Instead, *we imprison the injured part of ourselves with our destructive memories. Those who injured us in the past become the only relationship available to our hurt self.*

In other words, when we hide, we constantly relive our hurts over and over again. This further damages an already-wounded heart. And we can't find room for new, different, and healing relationships.

Angela's undeveloped need for separateness would have benefited greatly from her being with people who celebrated and relished her boundaries. People who could rejoice in her freedom to say no to them would encourage that part of her to reattach to the world. But the more she hid that part, the more she complied with the emotional memory.

Abuse victims are deeply affected by this pattern. When a

child's physical, sexual, or emotional boundaries are violated, hiding generally steps in, in some form or another. Then, when the hurt part is isolated, it's as if the child is left in a locked room, alone with her abuser.

As isolation deepens, memories recur and reinjure the child countless times over the years. Only when there is an intervention of safe attachment into that hurt, trusting part of the soul can there be relief from the repetition of the damage.

Jesus spoke about this principle:

> "When the unclean spirit goes out of a man, it passes through
> waterless places seeking rest, and not finding any, it says,
> 'I will return to my house from which I came.' And when
> it comes, it finds it swept and put in order. Then it goes
> and takes along seven other spirits more evil than itself,
> and they go in and live there; *and the last state of that man
> becomes worse than the first.*" (Luke 11:24-27; emphasis
> added)

Jesus' illustration points out that a spiritually empty heart—that is, one caught in isolation—is susceptible to being plunged back into the injuries of the past. We need to fill up our "empty house" with unconditionally loving, honest people. Then there's no room for more damage.

Notice what this passage does *not* say. It does not say the evil spirits returned to find the Spirit of the living God there. Instead, the heart is "swept and put in order." The person has not moved *toward* God, but has tried to deal with his heart in isolation from Him!

THE COST OF STAYING IN HIDING

The final aspect of harmful hiding is that our choices of hiding styles are related to what we are protecting in ourselves. In other words, our defensive patterns are specific to our injuries. Some hiding styles are used for attachment deficits, others for boundary injuries, and so on.

We can be a great help to ourselves when we learn which styles we use. That way, we can begin to identify the spiritual and emotional immaturities we need to work on repairing. Our specific hiding patterns are the subject of the chapters in the last part of this book.

Jenny's experience illustrates how easy it is to stay in hiding once it becomes a familiar place:

Jenny would sometimes find relief from these discussions by sitting quietly beside the stream that ran through the Deep Woods. It had taken her a long time to find it, because it was hidden in a remote part of the Woods. It had always been a safe place for her. She loved listening to the musical language of the water as it rushed over the smooth stones in the stream bed.

One afternoon Jenny's reverie was shattered when the sound of shouting again broke into her seclusion. Less than a hundred yards away was another group of several uniformed soldiers. Just as she spotted them, they noticed her and began shouting and running toward her.

The last frightening experience with soldiers had taught Jenny a lesson. Even during her meditation by the babbling brook, she had kept one eye on her possible escape routes. This time, though, her reactions were much faster.

Without stopping to deliberate, the little girl moved into a dodge-and-weave pattern, running away from the soldiers and straight for the thickest part of the brush. Stooping over, she disappeared into the dense foliage.

As she scurried through the brambles, Jenny stopped every few seconds to listen for the men's voices. Once again, they grew fainter and eventually died off.

After losing her, the soldiers stopped to rest. Jenny was much too far away to hear their conversation.

"Are you sure it was her?" gasped one of the older men, out of breath.

"Absolutely," replied the second soldier, obviously the leader of the group. "Jenny's here and she's alive. Her

parents were right about her escape route."

The first soldier stooped to take a drink from the stream. As he stood up he said sadly, "Jenny must not realize that we have turned back the enemy invaders, that our land is safe again. And if that's right, then she wouldn't know that her parents sent us to find her."

A third soldier turned to face the commander and asked, "There's something I don't understand, sir. Why did she run? We're her countrymen. We're here to bring her home. Why would Jenny be panicked by us?"

The leader remained thoughtfully silent for a moment. Then, raising his eyes to the brush where he'd last seen Jenny, Officer Josef said quietly, "A uniform is a uniform." Turning toward the last rays of sunlight that bathed the edge of the Deep Woods, he led his men out of the forest.

Just as Jenny could no longer distinguish her countrymen from invaders, our hiding patterns prevent us from being open to the people, truths, and experiences that God makes available to help us mature spiritually. The more we isolate our hurt and immature aspects, the more difficult it is to discriminate safety from danger.

In part 3, we discover hope and the potential for coming out of hiding. We'll look at specific hiding mechanisms that accompany injuries to the four needy parts of our soul. Learning to discern your own specific tendencies in hiding can give you important insight into your growth needs. Once this is accomplished, you'll learn ways to emerge from your own Deep Woods.

PART THREE

Hope
for Those
in Hiding

CHAPTER THIRTEEN

Hiding
from Attachment

✥

T HE STORY is told of a man who, ailing from several unexplainable symptoms, made an appointment to see his physician. After a thorough examination, the doctor sat down with his patient and said to him, "I need to ask you a question: Have you ever had this before?"

"Why, yes, I have, as a matter of fact," replied the patient.

The physician nodded his head slowly and sagely pronounced, "Then, in my professional opinion, you've got it again."

Like the unfortunate man in the story, we've all "got it." That is, we all hide in harmful ways in some form or fashion, many unknown to us.

But we need more than the knowledge that hiding is part of our lives and relationships. We also need to know what our specific hiding patterns, or styles, are. And just as important, we need to understand what our patterns mean for us.

Why should we learn our hiding styles? There are two basic reasons.

First, *hiding styles are a "road map" to our developmental needs.* Our protective patterns help point out to us what it is they're keeping safe. They give us valuable information about what's behind the door they're guarding. This knowledge can help us learn if we're defending a broken trusting part, an injured will, a hurt imperfect self, or a bruised authority need. Once we're pointed in the direction of knowing what's wrong, we can begin to plan for repair.

Second, *understanding our hiding styles helps us make sense of the loss of freedom that comes along with them*. The explosive person who allows others to take advantage of him until he reaches a "point of no return" has a sentry called a temper. It protects him, but he also says and does things he regrets later. At the time, however, all he experienced was a loss of control and reactiveness.

Because they are reactive, defenses don't always allow us time to deliberate over a prudent course of action when they sense danger. This loss of freedom often causes conflicts in relationships and regretful feelings later, when we gain more distance on the situation.

This effect frequently occurs in addictive persons, who sincerely feel remorse over their last bout, even though they haven't begun the preventive recovery process.

Again, we can't fault the sentries for doing their job of protection. That's why they're there. The problem is that sometimes they can't tell friends (grace and truth) from foes (evil).

KEYS TO UNDERSTANDING OUR STYLES

Before we actually look at our particular hiding styles we should examine several general truths about them. These truths are good reminders of how pervasive these strategies are in all our lives.

We all use a variety of styles. I won't list every harmful hiding pattern in existence, however, because such a list would detract from our purpose of understanding the most fundamental, pervasive, and representative patterns we use reactively to protect ourselves.

We are complex and creative beings. We creatively adapt protective measures for each individual situation. Ironically, defenses are actually a testimony to our intricate nature as creatures built in the image of God: "For you created my inmost being; you knit me together in my mother's womb. I praise you because I am fearfully and wonderfully made; your works are wonderful, I know that full well" (Psalm 139:13-14, NIV).

Some hiding styles overlap. We employ some patterns for more than one developmental need. These are "all-purpose" defenses as opposed to more individualized kinds, which pertain only to their "assigned" injury. Even these "all-purpose" hiding styles have different flavors, however, depending on the injury they're protecting.

For example, we introduced splitting, or the ability to make emotional distinctions between likes and unlikes, as one of the building blocks to personality development. Splitting, it turns out, is also a major defense. It can be used to keep our relational neediness away from connection—harmful hiding. At the same time, splitting can also conceal our ability to make choices—again, harmful hiding.

Our hiding styles are always opposite to the protected part of the soul. Some relational hiding styles "disguise" certain situations so that our tender part won't be "found out." The overdeveloped self-sufficient person, for example, unconsciously pretends not to have inadequate, frightened feelings inside. He reacts oppositely to what he feels.

This "principle of opposites" is a reminder to us that spiritual maturity is moving from darkness to light, from concealment in fear and shame to confession and repentance in love. Satan wants darkness for us, because there the truth of our loved state in Christ can be denied. The opposites of the lies of darkness are the love and truth of God's light: "Do not be bound together with unbelievers; for what partnership have righteousness and lawlessness, or what fellowship has light with darkness? Or what harmony has Christ with Belial, or what has a believer in common with an unbeliever?" (2 Corinthians 6:14-15).

Light and darkness do exist side by side in us, as we struggle against our own sin and the sin of others. Even so, the Scriptures tell us there is no harmony between light and darkness: "And the light shines in the darkness, and the darkness did not comprehend it" (John 1:5). This verse refers to the overwhelming, overpowering nature of darkness. It seeks to envelop us, in the same way that a life of hiding can consume our hearts.

Yet the darkness didn't "comprehend" or overwhelm God's love and truth. If it had attempted to assimilate God's character, its contact with Him would have destroyed it. So it simply attempts to counterfeit God by having us hide behind whatever defensive style imitates light.

For example, Christians who can't express discouraged feelings often hide behind a mask of "having it all together." They often do this with the *intention* of providing a light or witness to the world. In reality, however, the mask produces a *distortion* of God's light. And the person's "witness" actually turns out to be a false picture of the character of God. After all, He Himself says to weep with those who weep and mourn with those who mourn. God does not pretend to feel happy when He's sad.

It helps to be aware of this reaction of darkness to light. As we observe the principle of opposites operating in our defensive styles, we can better see the part of the soul that we're trying to disguise, hide, or conceal.

All harmful hiding styles have denial at their core. Remember, the essence of any defense is that it causes us to act, feel, or think a lie. *This lie is basically that a legitimate, God-ordained part of ourselves doesn't exist.* We deny some truth about ourselves. The hiding style results in our living as if that lie were true.

TWO GROUPS OF HIDING STYLES

We'll be exploring our hiding styles according to the developmental need with which they occur. To give perspective on the reason for the defense, we'll also look at the fundamental fear that surrounds each injury.

Our harmful hiding patterns fall into two groups: internal hiding styles, and relational hiding styles.

Internal hiding styles are those patterns we use to hide from our painful internal feelings, thoughts, or memories. For example, people who idealize themselves see themselves in an all-good light. They protect themselves from the painful realization of their own imperfections.

Our *relational hiding styles* are those patterns of dealing with the world that protect us from the perceived danger of the world. Another term for relational style is "character style." Either way, it means *a consistent but problematic way of interacting with people and tasks, enduring over time.*

Most of our own personal hiding styles have existed for the better part of our lives. Over time, and without intervention of some sort, they take on a fixed, rigid quality. It's more difficult to straighten the trunk of a mature oak than that of a sapling.

If the injury being protected by the relational pattern is deep enough and damaging enough, *the defensive style will be so much a part of the person's everyday life that it seems like a part of the soul.* "Oh, that's just the way Stan is," a loved one will sometimes say. "He's had that quirk as long as I've known him. I've learned to live around it."

While it's true that our styles are deeply entrenched in our hearts, it's not really part of the image of God in us. Personality disorders can be healed. That's in part the message of the gospel. We can become free to love and be loved, and to freely choose without our fearful, sin-influenced, and self-protective reactiveness.

The Bible mentions the "training" that must take place for us to have "proven character": justification, relationship (peace with God), tribulation, and perseverance — to name a few.[1] As our true character develops through God's maturity process, we need the defensive traits less and less.

One last important point before we look at internal hiding from attachment: This chapter and the three following (13-16) discuss our hiding mechanisms in depth. Not every aspect of these chapters will necessarily relate to your specific need — unless you're a counselor yourself and you're looking for new insights. I personally recommend you read all four chapters because of the insights you can get in each. However, if you're in a rush, just turn to the chapter that addresses the hiding mechanisms related to that part of your soul you're convinced is injured most deeply. For example, if you believe you have an attachment deficit, read this chapter, and then you could turn to the final chapter (17) to learn more specifically how to come out of hiding. If authority is your problem, then turn to chapter 16. Again, there's something for everyone in each chapter, but you may want to focus on your own need first, learn more about coming out of hiding, then return to those chapters you've skipped at a later date. It's your choice.

INTERNAL HIDING FROM ATTACHMENT

When our need for attachment, or our *"yes muscle,"* is injured, we tend to view relationship itself as the danger. Our ability to trust God and others may have been violated by abandonment, abuse, detachment, superficial family intimacy, and other injuries.

What gives rise to hiding in this area? *The fear that our needy parts will cause our emotional annihilation.* At some level, a person's ability to reach out emotionally is damaged. We become certain that if we risk further relationship, at least one of two things will happen: (1) our own needs and dependencies will engulf and overwhelm us; or (2) others will betray or hurt us because of our needs.

The overwhelming terror we experience when our unmet needs for connection and our needy parts come face to face causes tremendously powerful hiding patterns.

We can identify six styles of internal hiding from attachment: projection, introjection, splitting, perceived omnipotence, devaluation, and hostility.

The "Log and Speck" Style (Projection)
Jesus addressed our tendency to project in the principle of "the log and the speck."[2] When we expel our bad parts onto others, we see them as having the log that's actually blinding us. We are to learn to take responsibility humbly for our own log before correcting someone else's speck.

James also deals with such projection, this time onto God: "Let no one say when he is tempted, 'I am being tempted by God'; for God cannot be tempted by evil, and He Himself does not tempt anyone. But each one is tempted when he is carried away and enticed by his own lust" (1:13-14).

The "badness" projected here is our own innate tendency to deny our creatureliness and desire what God never intended for us to have. We're to take responsibility for that part, instead of making God the villain.

Projection is the emotional act of expelling, or throwing out, intolerable parts of ourselves onto others. Individuals who have attachment deficits have unloved needy parts. They have also learned to hate those parts of the self, and eventually, to deny that they exist at all.

The problem with the log and speck pattern is that our "hated" parts actually don't go away. In our mind, that part has simply been "relocated." It's safer to deal with the badness if we see it in another person.

Leigh was an active advocate of conservative politics. She felt that big government was wrong, and that people should be more responsible for themselves. She tried to strike a balance between individual responsibility and compassion.

Sometimes, however, Leigh was disturbed by her own extremely negative reactions to the poor and homeless in her city. Walking past a crippled man on the street, she would find herself thinking, *Get a job, why don't you?* Horrified, she would ask God to change her heart, but the hostile thoughts kept recurring.

Leigh was projecting her hated neediness onto others around her. She had been raised never to complain about her pains. To have genuine needs was to be "whiny." Leigh's hated trusting parts were protected from more hostility by emotionally residing in others around her.

Emotional Picture Style (Introjection)

As with the "log and speck" pattern, the "emotional picture" pattern is a cornerstone developmental process. While in projection, we place aspects of our soul on others. In introjection, we place traits of other significant people onto ourselves.

You've heard it said, "You are what you eat." In the spiritual world, we become very much like those we're closest to — for better or worse.

Good emotional pictures eventually create an internal place in the heart for a sense of constancy, stability, and security (the position of being "rooted and grounded in love"). Helpful introjection results in a state of object constancy—an emotional steadiness inside us—so that we don't have to operate in spiritual and emotional isolation.

The helpful emotional picture style is the starting point for more mature processes such as identification and modeling. The more loving, growing people we spend time with, the more we allow them inside, the more we become like them—and so, like Christ.

The harmful emotional picture hiding style is different. Here, a person may identify with the wrong character traits of another and take them inside. The result is like swallowing a toxic substance: the soul becomes poisoned by the harmful parts of the other. Just as we become more like the loving people we allow inside, the opposite can happen also. Remember, bad company corrupts good morals.

I had seen Barry for a chronic depression. He was in his mid-thirties, a successful developer, and active in his church. Though he deeply wanted to make attachments, Barry had always had problems feeling close to others.

When we took a deep look at his formative years, Barry described his parents as pleasant enough people. Yet when I asked him what dinner conversation revolved around, he was puzzled by my question. "We ate," he said. Exploring further, what emerged was a picture of nice, responsible parents who had no relational abilities themselves.

Individuals in Barry's family weren't treated harshly. But life fundamentally revolved around work. Parents worked at their jobs. Kids worked at school. Besides work, there were no other topics of conversation.

Barry had introjected a distorted picture of intimacy. For him, to be close meant to be pleasantly distant, with a few "survival" conversational skills. He had no concept of warmth and neediness. His introjection protected him from feeling the loneliness that actually did reside deep within. He was safe, but alone.

It required diligent efforts on Barry's part at beginning to trust others in order for his internal picture of distant love to be transformed. Gradually, a genuine trust and intimacy replaced Barry's distant politeness. To do this, Barry first started using a vocabulary that expressed his feelings rather than merely intellectual concerns or his job. Even more important, he found safe Christian relationships in which he was encouraged to share his emotional needs, both positive and negative.

Black and White Style (Splitting)

Without the ability to make distinctions between ourselves and others, decision-making would be impossible. Yet a black and white hiding style can be a way to "cut off," or remove, parts of ourselves from others who diminish us.

The Fall created a fundamental split in the universe, when we were separated from God, and each other, by sin. The alienation and isolation caused by this rift in closeness was solved on the cross:

> Remember that you were at that time separate from Christ, *excluded* from the commonwealth of Israel, and *strangers* to the covenants of promise, having no hope and without God in the world. But now in Christ Jesus you who formerly were *far off* have been *brought near* by the blood of Christ. For He Himself is our peace, *who made both groups into one, and broke down the barrier of the dividing wall.* (Ephesians 2:12-14; emphasis added)

This description of Christ's integrating Gentiles with Jews gives us the counterpart to splitting. *The antidote to splitting is reconciliation.*

For the individual with attachment injuries, love and limits are split. That is, our bonding ability and our aggressive parts are kept away from each other. We fear that our hatred toward our neediness (as illustrated in self-statements such as "Why don't you grow up!") will destroy those injured weak parts.

Elaine would talk about her own soul this way: "There's a

strong, independent Elaine, who's good. But there's also a weak, clingy Elaine who's bad." Elaine spent most of her time trying to keep these two parts away from each other, especially by keeping "weak Elaine" out of the picture entirely. That part of her was too much trouble. It made her do foolish things like fall in love, get close to the wrong people, and get hurt.

Another example of splitting in this area of attachment has to do with serious trauma, such as physical, sexual, emotional, or ritualistic abuse. When people have suffered this sort of severe injury, it's common for them to use splitting to a great degree.

Sometimes large segments of time, such as the abusive years, will be split off from memory entirely. And in extreme cases, sometimes the splitting is a fragmentation of the self into several or many "selves," as in multiple personality disorders.

Splitting protects us from having to remember and reexperience traumatic events that would be too destructive to handle at the time. It takes years, and a great deal of work, for people with this sort of background to develop enough trusting relationships for the split-off parts of the soul to come together within the attachments.

Do-It-All Style (Perceived Omnipotence)

As we mentioned in chapter 6, the Fall caused a sense of omnipotence in children in which they believe they are the center of the world. As we mature, we grow out of this into a position of empathy and sacrifice for others.

In cases where trust has been hurt, however, this same do-it-all-style causes us to believe that we truly can exist without others' help. What complicates things is that, quite often, under this distortion we can become extremely resourceful and competent at problem-solving, so that our "walk" appears to match our "talk."

Individuals with omnipotent detachment defenses have a hard time understanding the Bible's teaching about our mutual needs: "And the eye cannot say to the hand, 'I have no need of you'; or again the head to the feet, 'I have no need of you'" (1 Corinthians 12:21).

George had never experienced a serious failure in his life. He was the perfect picture of confidence. When George's wife left him, he was convinced that his "can do" attitude would pull him through, if he "looked on the bright side" enough. It wasn't until concentration, sleep, and energy problems caused serious work conflicts that he began questioning his omnipotence.

George began realizing how his perceived omnipotence kept him from true intimacy with God and others. As he found a loving community of other Christians he began to feel safe in admitting that he really couldn't do it all by himself. His limitations became a normal part of life, not a fearful enemy.

Sour Grapes Style (Devaluation)

This "sentry" causes us to minimize love. *If we don't believe caring people exist, or that we actually have a need to be cared for, we make our loneliness seem less painful.* The sour grapes defense is a way of minimizing pain by pretending that someone never mattered enough to us to hurt us—like the football coach who says after a losing season, "Well, this season didn't really matter; we were rebuilding."

The sour grapes style is especially difficult for those who care for the attachment-deficient person. They are often frustrated that the person doesn't believe they actually care. It's hard to understand that devaluation has helped this person survive a long time.

George also used devaluation to protect himself. He devalued his wife's love: "She never cared in the first place." He also devalued his own need for her: "I was never in love with her, either." Of course, both statements were untrue.

An interesting thing happened as George became more intimately involved with his small group fellowship. Gradually, his deep hurt over his wife's abandonment, as well as his deep longings for her love, returned to him. While this hurt George more, it was a critical turning point in his healing process. The safety of his fellowship's caring allowed George to begin grieving. Slowly but surely, he let go of the lost relationship. This left room in his heart for new relationships as he rebuilt his life.

Hostility Style

When individuals have experienced extreme detachment, or their loving feelings have been punished in some way, they often develop *reactive hostility*. People who use rage protect themselves from more hurt by using anger to provide the illusion of power. This helps defend against having helpless, hurt, needy feelings, which don't allow them to feel safe.

One of the factors that had distanced George and his wife was George's defensive hostility. Whenever he felt the need for her to comfort him, he became frightened of the feelings and would become sarcastic and biting toward her, hurting her and keeping himself at a distance.

It took a great deal of loving feedback from George's group for him even to recognize his defensive hostility. Statements like, "George, your sarcastic remarks interfere with my feeling close to you," opened his eyes to the isolation he brought upon himself. His remarks gradually became less caustic, and he became more authentic in his sharing with the group.

RELATIONAL HIDING FROM ATTACHMENT

Just as the internal styles hide us from our own needs for love, so do *relational styles* paralyze us in isolation from those who would love us the most. Let's look at the most prominent of these styles.

The Lone Ranger Style (Detached)

The detached relational style might be better described as a non-relational style. Individuals with this hiding pattern exhibit lives that are simply empty of deep relationships. They may be married, have families, and work in a social environment. Their relational connections, however, tend to be superficial or nonexistent.

The detached character seems not only devoid of attachment, but also in no need for relationship. He appears content in non-relational settings, such as hobbies, work or projects, or simply being alone.

This style masks the actual void inside the heart. In reality, detached individuals do not feel that they really belong in any relational setting. It's as if there's no "place" for them except isolation. They need people who can accept their detachment, yet at the same time persistently invite them to deeper levels of intimacy.

The Hermit Style (Avoidant)
Similar to the detached style, avoidant people also move through life alone. The difference is that they are emotionally aware of their need for connection. The attachment injury can be felt and is very painful. They feel deep longings for love and belonging, and they experience extreme isolation.

The problem for avoidance individuals is that *their fear of love is experienced as greater than their need for love.* Their terror of trusting keeps them in bondage to their aloneness. When they begin to allow intimacy, they tend to abruptly sabotage it or anxiously disconnect.

Just as Jesus comforted us with His assurance that He would always be with us, avoidance people need that same assurance from Jesus' people. They need to know that they can move either closer or farther away as they need to—but without the threat of abandonment. Just like a frightened pet bird learns to light upon the steady finger of its owner, avoidance people can gradually settle down on the extended connection with others.

The Rescuer Style (Caretaking)
Often, people who have unmet attachment needs will take responsibility for the emotional needs of others. They tend to be active in church ministry and charity, and are seen as a source of support by many hurting people. They are warm and caring. They're *caretakers.*

While caretakers seem quite connected to others, the nature of their relationships is overwhelmingly one-way. It's as if they are always on the "giving" end and seem to attract "takers" like a magnet. The sad fact is that they can be in the midst of several active relationships and still feel very alone.

Caretakers tend to use the log and speck style to maintain their emotional distance. They project their own needy, fragile feelings onto others and take care of them. In that way, they are nurturing parts of themselves in others, the way they would like to be loved but are afraid to admit to.

It's difficult for caretakers to receive love. The fear of neediness emerging is too terrifying, so they avoid their needs.

A coworker of mine strugggled with this trait. She was so careful at avoiding discussing her needs that when I would ask her, "How are you, Jane?" in the morning, she would quickly say, "Fine-how-are-you-what-are-you-doing-today?" It really was so fast that it seemed like one word.

Once I understood my coworker's avoidance, I showed up for work and said, "Good morning, Jane; you're fine, how am I?" After a few confused seconds, we were able to begin resuming a normal conversation that included her own struggles.

It's important here to distinguish between *caretaking,* or what is sometimes called codependence, and *love.* There has been an emphasis in the past few years in Christian circles on the problem of believers who enable the irresponsibility of others.

Those who unknowingly support the habit of an alcoholic spouse, for example, struggle with caretaking. The love they feel for the addictive person often keeps them in denial of the problem, or fearful of causing conflict. Instead of setting biblical boundaries on the behavior, caretakers remain silent.[3] The addiction then worsens until the consequences of the alcoholic's behavior causes a crisis of some sort.

The problem of codependency is a real one. However, in some circles it seems to give true biblical love and sacrificial caring a black eye. Sometimes when a caretaker tries to help a friend, she might think to herself, *Here I go, being codependent again.*

That isn't necessarily the case. The act of giving could just as well be true, grateful obedience to God. Many believers who struggle with enabling and boundary conflicts are, at the same time, genuinely loving people. Their actual caring should not be criticized as a sickness, because it isn't.

The best way to distinguish between caretaking and love is to ask yourself the following two questions:

1. "Is what I'm doing from a cheerful heart, or from fear or

guilt?" Our fear of others' rage, or our guilt over letting them down, is antagonistic to love.

2. "Will my action for this person help him grow spiritually, instead of promoting sin or irresponsibility in him?" Paul instructs us, "Laying aside falsehood, speak truth, each one of you, with his neighbor, for we are members of one another" (Ephesians 4:25).

If the answer to both questions is yes, it's likely that your act is a loving one. (See the section on "suffering" in chapter 8 for a more detailed look at this issue.)

The Porcupine Style (Hostile Distancer)

Using the internal hiding style of reactive hostility, hostile distancers keep people away by a chronic anger and mistrust that eventually may wear down the most persistently caring person. These individuals are "porcupines" to their closest relationships, caught in a cycle of loneliness and self-alienation.

Projection is another defense used here, in which the distancer projects his own negative feelings into others, causing him to feel persecuted and attacked by others. This is called *paranoid projection*, and it's quite destructive to relationships.

In his latter years, Saul projected his paranoia onto David, as David's blessing from God bore fruit:

> And the women sang as they played, and said, "Saul has slain his thousands, and David his ten thousands." Then Saul became very angry, for this saying displeased him; and he said, "They have ascribed to David ten thousands, but to me they have ascribed thousands. Now *what more can he have but the kingdom?*" And Saul looked at David *with suspicion* from that day on. (1 Samuel 18:7-9; emphasis added)

Instead of being happy for David's success, Saul placed his own envy and rage onto David and became wary and frightened of being usurped by him.

Passive-Aggressive Style

Passive-aggressive individuals tend to be highly resentful of others' supposed control over them, but they don't directly confront them. Instead, they show their anger in indirect ways, such as procrastination, sarcastic humor, "forgetfulness," and intentional inefficiency.

The passive-aggressive style protects individuals from admitting their rage at others. They're terrified that if their resentfulness is exposed, others will expose their aloneness and neediness. The conviction they feel on a deep level is that their detachment must be protected at all costs. Passive-aggressiveness defends them against the intimacy that often comes with face-to-face confrontations.

Antisocial Styles

In the antisocial pattern of relating, individuals live according to the law of the jungle: *every man for himself*. Antisocials have no place for the law of love, as they generally have never experienced true empathy.[4]

With no ability to empathize with the hurts of others, antisocial people do not develop a healthy conscience: they are "seared in their own conscience as with a branding iron" (1 Timothy 4:2). The result is a position of self-centeredness, with no deep concern over the injuries this may cause to others.

The antisocial style protects individuals from closeness in a peculiar way: *they never really had closeness to begin with*. They lack an emotional ability to conceptualize attachment, a capacity for empathy, an ability to feel others' pain. Love is seen only as weakness or vulnerability. The antisocial style hides them from this sense of vulnerability.

Antisocials may need to be confronted in a veritable frontal assault of the truth of how they are protecting themselves by exploiting others. Only then can they begin to understand how they hurt others, as well as themselves, and slowly move toward closeness.

Addictive and Compulsive Styles

Addictions to, or compulsive behaviors concerning, substances, food, sex, or work are a character pattern for individuals with attachment deficits. The object of the addiction or compulsion becomes a substitute for relationship.

Michael had never had a successful dating relationship because of his inabilities to attach to women. Now, in his mid-thirties, he was becoming more anxious about ever finding a marriage partner. Yet when his anxiety was at its height, it seemed to increase his work productivity instead of moving him toward relationship. He would spend twelve-hour days at the office, delighting his boss.

Michael's compulsive drive to overwork kept him from experiencing his grief and aloneness. At the same time, it also prevented making new attachments. These two results were a powerful motivator for his "overwork drive" to continue.

One night in a fellowship group, a friend told Michael, "Sometimes I feel like you're so driven—like a wound-up mainspring ready to break. How can we help you bring your anxiety to us instead of focusing it on work?" This penetrating but compassionate remark brought tears to Michael's eyes. For the first time in his life he began bringing his fear and loneliness to the place God had intended all along.

HIDING STYLES (A SUMMARY)

GENERAL:
- Hiding styles are a "road map" to our emotional injuries.
- Understanding them helps us understand our loss of freedom, love, or relation.

KEYS TO UNDERSTANDING OUR STYLES:
- We all use a variety of styles.
- Our styles are always opposite to the part of our soul we're protecting.
- Some hiding styles overlap.
- All harmful hiding styles have denial at their core.
- Don't condemn styles; learn to "outgrow" them by meeting undeveloped needs.

TWO GROUPS OF HIDING STYLES:
- INTERNAL HIDING—We use this to avoid painful feelings, thoughts, and memories.
- RELATIONAL HIDING—We get defensive or problematic when interacting with people.

JENNY'S HIDING FROM ATTACHMENT

Though our emotional "sentries" attempt to protect us from unloving people or other pains, they also keep us away from caring people and experiences that might heal and strengthen us.

As we understand what the "sentries" protect, however, we can learn what developmental need is being automatically, and reactively, guarded. With that information, we can take steps to heal the injured part of the self.

Jenny was unaware of the sentries her emotions had placed to protect her while she was in hiding. She used two defenses most prominently: the sour grapes defense and perceived omnipotence. Let's review how she posted these sentries:

> *By now Jenny had learned how to keep her life orderly and safe in the Deep Woods. Her daily routine included waking up at about the same time each morning, washing in the stream, eating, walking, and exploring.*
>
> *Jenny's routine also included all kinds of rules, even for the little things.* Wash in the stream until you count to two hundred, then come out, *she would remind herself. As she set out to explore she would recite,* Explore the Deep Woods one hundred more steps than the day before. *These rules became rather fixed and rigid, but they helped give her a sense of control over her life. She didn't feel quite so helpless inside now.*
>
> *At the same time that life in the Deep Woods seemed more familiar and routine, Jenny's heart was changing toward her memories of home and family. At first they had felt sharp and painful, and then receded into a dull ache. Now she had a new feeling—an emotion of pushing away.*
>
> *Each day now, Jenny felt less and less that she needed her old relationships, even with her parents and Officer Josef. The growing distance was replaced by a kind of strength, but with a hard edge to it. It gave her thoughts such as,* I never really needed them anyway. *Or,* I'm better off than I was before; we were never that close.

Jenny was somewhat concerned that the distance was widening between her formerly sad, needy feelings and her newfound strength. But it did seem to make things more peaceful in her heart.

You may find Jenny's "sour grapes" and omnipotent defenses somewhat like your own. These harmful hiding patterns only signaled how very much she hurt inside. The longer she hid, the more disconnected her emotions became. Jenny devalued her relationships with her parents (sour grapes). And, she began to believe she could survive without anyone else's help (perceived omnipotence).

In a similar way, the more you find yourself hiding behind some of the defenses we've looked at in this chapter, the more you should consider it a signal of the amount of pain you're facing.

Right now would be a good time to review these defenses and find one or two that most often characterize your own hiding. Are you devaluing relationships or feeling no need of others? In each defense pattern I've pointed out some helpful guidelines to follow to move back toward relationship with God and others. Begin taking small risks. Try one of these suggestions. You may find a way out of destructive hiding from attachment.

Now we'll turn to the second major developmental need in our lives, separateness, and the various styles of internal and external hiding that it triggers.

NOTES   1. See Romans 5:1-4.
             2. Matthew 7:1-5.
             3. See Matthew 18:15-17.
             4. Matthew 22:36-40.

HIDING FROM ATTACHMENT

CAUSES: •Need for attachment, "*yes* muscle" is injured.
SYMPTOMS: •Relationship itself is viewed as the danger.
•Ability to trust God and others has been violated by injury.
FEARS: •We fear the needy part of our soul will cause our emotional annihilation.
•Our own needs will engulf and overwhelm us.
•Others will hate or hurt us because of our needs.

INTERNAL HIDING FROM ATTACHMENT

STYLE	DEFENSIVE BEHAVIOR	RECOMMENDED STEPS
•Log and Speck	Projection of own "bad part" onto others.	Take responsibility for own log before correcting others' specks.
•Harmful Emotional Picture	Introjection: places wrong traits of significant others on self.	Learn to discern our own and others' harmful traits.
•Black and White •Do-It-All	Splits off parts of self from contact with own soul or other people.	Reconciliation of all parts of self with God and others.
•Sour Grapes	Perceived omnipotence in which we believe we can exist without others.	Humbly recognize our mutual needs for each other.
•Hostility	Reactive anger against having loving feelings punished by others.	Give up anger as an illusion of power and safety; allow sadness and weakness in self.

RELATIONAL HIDING FROM ATTACHMENT

STYLE	DEFENSIVE BEHAVIOR	RECOMMENDED STEPS
•Detached	Deep feelings of not belonging and of near total relational isolation.	Seek people who will accept detached style and help us develop intimacy.
•Avoidant	Fears love and attachment more than isolation; sabotages relationships.	Need assurance of acceptance from others in "safe relationships."
•Caretaking	Projects personal needs onto others and then cares for them.	Learn to distinguish our own and others' needs for genuine love.
•Porcupine/ Hostile Distancer	Becomes a "porcupine" to others, creating a cycle of self-alienation.	Take responsibility for negative feelings; allow needy parts to surface.
•Passive- Aggressive	Resentful of others' control, resulting in indirect display of anger by procrastination or forgetfulness.	Learn direct, face-to-face confrontation and appropriate expression of anger.
•Anti-Social	Sees love or acceptance as weakness and thus exploits others.	Learn how this behavior hurts others; be open to truthful, direct confrontation.
•Addictive- Compulsive	Substitutes need for attachment with some substance or activity in place of people.	Take loneliness to God and others rather than substituting false focus.

CHAPTER FOURTEEN

Hiding from Separateness

✛

O UR SECOND major developmental need is to become a person with will, boundaries, and an accurate sense of responsibility. This is our need for separateness. It can be damaged by relational experiences where either we say no to taking biblical responsibility for ourselves; or we say yes to taking unbiblical responsibility for another person.

These sorts of injuries may be caused by enmeshment struggles, boundary failures, abuse, or parental failure to encourage separation — to name a few.

The predominant fear of people with separateness deficits is that being separate will cause abandonment and isolation. In other words, the prospect of setting boundaries strikes terror that they will be forever alone.

Sometimes this fear of abandonment or isolation is experienced as emotional withdrawal from others. At other times it is felt as an attack by someone as punishment for saying no to a demand. Both types of fears work together to create hiding patterns that help ensure the isolation of our needs to make autonomous choices and judgments, set limits, and develop our "*no* muscle."

INTERNAL HIDING FROM SEPARATENESS

Log and Speck Style (Projection)

The boundary-injured individual also uses the log and speck pattern, but in a different way than the attachment-injured person. It's not *relationship* that holds the terror, but *aloneness*. What is projected, then, are the person's aggressive characteristics.

To stand against others on principle, to be righteously angry, or to refuse to tolerate the irresponsibility of another person are all aggressive parts of being created in the image of God. But for those who are hiding from separateness, these traits and feelings can be too dangerous to experience. Therefore, they must be placed on others instead, and experienced as others' characteristics.

Joyce was well-loved by her friends, but she had a tendency to apologize constantly for supposed "offenses" that had actually offended no one. She told her best friend, "I could tell you were angry last night when I didn't have time to talk to you on the phone." In reality, Joyce's friend had called for a trivial reason at 3 a.m. However, not feeling safe to express her anger at her friend's imposition, Joyce projected her anger onto her friend, attributing her own rage onto the other person.

Joyce denied her own anger by projecting it onto her friends. Then she would feel that they were put off by something she had done. It took some time in becoming less afraid of her own hostile parts for her unnecessary apologizing to diminish.

Emotional Picture Style (Introjection)

The person struggling with separateness issues takes on others' characteristics of closeness, but without boundaries. In other words, they will form a mental image of a relationship with continuous and endless nurturance. In this relationship, they emotionally swim in an ocean of fusion with the other person.

This emotional picture will become the model for all good relationships for them. Whenever conflict arises in a relationship, it threatens the connection and they become terrified of falling into an abyss of black isolation. Also, since no relationship can compare with the image of total connectedness in their mind, all present people in their life are a disappointment. Nothing is as good, they feel, as the introjection of love.

Sue was convinced that her greatest problem was her need for love. "If my husband and kids would only care about me the way I care about them," she would sigh, "I would be able to go on with my life."

When her family made changes to give Sue more caring, however, the attempt failed. Feeling more loved for a few days, Sue again fell into longing despair over the fact that there hadn't been enough tenderness, holding, appreciation, listening, and understanding.

There never would be enough, in comparison to Sue's introjection. She had been raised in a family in which her mother had unwittingly used Sue to meet her own loneliness needs. Her mom also encouraged passivity in Sue, by discouraging her spontaneous, active traits.

The result was that Sue kept in her heart a passive wish to be cared for, forever, in the same way she and her mother had been connected when she was a child. Her introjection of the way love should be prevented her from accepting adult relationships as they are.

Black and White Style (Splitting)

Boundary-deficient people often use splitting to keep love and limits apart. They fear that their rage will overwhelm and destroy their loving, tender feelings. So they keep appropriate anger and responsible boundaries away from their caring parts.

Burt had always felt that conflict meant hate. Seeing his parents in destructive battles resulting in a painful divorce had convinced him that any aggressiveness between people pretty much signified the death of the relationship. Whenever Anne, Burt's wife, became angry in a disagreement, he would experience a terrible fear that she was going to leave him, and would quickly change his position in the argument to avoid his terror.

Burt had emotionally split his wife into two halves: "Loving Anne" and "Angry Anne." "Loving Anne" couldn't be angry, and "Angry Anne" couldn't be loving. Burt's project was to keep "Angry Anne" out of the picture. He couldn't emotionally conceive of a wife who had both loving and angry features at the same time. As a result, his ability to be biblically intimate (speak the truth in love) with her was very limited.

Do-It-All Style (Perceived Omnipotence)

Often, separateness-injured individuals will believe they can keep others happy, or content, or loving. This sort of omnipotence keeps them from the frightening truth that anyone can leave them at any time. Becoming aware of the freedom God has given to others can be a terrifying revelation. It often results in a hiding style that requires a great deal of energy.

Trudy entered the hospital with a severe depression. After I spent some time understanding her emotional hurts and bruises, I discovered that most of her life had been spent devising ways to persuade her father to pay attention to her. Trudy had learned to listen attentively, to perform well in school and at work, and to be sensitive to others' needs. She would spend hours attempting to win praise from Dad for her efforts. What she couldn't factor into the equation was that her father was self-centered and distant. He didn't have the ability to respond to Trudy's needs.

Trudy's response to her dad's lack of attentiveness was to work harder and to try different ways of pleasing him. Her marriage to a successful man that she didn't love was one of her attempts. But her real problem wasn't Dad's lack of love; it was Trudy's do-it-all-for-Dad hiding pattern.

Trudy's style protected her from the deep sadness of accepting that she couldn't wring love from an unloving person. Her attempts to please him always kept a false, cruel hope burning that there was "something that will make him love me—I've just got to find it." Her depression was related to the fact that at twenty-eight, she was beginning to burn out with the effort.

For Trudy to heal, she needed a healthy sense of discernment about people. She became aware of two classes of people within the human race: those who would love her no matter what, and those who would not love her no matter what. Her tastes began to change and she found herself gravitating toward the first group, which was unlike her dad, and away from the second group, which was like him. In this way, Trudy was able to experience the love of the Body of Christ minus any requirement to do it all for them.

Self-Attacking Style (Turning Against the Self)

In this style of internal hiding from separateness, the aggression that can't be "owned" is redirected against the self. It becomes more acceptable to hate ourselves than to tell the truth about our rage at the sin of others against us.

In Christian circles, especially, the self-attacking style is often culturally rewarded. This is due to the fact that it's easy for people who are self-deprecating to be seen as spiritual, or under great conviction. The truth is, they are actually lying about their protest against injury.

It's also easy to mistake this hiding pattern as a defense. Since the hurting person seems to be openly dealing with his weaknesses, it appears that there is no concealment. At closer inspection, however, it's apparent that what the person is hiding is his actual separate, differentiated, justice-loving angry parts. The self-denigration protects him from dealing with the injuries to that undeveloped part.

Tom was a sales representative for a large, aggressive corporation. He was a conscientious worker, yet at times the productivity demands of the job were unreasonable.

Whenever Tom failed to meet a quota, he would enter a black depression lasting for several weeks. He would describe it as "feeling like I'm living under a cloud, that the world is gray with no color, and that there's nothing good for me under the sun."

For Tom, the depression was a result of his redirecting onto himself his justifiable rage at his job. The self-hate swelled into chronic blackness. Sometimes called a masochistic defense, turning against the self makes us punish the safest target: ourselves. What the self-attacker needs is a safe, relational context in which he'll be able to aim at the correct target, without fear of retaliation.

Safe Target Style (Displacement)

The "safe target" style occurs when a fear of confronting another person causes us to attack or criticize someone who isn't as threatening. We're not concealing our aggressive parts, but we are concealing the target they're actually aimed at.

This is also known as the "kicking the dog" defense. As the description goes, the office worker gets dumped on by his boss. He goes home and takes it out on his wife, who then yells at the kids. The last recipient of displaced anger is Fido, who gets kicked by the kids.

The biblical norm for confronting others is privately, humbly, and face to face, if at all possible.[1] The displacer is terrified of the imagined or actual consequences of such an encounter (job loss, humiliation, or relational loss).

Undoing

Undoing is a harmful hiding style based on the assumption that *there is actually something we can do to negate or annul something destructive we do, say, or think.* Undoers enter into all sorts of twists to repair their supposed harmfulness.

Sometimes what is "undone" is our own unacceptable thoughts or feelings. For example, to hide from her anger at a friend, a woman might find herself inviting the friend to dinner to "undo" her feelings. This can certainly be confusing to the friend!

I have my own "undoing" story: I was raised in a family who emphasized respect for authorities. One of the rules of etiquette was that children in our family called adults "Sir" and "Ma'am."

When I was six years old, I entered into a power struggle with my mother over the question of bedtime. After Mom had listened to my reasons for staying up later, she kept her limit on the hour I should be in bed.

Unhappy with the verdict, I crossed my arms and stood sullenly in my bedroom. "John," said Mom, "did you hear what I said?"

"Yes," I replied.

"I want you to say, 'Yes Ma'am,'" my mother pursued.

Defiantly, I raised my eyes to my hers and said, "No Ma'am!"

Immediately, Mom started across the room toward me to have a "hands-on" session. Quickly becoming aware of my situation, I started walking backward, saying as many times as I could, "Yes Ma'am, Yes Ma'am, Yes Ma'am!"

As in most cases, the undoing didn't prevent me from the consequences. At its core, however, the undoer believes that compliance *can* erase badness. It is actually an emotional legalism that prevents us from admitting our faults and bringing them into relationship, rather than trying to negate them.

Regression Style

Regression is a hiding style that returns the individual to an earlier stage of immaturity. Regression can occur in the form of emotional breakdowns, relational conflicts, impulsivity, and disruptions in carrying out responsibilities.

This defensive form of regression performs the function of keeping the individual away from his more adult, structured parts. This is at times due to a deep fear that being "adult" will bring isolation.

People who struggle with defensive regression are convinced, at some level, that the only way they can have relationships is to be childish around others. They've learned that neediness brings out nurturing in some people.

Laura was a kind of interchurch "project." She had an incredibly difficult background, with severe abuse and few emotional, spiritual, or financial resources. She was homeless, jobless, and isolated.

One local church, hearing Laura's story, felt a great deal of compassion for her plight. The members found her a place to live and paid for her counseling with a Christian therapist.

Things went well until Laura was ready to get a job on her own and become more self-sufficient. Just when arrangements were underway for her to work, she suffered a tremendous emotional upheaval and seemed to lose all the ground she'd gained.

The church, concerned and confused, began her recovery process again. And the same breakdown occurred again when it was time for Laura to go on her own. After the third time, the church threw up its collective hands and turned to another local assembly.

The process repeated itself several times, with several different churches, until Laura moved to another city. She seemed no better than when she had begun.

Laura was tremendously frightened of attempting to live as a separate adult. Her hiding place was a retreat to a crisis-oriented way of life that seemed to attract loving people.

It's important to distinguish here between *defensive* and *authentic* regression. Authentic regression happens when we find safe relationships in which to acknowledge injury. For example, a person who normally functions at healthy and productive levels may enter therapy and shortly begin experiencing more sad or angry feelings than she's felt in a lifetime.

This sort of regression is a result of the past being connected to the present. In other words, the person has soul injuries that have been suppressed—split off out of time, and now isolated from relationship. Once she feels secure in the safety of the connection with her counselor she brings the injury into the present, along with the pain it has been holding for years. Her feelings may be so intense that they affect present relationships and functioning abilities.

Authentic and defensive regression differ according to the basic honesty of the person. If it's evident that the individual is making every attempt to maintain her responsibilities, but the regression continues to interfere, it's probably authentic. But if great influxes of good-enough, caring, truthful resources are brought to the person over an extended period of time, and the person seems to make little effort to take responsibility for herself, the regression is likely to be defensive.

It's also common for regression to occur at times of loss and change in people's lives. Marriage, career changes, having children, moving locations, terminating therapy, and loss of relationships can all bring about regressive episodes. These are based on a fear of not being ready for the losses and changes ahead.

RELATIONAL HIDING FROM SEPARATENESS

Caretaking Style

As well as protecting us against having needy attachment feelings, caretaking can do "double duty" as a defense against being separate.

In this area, the caretaker has a built-in guarantee of a relationship of some sort. The dependence that he fosters in others carves out a place for him in their lives. Though it's rarely the kind of attachment that actually nurtures the caretaker, in the caretaker's eyes it beats being alone. For the caretaker, bad love is better than no love.

Caretaking breaks down, of course, when the caretaker begins asking for what he has been giving to others. When the response is minimal, the caretaker experiences great hurt, rage, and despair.

These feelings indicate that some of what seemed like love, given by the caretaker, was actually a "loan." When the caretaker called in the loan, the "loanees" didn't respond. They had never been aware of, much less signed, the emotional "loan papers."

We need to realize that when we employ this caretaking style, we're controlling others. This control of love protects us from our abandonment fears. When love is coerced, however, it becomes compliance instead. When we repent of "giving love to get it" and allow others to make free choices to move closer to or further from us, we begin to mature.

Dependence Style

This hiding style involves the internal defense of regression. Dependent people hide from their responsible, willing, choosing parts. They fear that if they make their own choices, others will leave them. So they relate to others like a child to a parent.

The dependent style tends to attract caretakers. However, those who are drawn to dependent individuals are motivated by feelings of obligation and guilt rather than by love. Even so, the dependent person readily accepts this compromise and attachment. Being an "emotional charity case" is preferable to isolation.

It is the neediness, not the relationship, that keeps people involved with this type of individual. The purpose of avoiding separateness, however, is fulfilled.

Dependent individuals are so frightened of aloneness that they will go to almost any lengths to keep others close by. This may involve compromising their principles, giving up their freedoms, or submitting to manipulation.

One woman with this relating pattern always had two boyfriends, never actually committing exclusively to either. Her thought was, *If one leaves me, at least I'll have the other.* For years, her fear of aloneness kept her paralyzed from being able to develop a deeply intimate relationship with either man.

It was only when she began taking risks by setting small limits with others that the dependency began to resolve itself. The dependent person needs to believe that her differences and opinions are not a guarantee of abandonment. She needs to experience the biblical truth that iron sharpens iron. She must realize that differences can enhance rather than destroy closeness.

Victim Style

In this relating pattern, individuals approach relationships from a position of blaming others. They see their own unhappiness and circumstances as the fault of others, and tend to look for others to take responsibility to repair their injuries.

The victim style removes responsibility and badness from those who use it. To take responsibility for one's own injuries would be extremely painful, so they avoid it by looking to others.

It's important to clarify the difference between the terms *victim* and *victim style*. *Victim* is a factual, historical designation. It refers to *a person who has been injured for the purpose of satisfying the evil purpose of another.* In a sense, we all are victims and victimizers, being products of the Fall.

A *victim style,* however, is a chronic relating pattern that denies the autonomy, choices, power, and responsibility of the victim. It virtually ensures re-victimization in the individual, sometimes throughout a lifetime.

In other words, not all historical victims have a victim style. Many who have suffered tremendous evil at the hands of others take conscientious responsibility for their lives. They are able to differentiate between "fault for the injury" (the perpetrator's part) and "responsibility to heal" (their own part).

Others who adopt the victim mentality remain in helpless positions and sabotage their recovery. Additionally, those who employ the victim mentality use it to keep themselves in a morally superior position to their victimizer (the perpetrator). The victim senses that the other is a "worse" person than himself.

This is a dangerous position, because it keeps the victim blind to his own contributions to the pain he's in. The victim externalizes all blame outside himself, and therefore can't be confronted about his own behavior. The victim can't get the log out of his own eye, which obscures his vision of everything except his victimization. As a result, he avoids responsibility for the sin in his own heart, the sin of perpetually insisting that others take responsibility for his recovery.

Wanda once asked her support group for "feedback." Given permission, several members pointed out characteristics in Wanda that distanced them from being close to her. Suddenly, Wanda jumped out of her chair and ran out of the room. By the time the session ended, she hadn't returned.

The next week, however, Wanda was back in group. When asked why she left, Wanda said, "I didn't want *that* kind of feedback." Upon more investigation, it became clear that for Wanda, "feedback" meant "positive support."

Wanda's victim style prevented her from being able to hear truth and still feel loved. Confrontation, even in love, felt like blame and condemnation to her. Gradually, with a great deal of work, she began to feel safe enough to accept criticism without feeling intensely attacked.

Manipulation Style

People with a manipulative character pattern use others to avoid taking responsibility for their own life. Often interacting with the antisocial style, people with this style use manipulation to hide from their separate, autonomous parts.

Rather than being able to undergo the training of learning God's law of consequences, manipulators may use any or all of several tactics to avoid responsibility:

- Not respecting the boundaries of others.
- Coercing others.
- Asking others to bail them out of jams.
- Continually borrowing money from others.

- Taking "short cuts" to responsibility, which eventually backfire.
- Using people in indirect ways without actually asking for help.

The Bible speaks against a "shortcut" approach to life:

> "As a partridge that hatches eggs which it has not laid, so is he who makes a fortune, but unjustly; in the midst of his days it will forsake him, and in the end he will be a fool." (Jeremiah 17:11)

God knows we need to learn self-control and delayed gratification to become adults. The manipulator style, however, attempts to control others to avoid that sort of autonomy.

Fred had never held down a job for more than six weeks, nor did he ever have to. He had the "gift of gab" and was able to meet his needs through others without working. He'd been able to live at home until his mid-thirties, when his indulgent mother finally developed enough boundaries to make him leave.

After that, Fred found a string of women who were susceptible to his coercive approach. He had lived with each until his welcome was worn out. By the time Fred entered a hospital program with a drug problem, his heart was so full of maneuvers that he actually couldn't tell when he was being "real" or "unreal."

It was only when Fred was confronted on his manipulations by staff and peers, clearly and often, that he began to change. A breakthrough for Fred was the day he admitted that he enjoyed controlling others for his purposes, and that most of the time, he felt no love for the people he was seducing. Saying that to the very people he was attempting to coerce was quite an uncomfortable confession for him. At the same time, however, the people in his group warmed to him because at last they saw truthfulness in him.

Chaotic Style

This character pattern tends to be impulsive, disorganized, and directionless. A lack of self-direction and the ability to focus, along with a predominance of harmful splitting, typifies this individual.

The person with a chaotic style splits his closeness and autonomy needs. That is, his needs for connection will draw him toward others in a dependent fashion. However, the connection cannot be sustained and the person distances by isolation or impulsive behavior.

The reason the chaotic person can't stay connected is generally one of two reasons: either the person he is close to disappoints him, and thus becomes "all bad"; or the individual's own fears of closeness cause him to sabotage the closeness to maintain protection.

The chaotic style, as you can imagine, disrupts not only the person's life but the lives of those close to him. He cannot sustain a sense of stability or focus because of the hiding pattern that keeps him away from closeness, yet also away from autonomy.

The person with a chaotic hiding style desperately needs consistent relationships, which provide structure in the form of support for his boundaries, assistance in clear thinking and decision-making, and an awareness of the consequences of his actions. This will give him a sense of stability and self-confidence.

Passive-Aggressive Style
Just as this relational pattern helps attachment-injured individuals from risking closeness, passive-aggressiveness also protects people from feelings of aloneness. Quite often, separateness-injured people will display this indirectly hostile pattern. It serves the purpose of punishing supposedly controlling people, but protects these individuals from having to take responsibility for the aggressive feelings they have toward others.

Vance and Gail had been married several years before they became aware of Vance's passive-aggressive style. Gail was a direct, sometimes overcritical person. She had no qualms about giving Vance frequent evaluations on his performance as a husband without waiting for Vance to request them.

Gail was also a gourmet cook, and she spent a great deal of time preparing meals just right. One night, after she had "evaluated" Vance, she then set out to make a souffle. When the oven temperature was perfect, Gail left the kitchen to answer the phone. When she returned, she found the oven was off, the souffle fallen and ruined.

Wondering if she were crazy, Gail walked to the living room and found Vance reading the evening paper. "I know this sounds weird," she said, "but by any chance did you turn off the oven just now?"

Setting his paper aside, Vance looked thoughtful for a minute. Then he said, "You know, maybe I did."

Vance had protected himself against his rage at Gail, and had avoided his fear of separateness. In this case, however, there was no protecting him against Gail's displeasure.

Histrionic Style

The histrionic pattern has three basic characteristics: a deep sense of dependency; seductiveness with the opposite sex to meet the dependency need; and deep contempt for the opposite sex for being "seduceable."

Individuals with this hiding style tend to have multiple romantic relationships. In a sense, they "live for" this type of love. Their lives feel empty if there is no romance occurring. They will take on same-sex friends "in between" romantic flings.

The true issue, however, is generally not a need for romance, but a disguised fear of autonomy. The histrionic hiding pattern protects the person from having to embrace loneliness.

Jessica came to treatment for help with "relationship problems." She was an extremely attractive, flashily dressed woman in her late twenties. Jessica wanted to know why she couldn't keep a dating relationship.

The pattern for her was consistent: she would quickly fall in love with men who had very masculine, strong traits. Sometimes those men would begin to become truly intimate and warm with her. When they "softened up," Jessica would feel bored with them and the relationship would end. Those men who stayed detached and emotionally unavailable stayed attractive to Jessica. The problem was, her dependency would wear on them, and they would leave her.

As we explored, we found that Jessica had come from a family in which she had been not only "Daddy's little girl," but also enmeshed with her mother. Her life had been complicated by an inability to separate from either parent.

Jessica's hiding pattern protected an undeveloped separating part that stayed isolated by her absorption with men. She had thought her problem was "men"—but actually, on a deeper level, she had a problem with an inability to achieve autonomy.

Addictive and Compulsive Styles

Just as dependencies on food, substances, and sex help people hide from closeness, addictions and compulsions also protect them from being alone. Addicts often use a substance in order to regain a sense of attachment and warmth that, for some reason, they don't find readily available in relationships.

JENNY'S SEPARATENESS

Jenny was living the nightmare of the person hiding from separateness: abandonment and isolation. Even though Jenny knew the external circumstances that had forced her away from her parents, the separation injury was so great she began looking for internal reasons to explain why her parents had been taken away from her.

Her conversations with Big Jenny and Little Jenny focused her internal struggles on whether Jenny had any responsibility for the separation from her parents. Big Jenny became the accuser and Little Jenny the accused. As Jenny played out this drama, she began to convince herself that her parents' capture was somehow her fault. She had no other protection against the separation injury, and she began to fall into self-hatred. Fortunately, Officer Josef's love stepped in to help her before it was too late.

Perhaps you find yourself in one of the patterns of hiding from separation. Like Jenny, you may be engaging in some form of self-attack, and this may cause you to see yourself as either more spiritual or more guilty.

HIDING FROM SEPARATENESS

CAUSES:
- *"No* muscle" is damaged.
- Sense of boundaries and personal responsibility is confused.

SYMPTOMS:
- We say no to taking biblical responsibility for ourselves.
- We say yes to taking unbiblical responsibility for others.
- We try to make others responsible for *us.*

FEARS:
- Being separate will cause abandonment and isolation.
- Setting biblical boundaries will cause us to be forever alone.

INTERNAL HIDING FROM SEPARATENESS

STYLE	DEFENSIVE BEHAVIOR	RECOMMENDED STEPS
• Log and Speck	Projects aggressive characteristics onto others.	Become friends with our own hostility.
• Emotional Picture	Creates an image of total merger with another person, resulting in disappointment when separateness is experienced.	Accept separateness as part of closeness.
• Black and White	Splits caring parts away from responsible boundary-setting parts.	Accept the reality that adults can be both caring and different at the same time.
• Do-It-All	Perceived omnipotence in relationships: keep everyone else happy and content.	Repent of omnipotence; recognize freedom of others to leave us, allow them to choose to suffer.
• Self-Attacking	Directs anger or aggression at others onto self.	Learn to aim aggression at the correct target, without fear of retaliation.
• Safe Target	Displaces fear of confronting another by attacking someone less threatening.	Confront the correct target biblically: privately, humbly, and face-to-face.
• Undoing	Tries to repair perceived destructive actions.	Recognize we can't "undo" or negate actions; accept the justified anger and hurt of others.

| •Regression | Childishness: returns to earlier state of immaturity, fearing that adulthood brings isolation. | Recognize and take responsibility for our own separateness; find people who love our separateness. |

RELATIONAL HIDING FROM SEPARATENESS

STYLE	DEFENSIVE BEHAVIOR	RECOMMENDED STEPS
•Caretaking	Fosters dependence in others.	Repent of *giving* love to *get* it.
•Dependence	Relates to others like a child to a parent, fearing abandonment if own choices are made.	Recognize differences can enhance rather than destroy closeness.
•Victim	Blames others for own injuries and unhappiness.	Take responsibility for personal healing.
•Manipulation	Uses other people and takes shortcuts to responsibility.	Learn self-control and delay of gratification.
•Chaotic	Impulsiveness, disorganization, and directionless; seeks dependence on others, but can't sustain connection.	Find safe, structured relationships; become aware of consequences.
•Passive-Aggressive	Indirect hostility toward others who supposedly control us.	Take responsibility for aggressive feelings toward others.
•Histrionics	Dependence, seductiveness, and deep contempt toward opposite sex, resulting in multiple failed romances.	Achieve personal autonomy by separating from parents appropriately.
•Addictive-Compulsive	Uses substance or activity as substitute for expression of separateness or rage.	Take resentment and powerlessness to God and others, rather than substituting drugs, alcohol, work, etc.

Again I advise you to review the defenses and look at taking some risks. Check to see if you're holding deeply felt anger about some personal injustice or injury. Ask yourself, "How do I protect myself from being separate?" Find some safe relationships and turn toward God's faithful lovingkindness to understand your own hiding better.

The more we hide, generally the more pain we're in. In the next chapter we will try to identify which hiding patterns we develop when we experience injuries to our souls in failing to understand the good and bad in ourselves.

NOTE   1. See Matthew 18:15-17.

CHAPTER FIFTEEN

Hiding from Our Good and Bad Selves

✛

W E CAN look at our needs for closeness and boundaries as the organs and skeleton of our bodies—the bone structure protects the vulnerable organs from injury.

Using the body as a metaphor, then, we can see that our ability to resolve our good and bad selves in part depends on how effectively we deal with infections that attack our inner selves. Do we deny those infections and attempt to hide them? Do we allow them to fester until they overtake the entire body system?

Our needs for adulthood are like one of our brain's important functions—that of decision-maker, in which it makes authoritative evaluations about where the body will go, what it will do, and how it will conduct itself. Who's in charge here? Is the brain taking responsibility for things, or is it referring all decisions to someone else?

By now a fundamental difference between the first and second pairs of spiritual and emotional needs should be clear: *attachment and separateness define the existence of our soul; good/bad deficits and authority conflicts determine the quality of life of our soul.*

Because of their importance to the functioning of our soul, it is paramount to understand how we hide from God's love in the recovery process in these two areas. In this chapter we'll deal with hiding from maturing our good and bad selves.

RESOLVING GOOD AND BAD

We have a need to accept the bad parts of ourselves and the world. This need is important because it helps us bring our own badness to a place of forgiveness. Our imperfect characteristics need to be brought into connection with God and others. What we fail to keep in relationship stays unforgiven and broken.

Our "*forgiveness* muscle" can be injured in many ways:

- A perfectionistic environment, or one in which failure is a cause for shame, can keep our goodness and badness split apart.
- Relationships and families that overstress the "excellent" parts of people, at the expense of the "mediocre" parts, discourage us from accepting our imperfections and bringing them to Christ.
- Over-positive environments that keep us from legitimate grief can also keep our badness hidden.
- Idealistic denial is a characteristic of some families who keep their members stuck in a naive position.

The predominant fear of individuals who are injured in their ability to resolve goodness and badness is that badness will annihilate goodness. People with this deficit are tremendously afraid that if they admit bad parts in themselves or others, they or others will forever be stuck in an "all-bad," shameful position.

INTERNAL HIDING FROM BADNESS

As we observed in the chapters on hiding from attachment and separateness, we hide in two basic patterns: *internally*—from painful internal feelings, thoughts, or memories—and externally, or *relationally*—in which we develop problematic ways of dealing with people and tasks, behaviors that endure over time.

First, let's look at internal ways we hide from our sinfulness and our perceived badness.

Log and Speck Style (Projection)

Terrified of being found out or exposed in their imperfections, forgiveness-injured individuals reject those characteristics of themselves that they consider imperfect and unconsciously place them on others.

Brenda had come from a high-achieving Christian family who provided a great deal of positive affirmation for the kids. However, failure in grades, sports, or student activities was an awkward subject in her home as well as school. As a result of these family and social pressures, the children tried to avoid failure as much as possible.

In college, Brenda became involved in a Christian campus group. She began leading Bible studies and helping other girls with their spiritual lives. After a few months, however, Brenda noticed she had a disturbing tendency to become impatient with Nancy, one of the girls in her group.

Nancy struggled a good deal more than other girls. She wasn't as "sharp" or "with the program" as the rest of the group. Often, Nancy wouldn't have her study assignments done, or would cancel because she was so overwhelmed with personal conflicts.

Brenda, who generally thought of herself as a warm person, found herself becoming critical and terse with Nancy. It took some time before she realized that Nancy reminded her of her own failures—the ones she couldn't show to others. Brenda began to understand that not only did she function better than Nancy, she also hid better than her friend.

When we don't feel permitted to admit our imperfections, we often project them onto other people. Brenda couldn't accept her own imperfections, because to do so would have risked great disruptions in her close relationships.

Failure in a dating relationship provided Brenda with an unexpected solution. She was unable to hide her feelings of loss and grief from her friends. However, instead of encountering criticism and coldness, Brenda was surrounded by friends who identified her failure with their own. Somehow, this made being imperfect seem normal to Brenda. As an added benefit, she found herself more able to empathize with Nancy.

Emotional Picture Style (Introjection)

People with good-bad deficits have taken inside themselves a distorted image of what people should be. The emotional picture becomes one of two extremes:

(1) an "all-good" picture of themselves; or
(2) an "all-bad" picture of themselves.

Generally, this picture forms as the result of thousands of interactions with significant relationships over the years, which bend the image one direction or another. In either case, part of the person's characteristics are split off and denied.

In high school, Martin had been a four-letter star athlete. His tremendous abilities had been a natural way of life for him. Going to work in business after college, Martin had gotten out of shape and had gained forty pounds.

When his twenty-year high school reunion came around, Martin made up an excuse and didn't attend. He was fearful that his internal picture of himself as slim and in shape was also the picture that his classmates had of him. Martin had introjected a grandiose picture of who he should be. This picture kept him hiding from his friends.

Black and White Style (Splitting)

Probably more than any other developmental injury, black-and-white thinking dominates people with good-bad deficits. These individuals have not experienced sufficient grace to be assured that they will not lose attachment if their faults are "exposed." They develop an inability to live by faith instead of works, the same pattern Paul censured in the Galatians: "Are you so foolish? Having begun by the Spirit, are you now being perfected by the flesh?" (Galatians 3:3). Because of this inability, these people constantly attempt to keep good and bad far apart in their lives.

Colleen, a junior in college, had a serious conflict. She had struggled with a binge-purge eating disorder—bulimia—since high school. When she was isolated or feeling pressure, the cycle would get out of control.

This was Colleen's "secret self," in which she experienced herself as "bad." The world could see "good Colleen," but "bad Colleen" was always isolated. Her terror of others seeing her in this difficulty kept her feeling that she was leading a double life. Her shame and self-hatred were tremendous.

For Colleen, the answer arrived in the form of a support group for other bulimic women. As she saw the other group members accepting the "bad" part of each others' disorders, for the first time Colleen could accept this destructive behavior as a part of herself. More importantly, she could now talk openly about her secret and still feel cared for. Instead of a "good Colleen" who was compliant and a "bad Colleen" who binged and purged, they were replaced by a "good/bad Colleen." She could now accept herself as both image-bearer and fallen creature.

Do-It-All Style (Perceived Omnipotence)
The good-bad deficient individual often maintains a false feeling of power over his badness. This power shows itself in two ways:

(1) "I can successfully hide my badness";
(2) "By hiding my badness, I can eliminate it."

Sadly, neither of these statements is true, for two reasons. First, *we're powerless to "will" away our faults without relationship*. In Romans 7:15-8:1 the Apostle Paul points out that we can deal with this inevitable reality of sin only through relationship with Christ. Second, *we can't conceal our bad parts perfectly, because they will be exposed by their fruits*. Many people, however, attempt to keep themselves hidden for a lifetime, believing that they can accomplish the impossible.

I once saw a boxing movie in which one fighter was hopelessly outmatched by the other. Yet, courageously, he kept approaching his opponent, time after time, round after round, taking tremendous physical punishment. After each round, his manager would say to him, "Why don't we stop the fight?"

"I can lick him," the boxer would say. "Give me another round."

The fight went on for fifteen rounds, and predictably, the weaker fighter was knocked out in the final few seconds. Carried off in defeat, he could be heard, saying to his manager through puffed and bleeding lips, "Give me one more round . . . I can lick this guy." The defeated fighter did his level best, but his best wasn't good enough to win. He couldn't accept his limitations in the match.

I often encounter Christians like this boxer. They try to eliminate their shameful parts by various omnipotent methods: willpower; discipline; self-denial; trying harder; looking at the "bright side."

All of these aspects are helpful traits. However, without acceptance of our limitations and recognition of our need for grace, all of our efforts are doomed to failure: "They are of no value against fleshly indulgence" (Colossians 2:23).

Most of us can identify with the experience of having a compulsive or addictive behavior or thought. We'll promise ourselves or God, "I'll never do this again" (it can be an unacceptable thought, sexual behavior, drug problem, or money impulsivity, to name a few). Then, after a period of hours to months, the behavior reemerges, causing us to fall into despair.

The problem is *the omnipotent promise*. The Fall guaranteed us that we are all capable of incredible destructiveness at any given moment. And there is no guarantee that we will abstain from destructiveness. Instead, we are to depend daily on the grace of God and His people to help us accept and mature through our badnesses. That's the biblical way.

Peak-to-Pits Style (Idealization-Devaluation)

It's common for people with a good and bad split to enter a rollercoaster cycle of wonderfulness to horribleness. They will start by tending to idealize and look up to others, which creates a pleasant attachment for a temporary period. But it definitely remains temporary.

The problem occurs when the idealized person lets his friend down in some way. When this happens, the "peak" relationship quickly turns to the "pits." The idealized person is often left confused and bewildered at the turn of events in the relationship, saying, "How can I be such a skunk today? Yesterday I was the best thing since sliced bread."

Individuals who need to avoid experiencing badness defend themselves by finding others on whom they can project perfection. They're terrified of the prospect that other people are just as marred and unfinished as they are. Their lives become a constant search for that special spouse, church, or job that won't let them down.

When they find the "perfect" person, idealizers then place all their hopes and dreams on that individual. Then, when the depravity or immaturity of the idealized other finally comes out, the idealizer becomes terribly disappointed and hurt by the "betrayal" of the other. This is often manifested in relationships by statements such as, *I thought I knew you. You led me to believe you were special.*

Even though the idealized person may have contributed to the deception, the idealizing person quite often unconsciously also contributed by *not noticing the humanness of his friend. And humanness always includes sin and badness.*

This hiding style is often unnoticed by idealized others. After all, being admired is seldom a painful experience. But idealization always contributes to disappointment and hurts relationships. In fact, *the greater the idealization, the greater the devaluation when it finally occurs.*

In order to work against the "peaks-pits" defense, it's often helpful for people in a relationship to try to list the negative qualities of the other. Honeymooners who haven't spent time struggling with the differences between themselves often wake up during the first year of marriage thinking, "What have I gotten myself into?" One woman described this creeping realization as follows:

My husband and I were the perfect couple. At least that's what everyone said. We were both student leaders in school, and had the same friends. I never really asked myself if we knew each other, much less if I loved all of him. I was just swept away by the perfection of the script.

It wasn't until after the wedding reception, and all the gaiety and friends were gone, that I noticed a problem. My husband and I had left to go to the honeymoon suite of the hotel for our wedding night. It was on the top floor of an expensive downtown hotel.

We entered the elevator by ourselves. The doors closed, and we were silent on the long ride up. I remember looking at my new husband, as if it was for the first time. And I thought, "Do I really know this man? What have I done?"

As it turned out, her questions were answered in the form of an extremely troubled marriage. She eventually forgave his badness, accepted her own sinfulness, and learned to fall in love with his strengths.

Soapbox Style (Reaction Formation)
Related to the projection style, soapbox hiding creates a passion against the "bad" part of the self we're concealing. This passion erupts in our personal vendettas or pet peeves. The result is that we react in an opposite direction to that bad part of ourselves.

In his church, Sam was noted for his ability to teach on sexual sin. As an elder, his teaching often seemed to unearth sexual misconduct in the church where no one would have thought it to be. Women's immodest clothing, off-color jokes, and teenage experimentation were frequent targets.

When his wife discovered his collection of pornography, Sam at first tried to deny its existence. Finally, with the help of a strong loving church group, he was able to take responsibility for the sexual part of himself that he'd preached against in others.

RELATIONAL HIDING FROM BADNESS

The Perfectionist Style
Probably the easiest character style to connect with injuries in

the good-bad area is the perfectionist—an emotional legalist. Just as the Christian struggling with badness attempts to correct it by rigid adherence to the law, the perfectionist experiences one failure as total failure. He desperately tries to keep good and bad apart by harsh and self-critical expectations of himself that no one could achieve.

Elizabeth's parents and siblings were acclaimed musicians. Several were professionals in the field, and others were award winners. Elizabeth herself was a talented singer. As the oldest child, she felt tremendous pressure to maintain the family standard of excellence in music.

Elizabeth's junior year in college was a difficult one with academic and career decisions, as well as a conflictual dating relationship. In the midst of this turmoil, her spring recital came up, in which she was to sing several solos in front of a large audience. Halfway through the recital, Elizabeth inadvertently coughed—a common problems for singers, especially when under stress.

The first cough was bad enough. When a second one came a few minutes later during another solo, Elizabeth could take no more and fled in tears from the stage. Her teacher found her sobbing in a corner. "I ruined it!" she exclaimed.

"Elizabeth," replied her professor, "if I'd taken a poll of the audience, after the coughs and before you left, no one would have noticed but you."

Elizabeth's head could hear the reassurance, but her heart couldn't.

The perfectionist lives in a world in which falling off the high wire of 100 percent—even one or two percentage points—means a long, long drop.

The Bible tells us that we have indeed all fallen off the high wire of perfectionism, but not in the sense that Elizabeth felt: "For whoever keeps the whole law and yet stumbles in one point, he has become guilty of all" (James 2:10). The fact is, those who live by the law of perfectionism are judged by it. But when we accept our failure to live up to the law, trusting instead in an attachment with God and others who can forgive us, we fall from the high wire of perfectionism into the safety net of grace.

The Admiration Addict Style

One style that attempts to hide badness presents a grandiose, "superstar" self to others, which is designed to accomplish two tasks:

(1) it draws attention to the person's strengths; and
(2) it conceals the person's perceived weaknesses.

Driven by a deep sense of shame, the admiration addict is continually in dread of one basic possibility: *that he will be "found out" and exposed as a fraud.* Though on the outside the addict appears to be extremely confident in his talents and abilities, he is quite frightened that he will actually be "known" by others.

Individuals who have learned to hide in this way are often legitimately gifted people who were only praised for their strengths — not for just being themselves, lumps, bumps, and all. They often feel a tremendous gap between themselves and the people who idealize them, sensing that they are being used and exploited by others' needs for a superstar.

The need to be entitled and special, however, takes precedence over being normal. The admiration addict can never relax. He is always vigilant to look and sound good to others.

It's easy to find this style in others. Those who need someone to idealize search them out like a beacon. Those who react against this sort of self-centeredness are quick to criticize the pretentiousness of the admiration addict, especially behind his back. This is true because of the show he puts on — the contrast between "real self" and "false self" is immense.

In actuality, the admiration addict is in tremendous pain and longs to be loved for himself. But he possesses a developmental inability to allow the imperfect self "out" to be loved.

Jim entered a hospital program with a depression and an alcohol problem. Yet in his sharing groups, he only presented stories of his great achievements with great regret that others couldn't see his specialness.

After a few days, one group member had begun feeling distant from Jim's "real self." In an honest confrontation, she told him, "I don't like to admit it, but sometimes I call you 'Prince Jim' when you aren't around"—referring to his airs of entitlement. Jim was quiet for a moment, then tears came to his eyes. "That's the nicest thing anyone's ever said to me," he said. Jim was so unaware of his hiding style, and so needy for affirmation, that he couldn't even hear the confrontation behind the statement.

When the true meaning of "Prince Jim" was explained to him, it took several days of love and support for him to recover from tremendous feelings of shame and humiliation.

When the admiration addict begins to allow others to see and love the "bad self," he loses the taste for admiration. This is a tremendous risk, however, for him to take. It requires a great deal of assurance of unconditional love from God and others.

The Pollyanna Style
This style refers to a tendency of some good-bad injured individuals to look only at the good side of themselves and others. They take a naive and idealistic view of life, expecting the best of it without being prepared for disappointment. Often, they come from homes in which badness wasn't discussed frankly.

One common result of this sort of character pattern is that the results of the Fall take this person completely by surprise. They can't conceive of others not being loving or trustworthy. Often, they will stay in denial about this for as long as possible before the evidence forces them to admit that they, or others, have self-centered and destructive parts. They are often shattered, crushed, and embittered by the contrast between an idealized childhood and a marred adulthood.

The Pollyanna character uses hope in an unbiblical way. Christians are to hope for good in a realistic manner. That is, we are to live in the hope that God's loving character will ultimately fill our hearts and lives:

> For in hope we have been saved, but hope that is seen is not hope; for why does one also hope for what he sees? But if we hope for what we do not see, with perseverance we wait eagerly for it. (Romans 8:24-25)

Pollyannas, however, take hope to mean an expectation that good things will always happen. They try to "think positive" and "hope for the best." The result, after many disappointments of this unrealistic hope, is heartsickness: "Hope deferred makes the heart sick" (Proverbs 13:12).

Many recovering Pollyannas go through a period of cynicism and bitterness as they begin to uncover the distortions they had thought were true all their lives. Some of these distortions include:

- When you expect the best, it happens.
- If you do your best, good results always happen.
- If you're nice to others, they'll be nice to you.
- Accentuate the positive and eliminate the negative.

Each of these statements is designed to hide the person from badness and failure. When this form of denial finally pans out in relational and work failures, Pollyannas begin painfully removing their rose-colored glasses and entering the "house of mourning."

The Romantic Style

Like the Pollyanna, the romantic style looks at only good things, but in a particular focus: Life is built on the excitement and passion of romantic love. For romantics, they can endure anything as long as they have an intense, emotional involvement in a dating relationship or with a spouse.

Much of the current popular music of our culture reflects this character style, with phrases such as: "You're everything to me"; "Life is empty without you"; "Loving you is all I need"; "I can't live without your love."

This kind of thinking confuses two types of God-given attachment: *romantic* love and *bonding* love. While romantic love is a specific connection meant for marriage, bonding love is deeper and broader. It's what the famous verses in 1 Corinthians 13 refer to: love is patient, love is kind, not jealous, bearing all things, and so on.

The romantic sees all attachment through the grid of romantic love. He does this as a way to be connected, yet without the mundaneness of everyday love. He fears that without the passion of romance, life will settle into an empty, boring routine. On a deeper level, he is terrified of his own "routineness."

Romantics are convinced that they are fundamentally boring people who have nothing interesting to say besides passionate exchanges. It is the romance, they think, that keeps others around them. They are deeply afraid that their uninteresting, meat-and-potatoes self will be exposed, rejected, and abandoned by others.

Sharon was one of the unhappiest people I've ever been around—an aging romantic. In her younger years, she had moved easily from relationship to relationship. Though this sort of instability had wreaked havoc on her family life, the gains of intense passion, seduction, and mystery had been a support for her.

Now in her mid-forties, Sharon could no longer attract men the way she had been able to. She began experiencing bouts of depression, weight gain, and relationships with men who were far beneath her standards. Finally, after a failed suicide attempt, she sought treatment.

Sharon's treatment was difficult because relating to men in non-sexual ways was foreign to her. She saw women as competition. Yet when she began moving underneath the desire for romantic passion to the deep, abiding love that the Body of Christ offered her, the seductiveness began to wane.

The All-or-Nothing Style

The all-or-nothing character style reflects an undeveloped ability to tolerate good and bad to the extent that relationships become almost impossible. It's as if there is no place in the person's head for both traits to exist. One man expressed it this way: "It's really very simple. When you agree with me, you're good. When you disagree with me, you must not understand me, so you're bad."

This character style tends to split good and bad within himself in the same way. If the all-or-nothing person feels loved, he feels "good." If there is conflict or frustration in the relationship, he often will experience himself as "bad." He simply doesn't have the ability to hold an internal biblical picture of being cherished by God and others during conflict.

One common characteristic of the all-or-nothing character is a consistent pattern of disruptive relationships. In order to protect against the feeling of badness, these individuals will often make themselves or the other person all-bad, so that negotiating disagreements is impossible. A conflict results in either self-criticism and withdrawal, or intense blaming of the other person. Sadly, this protectiveness of the "good self" ends up in a deepening cycle of isolation.

Addictions and Compulsions

As we've noted in previous stages, out-of-control behaviors, thoughts, and feelings are also protective in nature. In the area of the good-bad injured individual, these habits keep us from the shame of experiencing our perceived bad parts.

For example, one compulsive shopper thought she overspent to her credit card limits for no reason at all. As she explored the timing of her sprees, however, she found that they generally occurred just after her husband had been critical of her. Critical confrontations caused her to feel "all-bad." She had too little internal grace to hold on to her good traits when confronted. Overspending restored a sense of equilibrium to her injured "good self."

HIDING FROM EVIL, SEARCHING FOR TRUTH

Now we've looked at the problem of human nature: each of us has a sin nature; each of us is created in God's image. The practical problem that most often faces us is, "What do I do with my *actual* and my *perceived* badness?" Sometimes we deal with it constructively, and come out of hiding. Sometimes we treat it in destructive ways, and push ourselves deeper into the Deep Woods.

If we try to hide the fact of our imperfections, we'll end up in the sort of self-deception and hatred that Jenny fell into when she first attacked herself through Big Jenny. But if we deny that goodness resides in us, we'll believe the lie that Little Jenny started absorbing.

Of course, being created in God's image does not cancel out or override our sin nature—only Christ's death on the cross pays the penalty for our sin and makes new life possible. But the image of God is always within us, however tarnished.

David, king of Israel, fell into deep and destructive self-deception in his adulterous encounter with Bathsheba. David at first refused to acknowledge his sin before God, which plunged him into a terrible self-hatred that he took out on others around him—notably in having Bathsheba's husband, Uriah, killed.

The prophet Nathan pointed out David's sin and triggered David's repentance. Only then, when he fully acknowledged his badness before God, could David return to his status as an accepted servant of the Lord. David describes the process of repentance:

> How blessed is he whose transgression is forgiven, whose sin is covered! . . .
> When I kept silent about my sin, my body wasted away through my groaning all day long. For day and night Thy hand was heavy upon me; my vitality was drained away as with the fever heat of summer.
> I acknowledged my sin to Thee, and my iniquity I did not hide; I said, "I will confess my transgressions to the LORD"; and Thou didst forgive the guilt of my sin. Therefore, let everyone who is godly pray to Thee in a time when Thou mayest be found; surely in a flood of great waters they shall not reach him. Thou art my hiding place; Thou dost preserve me from trouble; Thou dost surround me with songs of deliverance. (Psalm 32:1,2-7)

Theologian Dick Keyes has written about this passage:

> David did not suddenly see himself as a wonderful person who had never intended to harm anyone, but rather accepted himself in a new way despite his sin. He had honestly faced it before God and God had forgiven him. . . .

HIDING FROM RESOLVING GOOD AND BAD

CAUSES:
- *"Forgiveness* muscle" is injured.
- Imperfections remain unconnected to God, self, and others.

SYMPTOMS:
- Failures bring deep shame.
- Inability to accept mediocrity or imperfections in ourselves or others.
- Denial of legitimate grief.

FEARS:
- Our badness will annihilate our goodness.

INTERNAL HIDING FROM GOOD AND BAD

STYLE	DEFENSIVE BEHAVIOR	RECOMMENDED STEPS
• Log and Speck	Rejects personal imperfections and unconsciously places them on others.	Ask God to "reach and know" my heart; ask loving others for feedback on imperfections; learn from what I react negatively to in others.
• Emotional Picture	Sees bad parts as corrupting goodness, splitting off a significant part of the soul.	Develop a wholistic picture of self, accepting both good and bad parts —realistic acceptance.
• Black and White	Keeps good and bad parts of self far apart.	Seek safe relationships, people who accept both good and bad in others.
• Do-It-All	Maintains false feeling of power over sin, thinking badness can be hidden, and by hiding it, can be eliminated.	Recognize sin can be dealt with only through relationship with Christ and His people.
• Peak-to-Pits	Goes from idealizing a relationship to devaluing it.	Accept own mediocrity and that of others.
• Soapbox	Creates a passion against the "bad" part of the self we're concealing, resulting in personal vendettas or pet peeves against others in that area.	Notice the humanness of our friends, which includes sin and badness; list good and bad qualities of self and others; take responsibility for the bad part we're concealing.

RELATIONAL HIDING FROM GOOD AND BAD

STYLE	DEFENSIVE BEHAVIOR	RECOMMENDED STEPS
• Perfectionist	Experiences one failure as total failure; keeps good and bad apart by harsh, unrealistic self-critical expectations.	Accept our failure to live up to the law; rely on "safety net" of grace.
• Admiration Addict	Presents a "superstar self" appearance to others.	Allow loving others to see badness and imperfections; the taste for admiration will diminish and the hunger for love will develop.
• Pollyanna	Looks only at the good side of self and others; thinks good things will always happen.	Recognize biblical hope in God's character; accept that we live in a fallen world.
• Romantic	Lives mainly for the excitement and passion of romantic love.	Discern the confusion between romantic love and bonding love.
• All-or-Nothing	Can't tolerate both good and bad in self or others; relationships become almost impossible.	Expose "meat and potatoes" self to others; develop internal biblical picture of being cherished by God and others during conflict.
• Addictive-Compulsive	Binges to protect self from criticism or to keep from dealing with "bad" parts.	Accept and respond to the forgiveness of God and others for our imperfections.

. . . By no longer hiding his sin from God (v. 5) he [David] was able to find a *hiding place in* God (v. 7). When he hid his sin from God, God seemed an enemy. When he acknowledged his sin, God became the one in whom he could hide from the trouble of this world. David's peace with himself and God was dependent on his honest recognition of what he had done.[1]

We don't know what Jenny's spiritual condition was, but we do know that she had come to a point of deep depression. Yet she was not developed enough to recognize her need for honest reflection on her own condition. As Keyes points out, this kind of honesty and self-awareness is essential to resolving our inner good/bad conflict:

Self acceptance and repentance are not in conflict, but are dependent on each other. This high level of honesty before God seems for a moment to risk our psychological safety, but brings with it the deeper peace that only integrity with God can yield.[2]

I hope you have the peace that comes from this acceptance of your good and bad selves. Accept yourself for who you are—a person created in God's image, capable of noble and selfless deeds; but also a person who is sinful, imperfect, and unfinished.

As we accept God Himself through Christ, we receive the grace that He bestows through forgiveness. Along with this unmerited acceptance and restoration, He also provides people of grace who can come alongside us and enflesh for us in our daily lives the reality of His forgiveness. This is the path out of the Deep Woods of the good and bad dilemma.

NOTES   1. Dick Keyes, *Beyond Identity* (Ann Arbor, MI: Servant Books, 1984), page 95.
2. Keyes, page 95.

CHAPTER SIXTEEN

Hiding from Authority and Adulthood

⟐

O UR FOURTH spiritual and emotional developmental need is to establish a biblical sense of our own adulthood and authority. When this part of our character remains undeveloped, it's often due to improper use of authority in the home.

Authority problems generally manifest themselves in three different ways:

(1) too-strict authority, also called *authoritarianism*;
(2) too-lenient authority, also called *laissez-faire parenting*, where no one is in charge; and
(3) *inconsistent authority*, a combination of both styles.

Individuals who have authority injuries experience *a basic fear of being attacked or criticized for taking adult authority over their lives*. They're frightened that they'll be "put down" by powerful figures if they are not approval-seekers. Authority-immature individuals generally hide from either aggressive or sexual parts of themselves.

The reason for this is that the initiative-taking and sexual parts of the soul are necessary parts of being an adult. By definition, an adult is someone who can take adult responsibility over his aggression and his sexuality. Authority-injured people are frightened of displeasing parental figures. Because of this, they are also frightened of these two aspects of the soul. Exposing aggression or sexuality could, they think, bring on criticism by a parental figure.

As with the three other primary areas of our soul already examined, authority injured people exhibit two general hiding patterns—internal and relational.

INTERNAL HIDING FROM ADULT AUTHORITY

Shoving Underneath Style (Repression)

With this defense mechanism, we attempt to remove intolerable thoughts and feelings by sending them out of our consciousness. An authority-deficiency makes us fearful of displeasing those we see as adult. As a result, when we become aware of parts of ourselves that might bring on disapproval, we "shove" those parts "underneath" our consciousness in order to forget them.

One woman suffered from sexual inhibitiveness and used a repressive hiding style. The picture of her parents on her bedroom wall hadn't gotten there by accident! Without realizing it, she had placed it there to keep a lid on the sexual feelings she was afraid of, because she had internal prohibitions against being a sexual wife. Her particular hurt was the result of critical parents; in other cases, it might come from school settings or other institutions in which sexuality was viewed as bad.

This woman's task was to accept sexuality as a natural, God-given part of adult married life—as God's gift to her and her husband. She would benefit greatly from a careful reading of the Song of Solomon (Song of Songs), which clearly presents sexuality as blessed by God.

Soapbox Style (Reaction Formation)

Just as individuals with good-bad conflicts employ this hiding style, it is also commonly found among authority-injured people. They develop an opposite reaction that hides them from a threatening adult part of the soul.

Many years ago, I was a unit director at a children's home. One of my jobs was to help orient new children to the cottage-style facility. As I took a teenager named Paul on a tour through the home one day, we began talking. While we were getting to know each other, I noticed that every sentence he uttered toward me ended in the word *sir*. "I'm from Idaho, sir," Paul would say. Or, "Where will I be going to school, sir?"

At first glance this seemed to be a positive departure from the usual authority-hating teenage boy we tended to take in at the home. Paul was quiet, compliant, and almost obsequious to adults. The conflict emerged a few weeks later when, over a minor disagreement, Paul beat up a houseparent.

Investigating further, the truth emerged. Paul had been removed from an extremely harsh home in which he had been beaten regularly by his alcoholic father. Overcompliance had been Paul's method of surviving this punitiveness.

When Paul was transferred to the children's home, the few weeks of a more permissive environment had allowed the "soap-box" defense to come down, and Paul's true feelings toward authority then emerged.

Eventually Paul learned how to talk about his resentful feelings rather than physically acting them out—a skill his father never taught him. More importantly, a houseparent who was very strong but loving befriended Paul. For the first time, he could argue with authority and still feel safe. Authority became his friend instead of an enemy.

Erasing Style (Undoing)

"Undoing" attempts to negate our supposed destructiveness. We use erasing as an emotional "sentry" to try to make up for our rebellious feelings by behaving in artificially loving ways toward others. In doing this, we hope that our rebelliousness won't be held against us.

Like perfectionism, undoing is a form of emotional legalism that operates against the "free gift" of God's love through Calvary. It's based on two factors:

(1) a *fear* that there is not enough forgiveness to allow us to be pardoned; and

(2) an omnipotent *fantasy* that we can erase our mistakes.

Scott, a high-level management professional, tended to be fearful that his subordinates would resent his position. He speculated that they thought he was snobbish. As a result, whenever he felt legitimately angry at them for some irresponsibility, the anger would instantly turn to guilt.

Scott acquired the habit of taking a subordinate out to lunch the day after he'd had a hostile word or thought toward the co-worker. This was his way of attempting to erase his guilt over feeling angry. Scott's subordinates, not being privy to his thoughts, thought Scott an easy boss.

Intellectualization Style

When authority-deficient people are afraid of assuming their own adult position, they often retreat to their head (logical thinking) instead of their heart (dealing with emotions). The goal of intellectualizers is *to stay away from feelings that might cause them to do or say something offensive.* Often, this hiding style protects them from intense sadness, longing, or hostility.

It isn't difficult to notice intellectualization, unless you have the same struggle. When the intellectualizer is asked how he feels, he generally responds with an opinion. This is usually not a conscious act, nor is it manipulative. It's simply a way to connect with others while attempting to hide seemingly dangerous feelings.

God doesn't ask us to make this sort of defensive distinction between the head and the heart. In fact, the Old Testament term for *heart* refers to both thoughts and feelings. God gave Solomon a wise heart, and Hannah's heart rejoiced when she found out God had answered her prayer for a son. The intellectualizer is fearful of that kind of integration of the soul.

Guilt Style

Guilt feelings are self-condemning emotions that cause us to criticize ourselves for real or perceived wrongdoing. These guilt feelings can become a hiding style for the authority-injured person, because *guilt is generally anger turned inward.*

Children who fear the criticism of a harsh authority figure (parent, teacher, pastor, etc.) don't feel safe to be angry at unfair or overly strict treatment. The risk of more criticism is too high. When this occurs, the child's anger becomes directed at herself, not at the authority figure, and is experienced as guilt. By feeling guilty rather than angry, the child protects her undeveloped authority aspects from further attack. Guilt feelings are very different from the "godly sorrow" Paul commended:

> I now rejoice, not that you were made sorrowful, but that you were made sorrowful to the point of repentance. . . . For behold what earnestness this very thing, this godly sorrow, has produced in you: what indignation, what fear, what longing, what zeal, what avenging of wrong! (2 Corinthians 7:9,11)

Godly sorrow is *authentic remorse for being unloving toward another,* and is not at all the same as the self-attacking of internalized anger.

Excusing Style (Rationalization)
This commonly used hiding pattern confuses "reasons" for "justifications." The authority-injured person will often find excuses for her impulsive words or actions that are in actuality used to prevent the anger of another toward her. Instead of providing reasons for her actions—which might explain what she did but might not get her off the hook—she instead offers excuses. She hopes that the excuse will justify the behavior, and so avert the anger of the parental person.

Jackie's family had prepared her to attend medical school. All her life her physician father had planned for her to follow in his footsteps. Jackie's testing and grades also showed she had the capacity to do well in that field. All seemed well until, unexpectedly, Jackie dropped out of her second year of medical school due to poor academic performance.

The reason Jackie gave her disappointed father was that she needed a break for a year and wanted to "gear back up." The truth was that Jackie hated medical school, and in her heart she knew she would never return. Jackie's fear of her father's disapproval caused her to excuse leaving school as a temporary measure, instead of facing him with her permanent decision.

People who hide with rationalizations are fearful of taking responsibility for their seemingly dangerous traits. Yet the excusing keeps those parts from being able to mature and develop in relationship with others. Facing up to their imperfections and learning to live with those human inadequacies will help excuse-makers become more honest with themselves and others.

Non-Medical Medical Problems (Somatization)

At times, authority-injured people will develop pains and symptoms that have no medical basis. Thorough testing will rule out any physical reason for such subjects as back and head pain, abdominal problems, and sexual difficulties.

Often, the cause of the problem is that the body and mind interact to protect the person from taking authority over his life. In other words, the body gets sick when the person is in a position to grow up in some area. This keeps the focus off the spiritual and relational issue.

Toni's job as assistant to a harsh and demanding boss was increasingly stressful for her. He blamed her for his own mistakes and expected more of her than was possible. Not a complainer, she didn't notice her headaches until they were blinding migraines.

At first, Toni made no connection between her job and the pain. After extensive medical testing showed no physical basis for her headaches, Toni began studying the effects of the stress of her job. She realized she was giving an undue amount of authority to someone who didn't deserve it—her boss. She needed either to stand up to her boss or to leave a job she otherwise enjoyed.

As her emotional issues unraveled, however, Toni began understanding her pattern of feeling intense rage toward her supervisor, shoving down the feelings, then developing a massive headache within minutes. Eventually Toni was able to set appropriate limits with her boss, to refuse his unbiblical authority and accept his biblical authority. As she began feeling like an adult in her job, her headaches subsided.

Just as our thoughts and feelings aren't meant to be isolated from each other, God meant the heart and the body to be integrated in a mysterious and complex fashion. David refers to this connection in reference to hiding his sinfulness:

> When I kept silent about my sin, my body wasted away through my groaning all day long. For day and night Thy hand was heavy upon me; my vitality was drained away as with the fever heat of summer. (Psalm 32:3-4)

RELATIONAL HIDING FROM AUTHORITY

The Approval-Seeking Child Style

People in an approval-seeking position have generally been in a one-down position with adults all of their lives and need a great deal of approval and permission from others to make decisions. They're frightened of breaking rules and tend to be overly careful, obsessed with making "right decisions."

This obsession often leads to paralysis in making important career and love decisions. They may find themselves in middle age feeling as unready to embark on life as when they were fifteen.

The difficulty here is for the person to see himself as an adult, without having to find a "parent" to approve of his decisions. He fears that he will be intensely criticized for failures, so he chooses not to choose at all—that is, unless the "parent" figure in his life gives permission.

Israel had the same "child position" problem. They wanted a king, and told Samuel the prophet to get them one. God lamented their rejection of Him from being King over them. God wanted to be their only king, but Israel would not relent and pressed their case with Samuel for a human king:

> Nevertheless, the people refused to listen to the voice of Samuel, and they said, "No, but there shall be a king over

us, that we also may be like all the nations, that our king may judge us and go out before us and fight our battles."
(1 Samuel 8:19-20)

Israel did not want a divine king, because they wanted to be like the rest of the kids on the block. A human king would make decisions for them. He would do their dirty work.

God granted Israel's wish and gave them a king, Saul. The next few centuries proved the system they had longed for did not work well.

Fusion with controlling figures is an addiction to human authority. It is basically a fear of taking responsibility for our own decisions and of answering to God for them. Israel wanted a fall guy to blame things on if they broke down—in the same way that Adam blamed Eve, and Eve blamed the serpent.

Jesus reinstated the rule of God over the parentalism of human leaders: "But do not be called Rabbi; for One is your Teacher, and you are all brothers. And do not call anyone on earth your father; for *One is your Father*, He who is in heaven. And do not be called leaders; for One is your Leader, that is, Christ" (Matthew 23:8-10; emphasis added).

Jesus was saying that whenever tradition, or human rules, break with God's, we are to "obediently rebel." This is why many families get worse when they finally decide to deal with emotional issues before they get better. They have unbiblical rules, which hurt all the members. Some member gets help, and starts living according to the laws of love and responsibility, instead of fusion, detachment, or overcompliance. Perhaps a spouse is confronted on drinking and deals with it. Often the family starts falling apart until all the members get help.

Jesus said that He came to bring division and that households would be divided.[1] Family situations like these reflect that principle. People who begin throwing off other people's inappropriate authority will make waves with rule-bound leaders. Approval-seeking children must seek this sort of help, though. They may rock the family boat for a while, but in the long run their own emotional health will be served.

The Controlling Parent Style

Often, an authority conflict doesn't emerge in a life as a "one-down" or childish perspective. It comes out more as being "one-up," or parental of others. This person has learned to identify with controlling figures to avoid challenging them. We met Phil in the beginning of chapter 7. Phil was compliant with his superiors so that he could feel in control of those below him.

This type of person has internalized a critical, harsh parental value system, and he has lost access to his spontaneous, adolescent parts. He will report never having had a "questioning" or rebellious period in his life; or if he did, he became frightened and ran back to the "traditions" of the parent figures.

Parental people tend to be judgmental of others, who represent the split-off adolescent in their own hearts. They aren't comfortable in adult-to-adult roles. They like to know "who's in charge" more than "who can I connect with."

Obviously, when a "parental" person meets a "child" person, they move into the cycle mentioned above, where the child gets needs met by asking permission and accepting judgment, and the parent gets needs met by constant advice-giving and criticism. Neither can get unstuck from their position until some sort of symptom occurs, such as a financial crisis, a depression, or an affair. It is only when either the "child" challenges the authority of the "parent" or when the "parent" repents of over-controlling that the impasse is resolved.

The Rebellious Child Style

This hiding character pattern has an advantage over the other two, though it has its own struggles. The rebel has an awareness of needing to question tradition. He questions and challenges whether the authority he's under is legitimate or not.

This isn't to say that this person has it easy. The perpetual adolescent has felt either that rules have injured him (the too-strict parent), or that he's never had appropriate rules. Either way, the problem is the same: *an inability to experience authority as constructive.* Authorities—in the form of parents, police, bosses, supervisors, and church leaders—are the "bad guys."

Relationship is severed when authority enters the picture.

Many of these individuals have "counterculture" characteristics, such as drug or alcohol abuse, radical lifestyles, and anti-
authority positions on issues.

People in this position tend to job hunt a great deal, because
the boss was "too controlling," when the reality is often that the
appropriate demands of the boss are perceived as those of a critical
parent. They sometimes have scrapes with the law because being
under authority takes away their adultness in their minds. They
can't conceive of the possibility that they can be under authority
and still be an adult. Jesus' example of that possibility is important to the rebel:

> Who, although He existed in the form of God, *did not regard
> equality with God a thing to be grasped,* but emptied Him-
> self, taking the form of a bond-servant, and being made in
> the likeness of men. And being found in appearance as a
> man, *He humbled Himself by becoming obedient to the point
> of death,* even death on a cross. Therefore also God highly
> exalted Him, and bestowed on Him the name which is above
> every name, that at the name of Jesus every knee should
> bow, of those who are in heaven, and on earth, and under
> the earth, and that every tongue should confess that Jesus
> Christ is Lord, to the glory of God the Father. (Philippians
> 2:6-11; emphasis added)

Jesus' "emptying" of Himself did not rid Him of His adultness,
though it led Him to suffering and death. Rather, it *confirmed*
His adultness. The rebel needs to experience being with strong
individuals who will help him bend to authority, yet without loss
of love or respect.

It's important to understand that, just like the child and
parental positions, the rebel also feels like a child around adults.
His reactiveness gives him away. *Rebellion is not freedom, because
it is simply a reaction to control.* It is not being an adult. When the
rebel learns to meet needs to be in control of his life, and not react
in hostility or defensiveness, he then becomes an adult.

People in the approval-seeking child position have felt their authority broken, and turned themselves inward: "Fathers, do not exasperate your children, that they may not lose heart" (Colossians 3:21). The rebel, instead of turning inward, acts outward with his defiance: "And, fathers, do not provoke your children to anger; but bring them up in the discipline and instruction of the Lord" (Ephesians 6:4). Both problems reflect an unbiblical authority structure in the family environment.

Obsessive-Compulsive Style
This character pattern tends to be unduly conventional, authority-bound, more comfortable with tasks than relationships, and has trouble making decisions. Quite often, the obsessive's preoccupation with details keeps him from arriving at larger-scale decisions that urgently need to be made.

Habits and rituals are an important part of daily life for those who are obsessive-compulsive. They establish routines such as certain routes to work or how their desk is organized in order to feel more in control of their lives. In addition, obsessives tend to be somewhat passive-aggressive, sabotaging their success by dawdling or procrastinating on responsibilities.

This style fits with the goal of protecting the injured authority characteristics of the soul. Obsessives are frightened of taking charge over their lives and making risky decisions that come with owning their behavior—confronting a superior, changing jobs, or requesting a favor from someone. They're frightened of the criticism that they feel this insubordination will bring. Often, the only criticism they experience is from their own internal harsh parent.

Addictive and Compulsive Styles
Substance abuse, overeating, overspending, sexual impulsiveness, and compulsive habits serve authority-deficient individuals by providing a place for their rebellious parts to emerge.

In this pattern, however, the addictive or compulsive behavior is a disguised form of rebellion, and is usually seen as uncharacteristic of the person: "Excessive drinking just isn't something I would do," is often the thought of the authority-bound person.

HIDING FROM AUTHORITY AND ADULTHOOD

CAUSES:
- "*Authority* muscle" is injured.
- Improper use of authority in the home:
  - Authoritarianism (too strict)
  - Laissez-faire parenting (too lenient)
  - Inconsistent authority (both)

SYMPTOMS:
- Approval seeking from authority figures.
- Unhealthy aggression or sexual behaviors.

FEARS:
- Displeasing parental or authority figures.
- Being criticized for exercising adult authority over life.
- Submitting to biblical authority.

INTERNAL HIDING FROM AUTHORITY

STYLE	DEFENSIVE BEHAVIOR	RECOMMENDED STEPS
• Shoving Underneath	Sends intolerable thoughts or feeling away from consciousness so we won't bring on disapproval.	Accept aggressive or sexual parts of self as God's natural order.
• Soapbox	Opposite reaction to injured part of soul resulting in passion against others in that area.	Learn to question authority and still feel safe so it becomes a friend, not an enemy.
• Undoing	Attempts to negate our supposed destructiveness by artificial love toward others.	Feel legitimate anger; recognize fantasy of erasing mistakes.
• Intellectualization	Retreats to head (logic) instead of heart (dealing with the emotion), hiding perceived dangerous feeling.	Realize God doesn't ask us to make such distinctions—feelings are part of the soul.
• Guilt	Turns anger inward when confronted by harsh, unfair treatment.	Develop godly sorrow: authentic remorse for being unloving toward another; allow anger toward appropriate object.

| • Excusing | Confuses "reasons" for "justifications," offering excuses for actions. | Bring fear of approval for decisions into relationship; ask for help, not disapproval, in owning mistakes. |
| • Somatization | Develops pains and symptoms with no medical basis when confronted with growth issues. | Make connections between pain and inappropriate treatment by authority figures; set biblical limits. |

RELATIONAL HIDING FROM AUTHORITY

STYLE	DEFENSIVE BEHAVIOR	RECOMMENDED STEPS
• Approval-Seeking Child	Seeks permission from others to make "right" decisions.	Take responsibility for own decisions; answer to God and biblical authority alone.
• Controlling Parent	Identifies with controlling figures to avoid challenging them; parental over others.	Repent of over-control of others; reevaluate critical, harsh parental value system.
• Rebellious Child	Questions and challenges whether the authority we're under is legitimate or not; reacts to control.	Recognize that rebellion is not freedom; learn to meet needs to be in control; learn healthy submission.
• Obsessive-Compulsive	Conventional, authority-bound; more comfortable with tasks than relationships; preoccupied with detail.	Confess anger and fear of authority; learn to see big picture without fear of disapproval.
• Addictive-Compulsive	Abusive addiction provides place for rebellious parts to emerge.	Integrate "subduing and ruling" aspects of life— owning rebellious nature —into relationship.

It would be closer to the truth to say, "I'm tired of being the elder son, and everyone else gets to be the prodigal. I've been compliant for the wrong reasons." But since the compulsive behavior has been "disowned," these individuals aren't able to integrate their "subduing and ruling" aspects into relationship. They tend to stay subservient with episodes of "uncharacteristic" destructive behavior. The hiding pattern becomes a false solution that compounds the authority-injury instead of solving it.

JENNY AND AUTHORITY

Fear of assuming authority is the starting point for many hiding patterns. As we have observed, Jenny's experiences often mirror our own:

> Eventually, Jenny became aware that the pieces of her broken heart were slipping away. Not that she wasn't doing well in her task of survival. In fact, if anything, she was more competent at finding food, catching fish, locating shelter, and staying warm. But the feelings that she had felt all her life were becoming more and more faint. Emotions such as love, tenderness, and joy seemed like words written in stone.
>
> It wasn't just the good feelings that had left. Even the bad ones—terror, panic, rage, and sadness—were a dull memory for Jenny. She never thought she would miss those feelings, but when they went, she knew something was wrong. Jenny was aware that feelings tell people they are alive.
>
> Now Jenny had become merely a creature of empty habits. She went through her routines of survival sluggishly, without the sense of spontaneity that had characterized her early days in the forest. She felt almost dead.

We've talked about how we keep the injured parts of our soul protected, and sometimes rightfully so. But if we continue in the sort of harmful hiding patterns we've looked at in this chapter, like Jenny our soul begins to suffocate. Our needy, immature parts will begin to atrophy for want of God's healing truth and grace.

Let's turn now to the final chapter that will help you resolve your hiding dilemma. Here we seek the key to opening the door of the heart without further injuring what lies within.

NOTE   1. Luke 12:51-53.

Chapter Seventeen

Coming Out of Hiding

✢

M Y OFFICE was silent for what seemed like an eternity.
Only a few seconds had passed, however, since Sally,
an attractive woman in her mid-thirties, had opened up
her session with these words: "Dan's furious at my dependence
on him. He wants to know if we three can have a session together
to talk about it."

You may remember that this scene is almost the same as the
one that I used to open chapter 2—except Sally's statement is
different here. Unfortunately, however, Sally never said to me
the words that are written above. I only wish it could have been
possible.

Had Sally's husband been able to address his resentment of
her neediness, they would have had to deal with one problem: the
question of needs and responsibilities in the marriage. But they
wouldn't have had to deal with the second problem: hiding from
true intimacy, which could have been painful, demanding, and
ultimately rewarding.

In this final chapter, we will look at ways we can move out of
our positions and styles of hiding. Whatever hiding patterns we
commonly use, and whatever injured and undeveloped parts of

the self we're trying to protect, *God desires us to be free from the isolation of our souls:*

> "The Spirit of the Lord is upon Me, because He anointed Me to preach the gospel to the poor. He has sent Me to proclaim release to the captives, and recovery of sight to the blind, to set free those who are downtrodden, to proclaim the favorable year of the Lord." (Luke 4:18-19)

Our spiritual and emotional hiding patterns keep us in a relational prison that God never intended for us. He has provided the resources to work through these patterns.

REMEMBERING WHY WE HIDE

It's an important step to be able to identify the defense mechanisms and character styles we use. This can provide us with perspective on how we sabotage our relationships and goals in ways we're not aware of.

Yet simply knowing our hiding patterns isn't enough for spiritual maturity to take place: "Knowledge makes arrogant, but love edifies" (1 Corinthians 8:1). We need more than understanding. In fact, one of the legitimate complaints about counseling or therapy is that some professionals seem to see diagnosis as the cure. It's as if individuals in treatment are supposed to become well automatically when the hole in their heart has been pointed out.

Identification of our hiding patterns is a first step to several others that are just as important: understanding the meaning of our hiding patterns, what needs they meet, what they protect, and what to do about them.

Hiding patterns exist as faithful sentries, set in position by our souls long ago. We need to remember that *they're there for a reason.* They exist because there was, and is, an injury to protect. They're doing the best job they can. While they may not be especially effective at discriminating the good guys from the bad guys, their number one priority is to prevent reinjury to our undeveloped parts. If only for that reason, *we need to respect our hiding defenses*. They didn't pop out of thin air.

TWO INCOMPLETE SOLUTIONS

Harmful hiding patterns keep us from the very resources God has provided for our healing: *grace, love* (relationship), and *truth*. But too often we try to take shortcuts to healing—we pick and choose among these resources instead of drawing on all of them.

We're going to look at two common shortcuts that are incomplete solutions to the hiding problem, because they don't take the full counsel of God into consideration. They fit the description in Proverbs 14:12 of "a way which seems right to a man, but its end is the way of death." These are *confrontation without relationship* and *relationship without confrontation.*

Confrontation Without Relationship

When I asked her to tell me her worst memory, Marie had no problem coming up with it. Shy and sensitive, Marie had always encountered problems adjusting to changes. When her family had moved to a new town in the middle of sixth grade, she had walked into a strange class in a strange school, not knowing anyone.

That was difficult enough. What had made the day especially traumatic for Marie, however, had been the cruel responses of several children. Their approaches had varied from simply ignoring her to criticizing her shyness in the way only sixth-graders can do: "Cat got her tongue? Maybe she's deaf and dumb." And so on.

When I asked her how those comments on her relational style of avoidance had affected her, Marie said, "I became a turtle. I just pulled my head farther into my shell."

Marie's situation is an example of a common approach to dealing with harmful hiding patterns: *confrontation without relationship, or truth without love.* In this solution, the individual is told about her hiding patterns with the confronter giving little thought to making a connection with the one confronted. She is then expected to "stop avoiding," or "stop being irresponsible," and so on. It happens with adults as well as with children.

The benefit of this approach is mostly for the friend doing the confronting. He can then say he has done his "duty" and told the truth. Whatever the hider wants to do with that information is now between her and God. The friend can walk off into the sunset, blowing the smoke off his "six-shooter of truth" and looking for another person who needs confronting.

I remember a Christian campus group I was involved in evaluating new members for their particular needs and gifts within the group. One of the more zealous leaders had picked out what he considered to be the "sharpest" person in the new group. As he discussed him, the leader said, "I've looked and looked, and I can't find a single sin in this guy."

I can imagine how the recruit would have felt had he known he was being spiritually evaluated in this vein. It wouldn't have been a very safe position for him. Such an evaluation sets up the individual, the leader, and the group for a big letdown when the "guy" eventually blows it — as we all inevitably do.

This is an incomplete solution to hiding problems, because *truth without grace leads to judgment.* When we're confronted on a problem, we need the safety of relationships to withstand the badness we have to face about ourselves. Taking a look at a destructive, sin-ridden part of our character is always a painful process. If we are securely anchored in loving, unconditional relationships, it's still difficult, but we can survive it. But if knowing our faults could lead to a loss of love, vulnerability becomes almost impossible.

The truth of God's Word exposes things that are in darkness and need to be corrected. But often this exposure only leaves us feeling opened up and condemned. Love, on the other hand, through relationships, provides an environment conducive to healing.

Painful, confrontational, exposing truth must be brought out in the context of relationship. The truth is like a car that transports people from one mountain peak to another. Grace relationships are like the bridge built between the peaks to handle the traffic. The important thing to know here is that the painfulness and confrontational nature of the truth we must transmit is *directly related* to the strength of our relational bridge.

For example, a mild confrontation requires less of a trust relationship than a major one. We don't need a lot of bridge for a subcompact-sized interaction. The need for safety still exists, but it's less. The problem comes when an eighteen-wheeler-sized confrontation is driven on a bridge built of kite string. The vehicle as well as the bridge are guaranteed to fall into the abyss.

This is why people who have developed long-term, safe, loving relationships can hear criticisms from their loved ones that might be quite wounding were they to be given by a mere acquaintance. There's a difference in bridge size. This kind of bridge can handle a big truck.

There are two fruits of the confrontation-minus-relationship approach:

1. *External compliance and an increase in hiding patterns.* Individuals who are excessively "truthed" often learn to *pretend* to be receptive to the information. They nod, sometimes take notes, and will even express gratitude. But their true opinion of the confrontation approach emerges in the fact that the injuries remain unhealed, and the hiding patterns stay or are simply switched around in a creative way.

Jesus' parable of a father and his two sons is an example of this compliance.[1] Asked by his father to work in the vineyard, the one son answered affirmatively but then didn't go. He remained compliant on the outside, but had an entirely different agenda of his own.

Ken, in the hospital for a substance abuse disorder, spent his first few days thanking group members for pointing out aspects of himself that were problematic. Finally, he used drugs while on a pass away from the clinic. When this was found out, the group again confronted Ken. This time he told them what he really thought of their criticisms.

Strange as it seemed to Ken, several members told him it was the first time they'd felt close to him. His compliance had been a barrier to intimacy. The loving acceptance of the group after a time helped Ken recognize his pattern of hiding through compliance.

2. *Open resentfulness and loss of relationship.* Although it's more honest than the compliant response to truth without love, the resentful response usually distances us from closeness. We sense that we're being pushed into an encounter that we're not ready for, and we react to protect ourselves. Again, the hiding pattern is only strengthened, not worked through.

The advantage of this reaction to unloving criticism is that at least we don't have to work through layers of false compliance to reach our anger at being bruised unrighteously. We stand a good chance of reaching out for relationship again in the future.

Relationship Without Confrontation

Marcia came to a support group with an anxiety disorder. As her story unfolded, it was apparent that she had been in several very destructive relationships, from family to friendships. She had been hurt a great deal by these relationships.

The group had responded to Marcia in a genuinely warm and accepting way. They had empathized without judging as she shared her pain; they had been there to lend a hand, or shoulder, when she needed it.

After several sessions, some of the members noticed a problem. Marcia was working very hard on dealing with the hurt and anger of her past injuries and was experiencing feelings she had shut off. But as time went on, it seemed that she was becoming fixated on reciting her injuries, over and over again, with very little thought as to how to create a better life for herself in the present. The more empathy she received, it seemed, the more she missed out on the relationships she had in the present.

Marcia's situation is an example of the second incomplete approach to helping people work through their hiding patterns. In her case, Marcia was receiving *love without truth.* It was difficult for her to finally hear, for example, that while she was genuinely a victim in her childhood, she was responsible for the destructive behaviors and relationships she had developed as an adult. Marcia would typically insist on silence or total empathy from the group when she shared, or she would withdraw, saying the group wasn't "safe enough."

The problem with the relationship-without-truth approach is that *grace minus truth leads to license, or irresponsibility*. Without a sense of our own responsibility to take active steps to heal our immaturities, growth becomes paralyzed. Paul addresses this conflict:

> And the Law came in that the transgression might increase; but where sin increased, grace abounded all the more, that, as sin reigned in death, even so grace might reign through righteousness to eternal life through Jesus Christ our Lord. What shall we say then? *Are we to continue in sin that grace might increase? May it never be!* How shall we who died to sin still live in it? (Romans 5:20–6:2; emphasis added)

Our unconditionally loved position in Christ wasn't intended to be an excuse for irresponsibility, but a motivator for grateful responsiveness. Our safety should lead us into becoming more loving people.

While the love-minus-confrontation approach does help us step forth from our hiding place, quite often one of three distortions occurs:

1. *Blaming.* As in Marcia's case, the focus permanently shifts to the injustices of the other person. Although it's important to uncover and expose those sins of the other, this sort of exposure is for the purpose of sifting out what is my responsibility versus someone else's in the development of my injuries.

When we ignore our own responsibility to enter recovery for our developmental injuries, we enter a fruitless place of perpetually blaming the other. This keeps us from moving on and taking hold of God's resources for growth. It is an external, rather than an internal, focus.

2. *Assuming a helpless position.* Often, the result of safety without responsibility leads us to see ourselves as powerless and unable to do anything to solve our injuries.

This occurs because we need a sense of responsibility to have a sense of power. Despair enters when we can see nothing in our problems except what we cannot control. Hope enters when, knowing we are limited, we see there are still some things we can make choices about.

3. *Apathy.* I once worked with Nick, a teenager whose family had given him an interesting picture of forgiveness. Nick had been arrested for multiple infractions such as driving under the influence, truancy, and vandalism. Each time, his parents would show up to support him. They would tell him they loved and forgave him. Then, to prove it, they would hire an expensive lawyer to fight the case, knowing Nick was guilty each time.

I asked Nick one day how he felt about the dangers he'd caused to others on the road, or to the victims of his vandalism. "I'm forgiven, so it doesn't matter," he said. There was no sense of responsibility or accountability on the boy's part. His parents had confused *forgiveness* with *licentiousness.*

Was Nick emerging from hiding? Certainly—he knew he was in need of limits. He was aware that he had an undeveloped sense of responsibility. But he had no reason to develop spiritually and emotionally. Everything was always taken care of by his enabling parents.

Apathy occurs when we're not aware of the cost of being forgiven. Some call this "cheap grace." We need truth as well as safety.

A DIFFERENT SOLUTION

Typically, the church has been identified with the "truth only" solution for hiding. Sometimes legitimately and sometimes not, Christianity has been perceived as a judgmental religion that excludes mercy and reinforces legalistic and fearful compliance to rules. Christians are often seen as hypocritical and controlling people.

On the other hand, psychotherapy has been identified with the "grace only" approach. Therapeutic solutions have been perceived as existing for people who "wanting to have their ears tickled . . . will accumulate for themselves teachers in accordance to their own desires; and will turn away their ears from the truth, and will turn aside to myths" (2 Timothy 4:3-4). The field is seen as providing permission for people to be self-indulgent.

The truth is that both groups have excesses on either side. Just as there are irresponsible Christian groups, there are also overly confrontational therapists. Another way to look at these two unsatisfactory approaches to helping people come out of hiding is that:

(1) "truth only" causes guilty concealment; and
(2) "grace only" causes irresponsible openness.

We need to help ourselves and others learn vulnerability about our defects, with an eye toward taking responsibility for our healing.

This brings us to a different solution from the two incomplete ones we've just explored. It's a biblical approach to solving the problem of harmful hiding.

God's heart is fixed on repairing the hidden, broken parts of our souls. The redemption of Christ's death for us is not just a philosophical treatise on our attachment to God. It is also a process, continuing daily in us. God wants to "make up to you the years that the swarming locust has eaten" (Joel 2:25). In other words, His plan of redemption for us is to finish our process of growing up, especially in those areas for which there has been little opportunity for growth.

What this means for us as Christians is that *God is a God of replacement*. He wants us to have a life of more than "coping" or "surviving." He actually intends for us to regain what has been lost.

For those who have been hurt in the area of attachments, He wants to provide safe, loving relationships in which we can learn how to trust. For those with deficiencies in separateness, He wants to help us learn how to repair our injured "*no* muscle." For those who keep goodness and badness split apart, He wants to help us find places of forgiveness for ourselves and others and a realistic understanding of a fallen world. For those who struggle with "one-down" positions, God wants to expose us to opportunities to become adults.

We are not able to change the past in which we were injured, but we can reach into the past to find and repair those frozen parts of our character.

STEPS TO A LIFE BEYOND HIDING

The following steps can lead us out of hiding and into the process in repair. I've organized these steps in sequence, but we repeat them in deeper and deeper levels throughout life. God uses them to restore His broken image in us by bringing us to a more Christlike image.

The key point to remember here is that *the solution to hiding is not ripping away our self-protective defenses; the solution is to make the defense unnecessary.* We accomplish that goal by meeting the need that the defense is protecting. The more we repair ourselves as image-bearers, the less concealment we need.

(1) Use Your Hiding Pattern as a Road Map to Your Needs.
Quite often, we're unaware of what our true spiritual and emotional needs are. This is because our hurt self withdraws and tries to make itself as invisible as possible. As one client told me, "If I get really small, maybe no one will ever see me enough to hurt me." The bonding-deficient person, for example, may be without a clue as to her lack of connectedness, much less the hurts that caused it.

Defensive styles are a directional arrow for us. They can't be hidden from view. Our "sentries" always leave clues to what lies behind the doors they're faithfully guarding.

Learn from your internal and relational hiding patterns. Ask trusted friends, "Do you see me doing this when I seem to be hurting?"

Remember the principle of opposites of harmful hiding patterns. The sentry always reacts in a different way than the part under protection. The person with split-off bad parts will make strenuous attempts, for example, to keep the conversation light and happy in order to keep her bad parts in hiding. The authority-deficient individual will often appear to be constantly seeking approval.

(2) Actively Seek Confessional Relationships.

As we begin the process of investigating our relational hiding patterns, we need to find safe relationships in which the immature parts of our soul can begin to emerge. *Relationship is the soil from which grace can enter the injured self.*

Even so, it's not enough to simply be connected to others. We also need to bring out our hurt parts to those people, releasing them out of darkness and paralysis in the limbo of the isolation of the past. This is called *confession,* or *agreeing with the truth.* The Bible says we are to confess our faults to one another to be healed.[2]

This confession may be of our own sins, or of the sins of others against us. *To confess is to allow others to see the part of us that we fear, hate, or are ashamed of.* This is exposing those thoughts, feelings, or behaviors that we fear are actually beyond being loved. *Developing caring attachments to God and others provides the balm for repairing injured parts.*

Emily had periods of such deep, intense despair that she had contemplated killing herself. This was her shameful secret, which pointed to a lack of attachment in the deepest part of her heart. When she joined a fellowship group, she had planned never to share that part of herself, because of her fears of rejection.

Finally beginning to trust the group, Emily took a risk and shared her struggle with episodic suicidality. Imagine her surprise when several other members came out with similar feelings. Emily's confession brought a lost part of her into a place of attachment. As a result, the destructive thoughts began to diminish.

It's important here to discern safe from unsafe relationships. If we confess our injuries to a critical person, we run the risk of further injury and deeper hiding patterns. Like Marie, we will simply draw our head deeper into our shell.

The following list of character traits, compiled by a study group I was involved in, provides helpful criteria in determining who is safe and who isn't. Look for:

- *People who react to you in a different way than those who injured you.* Use your memory to tell the difference:

"Now these things happened as examples for us, that we should not crave evil things, as they also craved" (1 Corinthians 10:6).

- *People who, over time, have a loving track record.* See if their walk matches their talk: "If a brother or sister is without clothing and in need of daily food, and one of you says to them, 'Go in peace, be warmed and be filled,' and yet you do not give them what is necessary for their body, what use is that? Even so faith, if it has no works, is dead, being by itself" (James 2:15-17).

- *People who can be observed from some emotional distance.* Take small risks in vulnerability before taking bigger risks: "Do not lay hands upon anyone too hastily and thus share responsibility for the sins of others; keep yourself from sin" (1 Timothy 5:22); "Test the spirits to see whether they are from God" (1 John 4:1). Many individuals are badly hurt by committing themselves to openness in relationships in which others can't handle that level of honesty—and thus become critical, defensive, or parental.

- *People with the ability to accept imperfections in others.* This refers to the difference between those who love the outside and those who love the inner self: "Let love be without hypocrisy" (Romans 12:9).

- *People who are no stranger to pain, yet are recovering.* Those who have suffered spiritually and emotionally can identify with developmental injuries: "so that we may be able to comfort those who are in any affliction with the comfort with which we ourselves are comforted by God" (2 Corinthians 1:4).

- *People who are aware of their own deficits.* Those who know their unfinished parts are more likely to be safe with the unfinished parts others: "First take the log out of your own eye, and then you will see clearly to take the speck out of your brother's eye" (Matthew 7:5).

- *People who have truth without condemnation.* It's easier to entrust our weaknesses to those who love us, and who will "[speak] the truth in love" (Ephesians 4:15).

- *People who have grace without license.* Attaching to others who see God's grace as leading to greater responsibility helps us to experience grace appropriately: "How shall we who died to sin still live in it?" (Romans 6:2).
- *People who bear good fruit in your life.* Ask yourself if your relationship with this person has made you more or less loving and responsible: "Even so, every good tree bears good fruit; but the bad tree bears bad fruit" (Matthew 7:17).

Overall, when you use this guide to identifying safe relationships, *look for "good enough," not "perfect."* Be willing to grow in these nine areas yourself as you look for them in others.

I just can't overstate it that *whatever is unconfessed is beyond the reach of healing.* The isolated injury that stays hidden feels "bad." The injury that is connected feels loved.

(3) Take Responsibility for Developing the Skills Needed for Repair.

Confession brings us into relationship, but we still need to shoulder the burden of providing our undeveloped aspects with what they need to "catch up" with the rest of our character. This means actively pursuing the skills dealing with our specific developmental injuries (see chapters 4 through 7).

Just as physical therapy, compresses, heat treatments, rest, and medication are part of repairing an injured tendon, these skills are our part in the sanctification process. Paul instructs us to work out our salvation with fear and trembling. God has His own part: "For it is God who is at work in you, both to will and to work for His good pleasure" (Philippians 2:12-13).

Upon leaving treatment, Sandra showed me her daily schedule book. I was amazed to see that she had penciled in at least one time each day for the following month, labeled "bonding." This entry marked a visit, meal, or phone call to one of a few safe people in her life. Sandra was taking an active responsibility for building relationships into her schedule until they became integrated in her heart.

(4) Let Go of Outgrown Hiding Patterns.

Harmful hiding patterns are like personal computers: they're vulnerable to becoming obsolete. Once we've repaired the deficits that caused the defenses, we no longer need the defenses. As a snake sheds its skin, so we can discard our "sentries" — instead of having them torn from our hearts before we are sufficiently matured.

We know we've created an environment in which defenses can be discarded when we've gathered around us sufficient safety, are working on skill-building and repair, and are aligned with the grace and truth of God and His people.

This is not to say that losing hiding patterns is an automatic process. It often takes work, humility, and asking others for help to let go of defenses we no longer need.

Tim had learned to overwhelm people with his aggressive "can do" attitude. Since he was a highly resourceful person, it was easy for him to hide his loneliness and sadness behind his talent.

As Tim began getting help, the isolation he had felt at not being able to have needs started to disappear. At the same time, he maintained his reflexive "urge" to become a workaholic when he was in need of comfort. He had to ask his friends to give him feedback when they saw him retreating to the more familiar pattern of aggressiveness, instead of the newer world of connectedness. As time passed and his attachments deepened, Tim's reactionary behavior diminished greatly.

(5) Maintain Helpful Hiding Patterns.

A woman I know became very excited about discovering that she had been hiding from her separateness by using a caretaking approach with her friends. As soon as she could, she rushed out of her group and called her mother, breathlessly exclaiming, "And Mother — I've learned that God wants me to be able to say no to people!"

"Well," came her mother's reply, "I always suspected you had a selfish streak."

It took some time for the group to support the woman after having her balloon burst so abruptly. The problem wasn't that she was coming out of hiding: It was that she had neglected to use appropriate hiding patterns to keep her connected yet protected. She had been vulnerable with someone who was opposing her attempts to stop hiding her separateness.

As we discussed in chapters 8 and 9, helpful hiding styles such as boundaries, anticipation, humor, and patience will continue to be necessary. We still live in a fallen universe, and a dangerous one as well. Even as we mature and grow, we'll need the kind of wisdom and discretion that the Proverbs tell us to develop. Helpful hiding styles are tools we need to keep at our spiritual and emotional disposal.

(6) Learn to Give What You Have Received.

Christians who are being loved and restored out of hiding learn something about the nature of love: It multiplies itself. Like a waterfall, when we are filled with the warmth of closeness with God and His people, we will spill over into the lives of others.

This is the grateful response to God's love mentioned in the Bible: "But thanks be to God that though you were slaves to sin, you became *obedient from the heart* to that form of teaching to which you were committed" (Romans 6:17; emphasis added).

The nature of allowing ourselves to move out of hiding, and into love, is that our lives bear fruit. Sometimes the fruit is in our own enlarged capacity to love and to develop Christlike character (the fruit of the Spirit). And sometimes it's the fruit of giving ourselves in service to others, be it teaching, helping, or just being a friend: "And this is His commandment, that we believe in the name of His Son Jesus Christ, and love one another, just as He commanded us" (1 John 3:23).

As we are restored, repaired, and matured, we are to help others find the same help we have found. This is the essence of the Great Commission, to make disciples of all the nations. It is both a responsibility and a natural outgrowth of being loved.

SAFE PEOPLE, SAFE GROUPS

We've already seen what safe people ought to look like, but aside from careful observation, how do we develop relationships with those folks? Quite often I get the question, "If safe relationships are such an important part of coming out of hiding, where are they?" Or I hear the comment, "I can't find those people! I don't think there are any!"

These are legitimate questions and concerns. My general answer is that such relationships are not obvious on the surface. But there are four ways of finding such safe people.

First, *evaluate and educate your current relationships*. Many people, realizing their lack of intimacy, automatically assume that the people they're closest to are not interested in growing deeper in attachment. Frequently, this is not the case.

Sometimes the people we're close to either don't know our emotional needs or don't know how to help. It's usually best to explain our struggles and needs first to those we're closest to, if these persons exhibit most or all of the traits mentioned earlier. We should have a high level of confidence in these relationships as safe, non-critical, and conducive to growth without reinjury. These are the people to whom we should offer "first right of refusal" in being part of our growth.

Second, *also seek new relationships*. Just as God allows us to "leave" Him (although He won't leave us), we must allow those who are not interested in being a part of our growth to be uninvolved. If some of those close to you indicate that they cannot handle such intimate details of your life, respect the place of growth at which God has them—their own hiding place.

Be prepared for the possibility that some you consider "close" to you will *not* be able to handle helping you grow. When this occurs, strive to be neither offended nor hurt—possibly these individuals are arrested in their own development in some area, or they just don't have enough time. In this case, it becomes your responsibility to seek out accepting, forgiving, gracious, and truthful friends who want to promote mutual growth.

I think there are some places to find such folks, but it requires the willingness to take risks. This leads to our next point.

Third, *join an organized, relationally focused group*. Even if you get a "yes" from someone close to you who wishes to help you grow, or from someone you meet in church or in a Bible study group, it's still (always) a good idea to become involved in a support group.

A support group can arise from many different contexts: a church-related small group, a professionally staffed support group, or an informally gathered group of friends or acquaintances. In any case, the primary focus should be growth and intimacy.

Bible studies and other "activity" groups that people often join are usually concerned with agendas other than closeness; if closeness is achieved in these settings, it's usually a byproduct rather than an intentional goal. Although study groups, softball teams, hobby groups, and clubs certainly have a valuable presence in our lives, they usually don't provide the best place to grow out of sinful hiding patterns, helpful self-protective behaviors, or deep hurts and immaturities.

Look for a support group, a small-group fellowship focusing on intimacy, or a therapy group *that has as its primary goal the growth of the individual toward closeness within the group.* If there is a clear movement in the church today, it's toward intimate small group fellowships in which people can safely reveal deep hurts and needs. If you can't find a group like this, seek out a Christian counselor or therapist who can recommend a safe place to grow.

Fourth, *be willing to make economically disadvantageous decisions to find closeness.* In some rare cases, when the first three steps above prove unsuccessful it's a sign that your geographical area may not be conducive to your coming out of hiding. If you discover this is true, it may indeed be worth the difficult choice to pull up stakes and actually move to an area in which genuine relationships can be cultivated.

Even though it may mean paying a high price, it is an urgent necessity to find a safe place to repair your injured parts and grow.

EXCHANGING HIDING FOR RELATIONSHIP

The Sun and the Wind were having a discussion one day over who was stronger. Then they spied a man walking along the road who was wearing a jacket. "Let's decide the issue this way," said the Wind. "Whichever one of us makes that man remove his jacket is the more powerful." The Sun agreed.

Winning the coin toss, the Wind began to blow at the man. At first he blew just steady breezes, but to no avail. Increasing the force, he began moving stronger gusts around the man. The walker simply wrapped his jacket more tightly around himself and kept going. In frustration, the Wind hurled hurricane-force gales at the man, almost sweeping him off his feet. Still clutching his jacket, although bent over backward, the man held on.

"I believe it's my turn," interrupted the Sun. Pointing toward the disheveled figure, he began gradually and gently to warm the air surrounding the man, a degree at a time. Within a few minutes the man had straightened up, continued walking, and begun to perspire. After a few more minutes, he took off the jacket and slung it over his shoulder, continuing on his way.

When we're attacked because of our hiding patterns—by others or ourselves—we simply hold them more tightly. If our defenses are our only friends, we will go down with them rather than abandon them and risk reinjury. It takes the warm light of grace and safety, with honest truthfulness, to help us outgrow our concealments.

The heart of this concept of outgrowing defenses can be seen in a phrase from 1 Corinthians 13:11—"when I became a man, I did away with childish things." Many Christians have been hurt by an incorrect understanding of this passage, paraphrased something like, "when I did away with childish things I became a man."

Telling people to do things they don't have the ability to do is like ripping a child's security blanket away from him before he's ready to give it up. The child will panic, and frantically search for his comforting possession. Sometimes he may search for another blanket, or withdraw into a heartsick hopelessness.

But if the child gets what he needs over time and is actively involved in his own maturing process, one day he forgets the blanket. He's just too involved with playing with his friends now. The blanket served its purpose and was relinquished in the child's personal, timely fashion.

God wants us to be involved in our own process of growing up into His image. That means *progressively redeeming* the injured, hidden parts of ourselves that cause us pain and difficulty. As we experience the unconditional attachment of God and His people, along with the appropriate kinds and quantities of needed truth over time, we fulfill that redemptive process.

Because "the kindness of God leads you to repentance" (Romans 2:4), a transformation can occur in the form of an exchange. *A life dedicated to self-protection and hiding can be exchanged for a life full of love, meaningful accomplishments, acceptance, and direction.*

Remember how Jenny came out of hiding?

There it was again: "Jenny! Jenny! Where are you?" When she heard the man's voice calling her, Jenny crawled to her safest spying tree and scurried up to her well-concealed look-out post to watch. This was the twentieth day in a row—why did this same soldier keep coming back every day?

Jenny didn't know much except that he was one of the terrifying men in uniform. That was reason enough to stay away. She recognized him from the last scare. But for these last several days, he'd always come alone to the Deep Woods, which was no small feat. The Woods weren't especially friendly to strangers.

Today, something was different about the soldier's approach. Jenny noticed that he didn't seem in any particular hurry. His voice and mannerisms seemed enticingly calm and appealing to her. He just sat there in the same place, near a large maple tree, calling for her every few minutes. After about an hour he left.

The soldier returned at the same time the next day. Now Jenny felt that he appeared kind and patient. And strangely enough, the animals were befriending him the way they had befriended her when she'd first come to the Deep Woods. The squirrels, rabbits, and deer slowly approached him as he sat under the maple, eventually coming close enough for him to touch them.

After thirty consecutive days of the soldier's appearing, Jenny decided to take a small risk. She positioned herself about a hundred feet away from him, next to a secret entrance to the deepest part of the forest. Poised to melt instantly into the woods, Jenny coughed in the soldier's direction.

As he peered toward her, Jenny caught her first full glimpse of his face. It seemed vaguely familiar. The solider began to smile without making a move or even getting up. Jenny's dim recollections of him began to well up inside until she recognized the kind face of her old friend.

"Jenny," he called out warmly. "It's me, Josef. I've come to take you home."

"I don't have a home," she replied. "Didn't you know about Mother and Father being taken away? I live here now. I live in a cave. It's my home."

"It's true," Josef went on, "your mom and dad were taken away by soldiers from another land. But your countrymen fought back and freed our land. Their soldiers are gone. The whole country is safe now and so are your parents. They're in the hospital, but they're doing very well and will be home soon. They want you to come to see them. Your mother and father miss you very much, and they sent me to find you."

Hearing this news created a multitude of mixed emotions in Jenny. Conflicting feelings surged through her. She felt a tremendous sense of relief at knowing her parents were safe and wanted her back. Deep within her was the little girl who longed to be held in their arms again.

But Jenny also felt a sharp tug of fear at the prospect of leaving the safety of the home she'd made for herself in the Deep Woods. For many months now, the dark places had been good to her. They had kept her safe and protected during her times of sadness and moments of terror. They had been her only comfort in endless lonely nights.

Jenny realized that staying in the Woods meant being alone forever. "Should I go with Officer Josef? Or should

I stay here?" The difficult dilemma brought back her old confusion.

To make matters worse, there was the problem of Officer Josef's uniform. For so long, the sight of military-style outfits had kept her terrified, reminding her of the horrible day her parents had been taken away. For Jenny, seeing a uniform had become a warning signal for danger.

Jenny gazed at Officer Josef's uniform, then looked at his kind face. Back to the uniform, and again to his face. The kind features and warm smile brought back memories of their close times in the village, their talks on the street corner, and their laughter together on her small playground. The memories flooded back.

Jenny waited, agonizing. His face, she told herself. I think I remember his face. Then she took a deep breath and made the hardest decision of her life. She slowly approached Josef and took his outstretched hand. Together, they walked out of the Deep Woods. Toward home.

Just as Jenny took a difficult step toward relationship, God wants us all to find a safe place to learn the ways we hide from love. In that place, we're destined to begin the often exciting, often painful work of resolving our hiding patterns, meeting our undeveloped needs, and moving further into Christlikeness.

And, as we experience restoration, we will experience and develop more of the kind of loving sensitivity that Officer Josef demonstrated when he won Jenny's confidence again. After the first time he and his fellow policemen discovered Jenny in the Woods and lost her in the chase, Josef could have returned shortly with a huge search party and exhaustively combed the Deep Woods. Her parents, still in the hospital healing from wounds inflicted by their captors yet desperately wanting the presence and safety of their beloved daughter, would likely have sanctioned such an effort!

But Josef recognized the terror the little girl had experienced already, and he imagined the fright Jenny would feel as such a search party closed in on her. So he set himself toward rebuilding

Jenny's confidence in her old relationship with him. He created a safe, non-threatening environment in which she could take the risk of approaching a person in uniform once again. Once Jenny recognized the safety, her redemption from the Deep Woods of hiding was ensured.

Our redemption is accomplished as we hide *in* God rather than hide *from* Him. It is God's love that comes looking for us in our secret hideouts.

My prayer for you is that as you turn away from the dark places of your own shame, fears, and anxieties, you will look first at the kind face of an Officer Josef whom God has provided to help you to safety and growth.

May we all become such restored loving, imaginative, and observant people. And may you find God and others walking with you as you come out of hiding!

NOTES   1. Matthew 21:28-32.
        2. James 5:16.